# THE PROTESTANT REFORMATION

*Belief, Practice and Tradition*

## The Sussex Library of Religious Beliefs and Practices

This series is intended for students of religion, social sciences and history, and for the interested layperson. It is concerned with the beliefs and practices of religions in their social, cultural and historical setting. These books will be of particular interest to Religious Studies teachers and students at universities, colleges, and high schools. Inspection copies available upon request.

<u>Published</u>

*The Ancient Egyptians*   Rosalie David

*Buddhism*   Merv Fowler

*Christian Theology: The Spiritual Tradition*   John Glyndwr Harris

*Gnosticism*   John Glyndwr Harris

*Hinduism*   Jeaneane Fowler

*Humanism*   Jeaneane Fowler

*Islam*   David Norcliffe

*The Jews*   Alan Unterman

*The Protestant Reformation*   Madeleine Gray

*Sikhism*   W. Owen Cole and Piara Singh Sambhi

*Zoroastrianism*   Peter Clark

<u>In preparation</u>

*You Reap What You Sow: Causality in the Religions of the World*   Jeaneane Fowler

*Hindu Goddesses*   Lynn Foulston

*Jainism*   Lynn Foulston

*Taoism*   Jeaneane Fowler

*Taoism and T'ai Chi Ch'uan*   Jeaneane Fowler and Shifu Keith Ewers

*Zen*   Merv Fowler

<u>Forthcoming</u>

*Bhagavad Gita (a student commentary)*      *Confucianism*

# The Protestant Reformation

*Belief, Practice and Tradition*

——

MADELEINE GRAY

**sussex**
ACADEMIC
PRESS

*BRIGHTON • PORTLAND*

2 4 6 8 10 9 7 5 3 1

*Published 2003 in Great Britain by*
SUSSEX ACADEMIC PRESS
Box 2950
Brighton BN2 5SP

*and in the United States of America by*
SUSSEX ACADEMIC PRESS
920 NE 58th Ave          Suite 300
Portland, Oregon 97213-3786

*British Library Cataloguing in Publication Data*
A CIP catalogue record for this book is available from the British Library.

*Library of Congress Cataloging-in-Publication Data*
Gray, Madeleine, 1950–
The Protestant Reformation : beliefs, practice, and tradition / Madeleine Gray
p   cm.
Includes bibliographical references and index.
ISBN 1–903900–11–5 (pbk. : alk. paper)
1. Reformation.  I. Title
BR305.3 .G73  2002
270.6—dc21          2002066935

Printed by TJ International, Padstow, Cornwall
This book is printed on acid-free paper.

# *Contents*

———

# Preface and Acknowledgements

To the question, "why yet another book on the Protestant Reformation", I have two answers. The first is that research and scholarly publication on the subject continues to occupy the attention of theologians, historians and social anthropologists. Controversy still rages over the state of the late medieval church, the extent to which the Reformation was driven by theological or political concerns, and the impact which it had on the lives and beliefs of ordinary people. There will always be a need for summaries of the state of the debate.

The second reason is one which arises from my own experience as a teacher of late medieval and early modern history. Undergraduates are increasingly uncertain about the basics of the Christian faith, and they find that many books on aspects of the history of the Christian church assume a level of knowledge which they do not possess. They do not all go as far as the young man who admitted to me a few years ago that he could not exactly remember which one was Jesus and which one was Buddha, but his problem was a real one and needs to be addressed. While this book is not intended for the complete novice (who might do better to start with the chapter on Christianity in Jeaneane Fowler's *World Religions: an introduction for students*), I have tried not to assume too much knowledge of Christian belief and practice.

In the preface to any book on the history of religion, it is customary for the author to explain her own religious standpoint. I was brought up in the Church in Wales and would now describe myself as a semi-detached Anglican. I have a great deal of sympathy and affection for the rituals of late medieval Catholicism, and I am a member of a pilgrimage study group which walks every year along a medieval route to a shrine dedicated to the Virgin Mary in the hills above the Rhondda in south Wales. But I also have a great deal of sympathy and admiration for those who saw the grave faults in late medieval spirituality and were prepared to risk their own lives to reform them. They may have destroyed much that was of value, but they destroyed to build anew. They had a vision of a church of educated and informed believers, each of whom could give a reason for their faith.

It is also customary in a preface to recognize help, support and encouragement from colleagues and others. I have many debts of gratitude which it is a pleasure to acknowledge here. The Protestant reformers are famous for revaluing marriage and family life as part of human spirituality. Luther owed a great deal to his Katie Bora, Calvin to Idelette de Bure; I owe more than I can say to my husband Steve, who is a far better theologian than I am. He, our daughter Rachel and my mother Betty Bennett have put up with my state of general abstraction while I was writing this book. My discussions with them have clarified much of the argument. I could not have done it without them.

My colleagues at the University of Wales College, Newport, have been unfailingly helpful and supportive in spite of all the pressures of modern higher education. It was Mervyn Fowler, head of the Philosophy and Religious Studies team at UWCN, who suggested my name to Tony Grahame of Sussex Academic Press, when he was looking for someone to contribute a book on the Reformation to the *Belief and Practice* series. I have discussed some of the material in the book with successive generations of students. They have all made perceptive and illuminating comments, and have added to my understanding. The Inter-Library Loan service at our library has produced a steady stream of books and periodical articles.

My then head of department, Dr Ian Fisher, listened with wry amusement to my analogies between Martin Luther's Wittenberg and our own institution: a new university, locally-based and uncertainly funded, with some brilliant teachers but struggling to acquire the necessary resources for our ambitious teaching and research programme. Like Luther's lectures on the letters of St Paul, our classes are interrupted by the sounds of building work as our buildings are extended to meet the needs of a growing body of students. But as Dr Fisher pointed out, at least Luther did not have to contend with modern bureaucratic requirements for the approval and validation of new courses. Academic planning was simpler in his day: the whole curriculum of the theology department at Wittenberg was revolutionized at a single meeting at Karlstadt's lodgings in March 1518.

Dr Fisher suggested that I should write the paperwork for the validation of Luther's new module on "Justification and Salvation in the writings of Paul and Augustine". Unfortunately, the challenge defeated me – as, who knows, it might have defeated Luther. This book is all I can offer as a substitute.

For Helen Miller
who taught me to think critically about the
Reformation.

# Introduction

Here are two stories about the Protestant Reformation. The first is told by the historians of the Protestant tradition, men like Jaroslav Pelikan, Steven Ozment and A. G. Dickens, and by theologians like Alister McGrath:

> The late medieval Catholic church was irredeemably corrupt. Clergy and church officials exploited the credulity of a lay population who they deliberately kept in ignorance of the true meaning of Christianity. Clerical standards of education and morality were deplorably low; priests demanded standards of behaviour from the laity which they were unable to follow themselves. Repentance and salvation were reduced to a cash transaction –
>
> > As the coin in the cash-box rings
> > The soul from purgatory springs.
>
> All attempts at reform were brutally suppressed, though dissident groups like the Lollards in England and the Hussites in Bohemia and Moravia kept the flame alight in secret.
>
> The floodgates of popular demand for reform were opened by the actions of one brave man, the friar and university lecturer Martin Luther. By his courageous and public opposition to Papal indulgences, his insistence that salvation was by faith alone and that the Bible was the sole source of spiritual authority, and his determination that the Bible should be available in the everyday language of the people, he initiated the movement which we know as the Protestant Reformation. He was followed by other charismatic spiritual leaders – Huldrych Zwingli, Martin Bucer, John Knox – and above all by John Calvin. They developed the basic concepts of salvation by faith alone and Biblical authority, sometimes taking them in directions of which Luther disapproved.

The second story is more complicated: it is told by "revisionist" historians like Christopher Haigh, John Scarisbrick and Eamon Duffy, and by Bob Scribner and the social anthropologists.

> While the late medieval church had its problems (and what large organization does not?), it catered well for the spiritual and emotional needs of the vast majority of the population. Peasants and labourers were educated in the basics of the faith as adequately as practical circumstances allowed, and a rich and complex spirituality was available for those able to take advantage of it. The church was sufficiently flexible to accommodate a wide divergence of theological standpoints and to absorb and Christianize beliefs and practices which we would now regard as superstition.

> However, the changing political circumstances of the sixteenth century led many heads of state and local rulers to seek independence from the hegemony of the Church and the Holy Roman Empire. They could articulate their desire for independence by using the ideas of a small group of university intellectuals who were pushing neo-Augustinian orthodoxy on the doctrine of salvation to its logical extreme and had thus incurred the wrath of the ecclesiastical hierarchy. This Reformation had nothing to do with democracy or popular belief. Indeed, when reformed ideas were used as a rallying-cry by the German peasants in the 1525 uprising, Luther disowned them and his supporters among the local German rulers crushed the uprising with the greatest brutality. The ideas of Luther, Calvin and the other reformers were used to reinforce magisterial control over the majority of the population. Women lost the power and scope for independent action which the medieval Catholic church had allowed them and were officially confined to the ghetto of "kids, kirk and kitchen".

> But the needs and beliefs of ordinary people could not so easily be suppressed. Popular folk traditions continued as powerful as ever. In some regions, witchcraft and magic actually became stronger, as people could no longer turn to the Church for help with their problems. The Protestant Reformation was a failure – indeed, there was no such thing as a Protestant reformation. Rather, there was a series of attempted reformations – radical, magisterial, popular, negotiating and renegotiating the implications of theological argument. Meanwhile, the great states of Europe – France, Spain, the Holy Roman Empire – remained Catholic, and it was Catholicism which was taken by Spain and Portugal to the New World and the Far East.

These conflicting accounts are bound to confuse students of the Reformation. Is one right and the other wrong, and if so, how can we tell which is which? Or are they both right in different ways, at different times, for different parts of Europe? It is difficult to write a book about the Reformation when the experts cannot agree on what the Reformation was. It is even more difficult when the experts are arguing about whether there was ever such a thing as the Reformation.

In some ways, paradoxically, the argument is part of the answer. The Reformation was different things at different times. It was a matter of intense personal conviction for Luther in his little German university in 1517, a matter of pressing national politics for Henry VIII in England in 1533. It was allied with political radicalism in Münster and with authoritarian despotism in Saxony. In England, it was welcomed in Yorkshire and rejected with civil unrest in neighbouring Lancashire. It was multi-faceted, with many causes and incalculable consequences.

There were many reformations – but historians still write of one Protestant Reformation. Even if they sometimes qualify the phrase virtually out of existence, most of them admit that something happened which broke the mould of medieval Christendom. After 1517, there would always be an alternative. The book I have written is a study of "the Protestant Reformation": but it will have to look at all these different reformations and consider how they contribute to the whole picture.

It is easier to say what this book is not than what it is. It is not an analysis of the origins of the Reformation, or an account of its precursors. This is not because the origins of the Reformation are unimportant or uninteresting. I am fascinated by the orthodoxy of Luther's early Augustinianism and the reasons why it was perceived as such a threat by the Catholic church when the very similar ideas of (for example) Gregory of Rimini were not; but that is material for a whole book, or a series of books.[1] Nor will the present study have much to say about the late medieval Catholic church or late medieval piety and spirituality. Again, this is a fascinating subject and one on which a great deal of research is currently being done; but this is not the place to summarize that research. Some of the texts for such a study will be found in the suggestions for further reading at the end of this book. It will be necessary here to give a brief outline of traditional Catholic doctrine and practice in order to place the changes initiated by the reformers in context, but that is all.

Finally, this book is not a narrative of the Reformation: it is a study of religious belief and practice. A narrative history of the Reformation would have to interweave the stories of religious change in virtually every one of the German and Swiss Protestant cities and states, as well as France, the Netherlands, England and Wales, Scotland and Scandinavia. We would also need to look at the Reformation in eastern Europe, where reformed ideas were initially successful but where most of the Protestant churches were crushed in the early seventeenth century.

There are a number of interweaving narrative histories of the Reformation now available, as well as detailed accounts of the Reformation in single states or cities and during shorter periods of time. What I hope to do in the present book is to step back from these narratives and to focus again on some of the common themes in changing religious belief and practice, in the light of the detailed research now available. The student should be aware that my chosen approach is to some extent at the expense of an awareness of distinctive local traditions. Although it was originally a religious movement, the progress of the Reformation was influenced by local conditions, and Reformed ideas developed in different ways in different states and territories. Differences in the reception of Reformed ideas could be even more localized. In England, the weaving communities of Yorkshire included a number of early converts to Protestantism; but just across the Pennines, Lancashire was the heartland of Catholic resistance. I have tried to take account of these local variations while concentrating mainly on the general picture.

I shall also provide an overview of some of the recent research on the social anthropology of religion in the sixteenth century. It is time we stood back from the ideas of the reformers, most of whom were professional theologians, in order to consider how ordinary people structured their spiritual lives and responded to the changes which took place in their churches. In particular, as this is a series devoted to religious practice as well as belief, I want to consider changes in church services and other religious rituals and in the fabric and decoration of church buildings. Social anthropology teaches us how we can "read" rituals and buildings in order to arrive at a better understanding of the beliefs of people who have left no written record of their own ideas.

A study of the Reformation in the broadest sense would have to include the Catholic Reformation. This is sometimes called the Counter-Reformation, but it had its origins earlier than the Protestant Reformation with the work of leaders like Cardinal Ximenes in Spain in the late fifteenth century. The intellectual movement which we now call the Renaissance had its effect on the intellectual expression of religious belief. New universities were founded in a number of European centres, and key theological texts were subjected to critical scrutiny. There were many reformers like Guillaume Briçonnet, bishop of Meaux in the 1520s, and Jean du Bellay, bishop of Paris from 1532, who wanted to introduce new ideas but were prepared to do so from within the structures of the Catholic church. The general movement for reform and renewal in western Christianity in the late fifteenth and early sixteenth centuries also led to an intensification of lay spirituality, with organizations like the Brethren of the Common Life emphasising the importance of the inner spiritual renewal of the individual. It could be argued that the Reformation as we know it grew out of these movements, but eventually found itself in opposition to them.

Recent studies have argued that the aftermath of both Protestant and Catholic Reformations resulted in similar and parallel processes which have been called "confessionalization". All the major churches – Catholic as well as Lutheran and Calvinist – developed distinctive institutional structures. They all enforced doctrinal systems and ritual practices. All three used propaganda and polemic, education and social discipline in the attempt to create cohesive social groups. All three had political implications and were used by the states of early modern Europe to consolidate their boundaries and create loyalty among their inhabitants.[2] This book, however, is confined to the Protestant Reformation – or more properly to the Reformations. The Catholic Reformation really needs another book to itself.

I shall, however, say a lot about the Reformation in England and Wales. These countries are often relegated to a short section in outline histories of the Reformation, if they are covered at all. It is my belief that the established church of England, for all its traditionalism in organization and its doctrinal fudges, deserves to be considered as a Protestant church for at least a century after Henry VIII's break with Rome. It was the Restoration of 1660 and the Oxford Movement of the nineteenth century which created the Anglican Church of the modern world with its vestments and rituals, its incense and candles and its tendency to hesitate over anything which might imperil relations with the Vatican. With their chequered confessional history, England and Wales also provide us with a test-bed for many of the ideas of the Reformation. Vitriolic debates over issues like the use of leavened or unleavened bread in the Communion service and the wearing of distinctive clothing by the clergy indicate how important these matters were to sixteenth-century believers. The history of the English Book of Common Prayer, with its shifts in the vocabulary of prayer and ritual, suggests how belief was made concrete in the patterns of worship.

While I have tried to structure this book so that it provides an analysis of the most important themes in religious belief and practice in the Protestant reformation, I have had to bear in mind the differences between different groups of reformers. These differences could be quite marked and could lead to acrimonious disputes. My own belief is that it really is more accurate to speak of "Reformations" than "*the* Reformation". The Reformation, so-called, was really a series of discrete developments which found much common ground but never fully coalesced.

Its complexity is certainly one of the reasons why the Reformation(s) succeeded where previous breakaway reform movements had been crushed. There were so many aspects to the campaign for reform that it attracted widespread support. Nevertheless, its breadth of appeal had inherent weaknesses. The textual critiques of the humanists, Luther's personal revelation of the importance of faith for salvation and Zwingli's attack on the increasingly restrictive practices of late medieval devotion were interwoven with popular anticlericalism and political hostility towards the secular powers of the church and the Pope; but the fabric was always liable to unravel under pressure.

Historians have conventionally divided the Protestant reformation into two or three separate movements – Lutheran, Calvinist or Reformed, and radical. The first two of these groups take their names from the two outstanding leaders of the Protestant Reformation. Martin Luther's outburst against the sale of "indulgences" (remissions of the penalties for sin) at the little German university town of Wittenberg in 1517 is generally regarded as the beginning of the Reformation. Luther's main concern was with the importance of faith rather than human action as the way to heaven. It was his successors who systematized his ideas and established the church named after him. John (or Jean) Calvin was one of the second generation of reformers who settled in the Swiss city of Geneva. There he and the ruling council of the city established a church whose beliefs and organization were based as far as possible on the Bible and the model of the early church.

It is necessary here to say something about the words used to identify these groups. Terminology is something that historians worry about from time to time. All the words we have at our disposal bring with them a range of implications which may not be exactly what we want to say. There really is no alternative to the word "Lutheran" for those churches which followed the idiosyncratic and forcefully-expressed ideas of Martin Luther. But "Calvinism" has developed in ways which take it far beyond the ideas of John Calvin – in its emphasis on the doctrine of predestination, for example (see pp. 30–4) and in a tendency towards Biblical fundamentalism which is in contradiction to Calvin's own ideas (see p. 67). For this reason, some historians of the Reformation prefer the word "Reformed" (with a capital R) to describe the churches which followed Calvin's ideas. This is logical, since they considered themselves to have gone beyond Luther's ideas and to have reformed the church further. Unfortunately, if we speak of these churches as Reformed, it leads to endless confusion with the churches of the Protestant Reformation as a whole and even with some of the more thoughtful leaders of the Catholic Reformation. I have therefore decided to revert to the old practice of describing these churches as "Calvinist". They regarded themselves as following Calvin's ideas, even if they had gone beyond him in some respects. After all, there is a lot in Christianity which its founder Jesus Christ would find it difficult to recognize.

Some historians are even reluctant to use the word "Protestant" to describe the churches of the Reformation. The word has no validity before 1529, which is when it was coined to describe the German princes who protested against the decrees of the Catholic majority at the Diet (the Imperial Assembly) at Speyer. Unfortunately, the alternatives to the word "Protestant" – words like "Evangelical" and "Reformed" (again) – all have other connotations and can be equally confusing. Words change and develop in their meanings, and we always need to remember that the words we choose to describe people in the past are not necessarily the words they would choose for themselves. I will therefore be using the word "Protestant" to describe all these churches, even for the period in the 1520s when it is really an anachronism. I have tried to avoid using the word "Reformed" (capital R) to refer to the specifically Calvin-inspired group of Protestants. Instead, I have used it to refer to all those who wanted reform in the church, whether or not they would have gone so far as to have used the name Protestant for themselves.

It is therefore legitimate to speak of the Lutheran and Calvinist Reformations. However, we need to remember that not all groups of moderate Protestants will fit into these neat boxes. A pattern may emerge with hindsight, but many moderate Protestant groups of the mid-sixteenth century took their own line, using (for example) Luther's ideas on worship or church government but accepting Calvin's ideas on the spiritual meaning behind their worship. (I discuss this in more detail on pp. 203–5.)

The radical reformers were even more diverse in their origins and ideas. Their ideas ranged from the violent millenarianism of Niclas Storch and Thomas Müntzer (both of whom accepted the need for physical force to bring in the promised kingdom of Christ) to the uncompromising pacifism of Conrad Grebel (who admired Müntzer but rejected all forms of violence); from the Biblical fundamentalism of the early Anabaptists to the spiritual mysticism of Caspar Schwenckfeld and the rationalism of the Unitarians and Socinians.

The radical reformers are sometimes called the *Anabaptists* (literally, the Re-baptizers) because most of the radicals came to the belief that only adults who understood the meaning of their faith could be baptized and admitted to full membership of the church. Like Luther and Calvin, they based their teaching on the Bible, but they were more uncompromising in following Biblical ideas to their logical conclusions. What made them politically radical, though, was their idea that true Christians had to separate themselves from a sinful world. They rejected the authority of the state – refusing, for example, to swear oaths of allegiance or to do military service. This made them fiercely unpopular and they were persecuted even by Protestant rulers. Luther and Calvin both tried to distance themselves from these radical reformers. Calvin wrote the first version of his *Institution of the Christian Religion* in part to convince the king of France that the French reformers were not Anabaptists.

There were other, even more radical reformers. The spiritualists rejected the authority of the Bible, believing instead that God's spirit could speak directly to them and guide them. The antinomians rejected all legal and moral codes. They believed that, once they were in a state of grace, they could do no more wrong. Some of the most extreme reformers even challenged the fundamental Christian doctrine of the Trinity, the one God who nevertheless has three persons. This anti-Trinitarian group originated in Italy with Italian radicals like the Sozzinis who eventually travelled to eastern Europe. It is often called "Socinianism" after the Latin form of Sozzini.

The Lutheran and Calvinist reformations are sometimes grouped together as the "magisterial" reformation – that reformation which was supported (and in some places enforced) by secular authority, as opposed to the radical reformation which was generally seen as a challenge and a threat to secular authority. It is inevitably easier to write about the magisterial reformers. Their ideas are more coherent, and their organizations better documented. Often, we know of a group of radical reformers only from the writings of those who attacked them.

Nevertheless, it is important to study them because they give voice to ideas which have been influential in the subsequent development of Christian thinking.

These diverse groups of Protestant reformers have given rise to the range of Christian denominations in the modern world: the magisterial reformers not just to the Lutheran and Calvinist churches but to the Presbyterian churches, the Kirk of Scotland and (arguably) to the Anglican/Episcopalian churches. The radical reformers produced, as well as the Baptist churches, the Independents and the churches which call themselves Brethren. The Methodists belong to a slightly later tradition. The Calvinistic Methodists were clearly in the tradition of Calvin's Geneva; the Wesleyan Methodists are Presbyterian in their church organization but Arminian in their beliefs.

A book in a series on religious belief and practice must of necessity emphasize the importance of religious motivation in studying the Reformation. We will therefore have to deal with the technicalities of Christian theology in order to explain the ideas of the reformers, most of whom were professional theologians. For all his popular image as the bluff man of the people, coarse in his expressions and fond of a pint or two, Martin Luther was a university academic who worked out his theology of salvation in the lecture theatre and the common room. The language of Christian theology is often unfamiliar in a multi-faith society, and the concepts which it embodies are becoming alien to an increasingly secularized readership. This book attempts to provide a brief introduction to Christian ideas on the issues which most concerned the reformers. Technical terms – "justification", "sacraments", "eucharist" – will be discussed when they become significant in the text, and can also be found in the Glossary at the end of the book.

Even if we accept that the Reformation was initially a movement for religious reform, the extent to which reformed ideas were accepted, rejected or manipulated in different communities and states was influenced by the social, economic and political framework of sixteenth-century Europe. This accounts for some at least of the diversity of responses to the initial religious impulse. The Reformation may have started with a disagreement over religious belief and practice, but the success or failure of doctrinal reform had to do less with the force of those beliefs than with the context in which they were expressed and the secular use which could be made of them. It makes no sense to treat religious ideas as epiphenomena, mere froth on the surface of the really important long-term changes in social and economic trends; but nor does it make sense to treat religious changes in isolation from their historical context. While this book is intended as a study of the beliefs and practices of the Protestant Reformation, we have to remember that the Reformation took place in historical time. The beliefs and practices we are looking at are the beliefs and practices of real people in the past. We cannot understand them if we take them out of that context.

What we have to do, then, is to take these Protestant Reformations on their own terms, as movements which were primarily religious in their origins but which took place at a particular time and in a particular context and which had profound implications for the political, social and economic life of the societies in which they were rooted. We need to remember that we are looking at a period when questions about salvation and the fate of the individual after death were crucial for the majority of people. Right living meant less a moral code for dealing with neighbours and more the rule for a relationship with God. At the same time, we need to be aware that the language of religion could be used to articulate very different concerns. The students of Wittenberg who demonstrated in the streets in the autumn of 1521 claimed they were demanding changes in the liturgy of the Mass, but they were probably exercising the right which all students have claimed down the ages, to challenge established authority on principle.

*             *             *

Some misconceptions will need to be cleared away. The early reformers had no wish to found new churches. They wanted to reform the thinking of the universal, Catholic, church on such crucial doctrines as the meaning of its sacraments and the means of salvation. However, the intransigence of the Catholic church forced them to split away from it. The early Reformers asked repeatedly for a church council before which they could defend their ideas. Luther is famous for his principled stand at the imperial assembly at Worms, but most of the reformers were surprisingly willing to compromise. Consequently, until at least the middle of the sixteenth century, it is misleading to think of Europe as divided into two distinct blocks, "Catholic" and "Protestant". Instead, there was a whole spectrum of viewpoints, embracing the humanistic liberalism of the followers of Erasmus and the ecumenism of Hermann von Wied, the evangelical Archbishop of Cologne, as well as the hard-line traditionalism of the theologians of the Sorbonne and the equally hard-line Protestantism of John Knox and Calvin's followers in Geneva.

Nor was the Reformation a united, self-aware movement. Its origins were too diverse – the classical humanism of Bucer and Melanchthon,

Luther's move from scholasticism to the Bible, Zwingli's concern for ethical reform. Because of this, and because of the early reformers' reluctance to divide the church, there was no coherent strategy for change. Instead, there was a series of campaigns for reform in different aspects of church life. As the Catholic church rejected these and moved against the reformers with varying degrees of severity, so the reformers' responses became more radical. However, it would be many years before there was any underlying plan. Francis Higman has described Luther, Zwingli and the other early reformers as "firemen" – always responding to the latest emergency, and with no time to develop a coherent strategy of their own.[3]

Luther never intended to found the Lutheran church. Indeed, Luther never intended to found a church at all: he simply wanted to reform some errors into which the Catholic church of which he was a member seemed to be falling. His great priority was to prepare individuals for the end of the world (which he thought was imminent) and the Last Judgement. All other issues paled into insignificance in the face of his belief in the primacy of faith as the only way to salvation. He was quite prepared to compromise with any other aspect of the Catholic church if it would return to what he believed to be the truth about the way to be saved. Nor did Calvin want to found the Calvinist church. He wanted to lead the whole Reformation in the direction which he felt was the right one, and he must eventually have hoped that the whole of the Christian church could unite in recognizing the truths which seemed so fundamental to him.

As their ideas developed, so the reformers themselves became divided, in ways which created the preconditions for the plethora of modern denominations. The fault lines for these splits were the basic doctrines of the reformers – the nature of the true church, the significance of its sacraments (and especially the Eucharist), the implications of the Reformed doctrine of salvation. However, groups also split on geographical lines, especially in the city-states of Switzerland and the Holy Roman Empire. As the reformed churches spread and became more powerful, and as opposition to their ideas became weaker in some areas, so they had more scope to develop their thinking, and in general they developed away from each other.

The series of confessions and catechisms produced by different groups of reformers – the (Lutheran) Augsburg confession of 1530 and Melanchthon's revision in 1540, the confessions of the Swiss cities, Strasbourg, Basle and Zürich, Calvin's 1541 Geneva catechism and the (slightly different) confession he wrote for the French in 1559, and many more – testify to the extent of their divisions. The fact that we can now talk about "*the* Protestant reformation" can blind us to the savage hostility which marred relations between different groups of Protestants. This was not what any of the reformers wanted. They all believed in the unity of the church – but they found it impossible to agree on a basis for that unity. In their attempts to define and defend their different standpoints, they took the Reformation away from its roots in the search for spiritual renewal and made it as rigid and doctrinaire as the medieval church they were attacking.

We must always remember, though, that this rigidity, like the fragmentation of the church, was not what any of the early reformers wanted. In many cases, the refinement and rigidity of doctrine was not the responsibility of the first generation of reformers. Luther was not a Lutheran; Calvin would have found much to disagree with in the Calvinist church as it had developed by the end of the sixteenth century. Virtually all the mainstream, "magisterial" reformers were prepared to attack the ideas of the radicals and the Anabaptists. But the split between Lutheran and Calvinist orthodoxies did not become irreconcilable until the mid-1570s.

Nor did the reformers claim that their ideas were new. Our modern enthusiasm for creativity and innovation would have been anathema to the medieval mind. Truth was grounded in authority, and authority was located in the past. The reformers' opponents might accuse them of innovation, but they claimed that their thinking was rooted in the Bible and the work of the early fathers of the Church. The Reformed thinkers were not forward-looking. They still thought in terms of a continuing decline from an ideal golden age in the past, and it was their hope that they could return to this golden age of the primitive church by re-establishing the authority of the Bible and the purity of its text. In his *Institution of the Christian Religion*, Calvin went so far as to argue that it was the Catholics who were guilty of innovation, while both the Gospel and the tradition of the early church was on the side of the Reformers.[4]

The Reformation had nothing to do with freedom of thought or freedom of conscience. When Guillaume Farel persuaded Calvin to remain in Geneva at the request of the town council in 1536, the two men drew up a detailed confession of faith to which they expected all the townspeople to swear allegiance. The town council backed them, but their demand was met with widespread hostility among the inhabitants. The people of Geneva thought that in choosing the Reformation they had chosen freedom, and they complained that Calvin was trying to bind their consciences far more tightly than the Roman church had done.[5]

In the famous speech with which he is credited at the Diet of Worms, Luther proclaimed that his conscience was bound by the Bible as much as it had been by the monastic rule:

> I am overcome by the Scriptures I have quoted. My conscience is captive to God's word. To act against conscience is neither safe nor honest. Here I stand: I can do no other.

But what really constrained Luther was his own interpretation of the Bible. The right which he claimed for himself he was unwilling to allow to those who interpreted Scripture in other ways. Calvin, too, made it clear in his *Institution of the Christian Religion* that Christian liberty meant the freedom of the Gospel, the freedom to serve and praise the Lord. Neither Luther nor Calvin was prepared to extend toleration to the Anabaptists and the other radical reformers.

Ironically, for a movement which was in part triggered by anticlericalism and inspired by Luther's doctrine of the priesthood of all believers, the Reformation probably reduced the influence of the laity in the church. The network of religious guilds and the establishment of private chantries and lesser endowments which underpinned the later medieval church gave a surprising amount of control to the laity, who might well be responsible not only for maintaining the fabric and decoration of their church but also for organizing ceremonial and even appointing some of the priests.[6] Ultimately, it was the laity who dictated the distinctive spirituality of the later middle ages, with its emphasis on pilgrimages, miracles, cults of the saints, and the humanity of Christ and his family. All this ended at the Reformation. Hsia has described the process as *desacralisation*.[7] Religious belief was brought back under the control of the professional clergy. The sacred was officially removed from everyday life and replaced by social discipline enforced by the state church.

For the magisterial reformers, the doctrine of the priesthood of all believers did not give every believer the right to establish and preach doctrine or administer the sacraments. They no longer believed that the process of ordination gave the clergy special powers, but they still believed in the importance of a properly trained and appointed ministry. The radical reformers were prepared to allow individual congregations to choose and appoint their ministers, and in many radical congregations lay people could lead the central rituals, the sacraments. Nevertheless, most of them still insisted on the need for identifiable individuals to lead the congregation, to instruct in doctrine and to enforce discipline. It was not until the seventeenth century that groups like the English Society of Friends (the "Quakers") were prepared to dispense with the whole concept of a separate ministry.

Even during periods of persecution, few even of the most radical reformed groups would allow women any degree of influence in the church. Women had had an accepted if secondary rôle in the medieval church. They were not allowed to be ordained, but as midwives they were frequently expected to administer the crucial sacrament of baptism to new-born infants who might be too weak to survive. As nuns they could offer spiritual inspiration and might even exercise a measure of spiritual leadership through their advice and counsel. As members of religious guilds they could influence church life at parochial level. Many parishes had guilds of women responsible for maintaining church lights and parish activities.[8]

Female participation in these aspects of in church life was wiped out by the Reformation. Changing views on the sacraments meant that baptism by midwives was increasingly disapproved of. The medieval framework of intercessory prayer which underpinned both monastic life and parish guilds was swept away. The Reformers drew much of their inspiration from the Biblical letters of St Paul. And Paul had said "It is a shocking thing that a woman should address the congregation . . . A woman must be a learner, listening quietly and with due submission. I do not permit a woman to be a teacher . . . " (1 Corinthians 14:35; 1 Timothy 2:11–12).

There were a few exceptions. The radicals in Zwickau included a number of women who are known to have been active in promoting their beliefs. Mrs Teucher, a follower of the Zwickau radical Thomas Müntzer, admitted when questioned that she had been a preacher. Two of her fellow Anabaptists, Mrs Kratzber and Mrs Vetter, were expelled from Zwickau in 1528, not so much for their beliefs as because they had been converting others.[9] However for most Protestant congregations, certainly those in the Lutheran and Calvinist traditions, the ideal of womanhood was exemplified by women like Luther's own wife Katherine Bora. Herself a former nun, she kept house for Luther and raised his children, and is said to have done her housework on her knees when she was too weak to stand after childbirth. Some of the Radical groups were even more repressive. The Münster Anabaptists saw gender subordination as part of the spiritual order, proclaiming that the authority of the husband over the wife was like Christ's authority over the husband. The Münster experiment in polygamy had practical reasons – too few men in the besieged community – but it was also a powerful demonstration of their belief in patriarchal authority.

Nor was the Reformation necessarily linked with political radicalism or democratic control. The Reformation was not always popular. Ordinary people were generally happy with the action-based piety of medieval Catholicism. It was usually the intellectuals who saw the problems with it. Geneva has become a byword for the rigorously reformed Protestantism which takes its name from Geneva's religious leader Calvin. However, it is worth remembering that Calvin was twice thrown out of Geneva by popular demand, and that he always faced considerable opposition to his ideas from the ordinary people of the city.

It is tempting to read Luther's doctrine of the priesthood of all believers as a blow against the authoritarianism of the medieval church hierarchy. However, the successes of the early Reformers – Zwingli and Bucer as well as Luther – were closely linked with their ability to win over the secular power and to use its support. Princes and town councils alike used the powers that Luther offered them to extend their authority in secular as well as ecclesiastical matters. The Reformation may thus have enhanced the power of *some* of the laity in church and state – but it did so at the expense of wider lay participation.

On the positive side, there was nothing puritanical or killjoy about the early reformers. The Reformation in the Swiss town of Zürich was sparked by an episode in which a group of printers working on an edition of the letters of St Paul ate some sausages during Lent. The academic responsible for the book, Huldrych Zwingli, went on to campaign for the clergy to be allowed to marry, and he himself married his mistress.

Martin Luther had taken his religious vows compelled by his early fear of death and damnation. Prone to depression, he eventually concluded that the devil was to blame and that the devil led people to retreat into isolation and loneliness, making them more vulnerable to the temptation of despair. He therefore decided to fight the devil not with monastic austerity but by seeking company, playing music (he was a competent lutenist and flautist) and by getting married – as he said, "to spite the devil". Clerical marriage was one of the early touchstones of Reformed identity. For some of the earlier reformers marriage was a doctrinaire move, for some it was the result of emotional compulsion; but for Luther, who did not marry until 1525, it seems to have sprung from a conviction of the importance of human contact.

The Genevan leader John Calvin and his followers are traditionally portrayed as ascetic puritans, determined to eradicate all pleasure from life. In fact, Calvin repeatedly stressed that the beauty of nature is given by God the creator for humans to enjoy. Food is meant to taste good; wine is meant to "nourish, refresh, strengthen and gladden". Nor was Calvin a fundamentalist in the modern sense of the word. His attitude to the Biblical story of the creation of the world in six days, for example, was that it was a story designed to convey simple truths to those who could not understand anything more complex.[10]

The Reformation has traditionally been presented as an attack on the deplorable state of the late medieval church. It is debatable, however, how far the Reformation improved conditions, and how far the Reformation itself was responsible for such improvements as took place. Standards of clerical education and discipline were raised, though it was a slow process. The state-controlled churches of Protestant Europe were no better funded than the medieval Catholic church had been, and many parishes were still too poor to attract high-calibre ministers. The disruption of the Reformation was in itself part of the problem. Churches which were devoting much of their energies to propaganda wars against other churches were in no position to educate and inspire their congregations. Meanwhile, the spread of lay education probably had more to do with economic change, and with technological advances like improved printing techniques, than it did with Protestantism. Records of parish visitations in Lutheran Germany repeatedly testify to the extent of lay ignorance. Ordinary people were shockingly ignorant of even the most basic Christian doctrines. None of the church elders in Notenstein in the 1560s could remember the Ten Commandments. In Vierzehen Heiligen, villagers were unable to say who Christ was.[11]

The present survey of Protestant belief and doctrine will necessarily blur many fine distinctions and compress chronological developments. We will consider in turn the main features of Protestant belief and practice: the nature of salvation, the sacraments, rituals and organization of the church, and the response of ordinary people to these changes. We will begin with the Reformers' doctrines of sin and redemption since it was Luther's crisis of belief over his own salvation, and his crisis of conscience over the debased (as he saw it) prospect of redemption being offered to his parishioners, which sparked his initial challenge.

# 1

## Sin and Salvation

Much of the recent historical writing on the Reformation has concentrated on the debate over the alleged shortcomings of the late medieval church, the extent to which it served or failed to serve the needs of the majority of the population, and the extent to which the spiritual lives of ordinary people were affected by the changes of the sixteenth century. For many of the early reformers, this would have been to mistake the incidentals for the central issue. Martin Luther was initially a loyal member of the Catholic church, a monk who taught theology in a fairly traditional university. He had no fundamental quarrel with the personnel or administration of the church. At the outset, his concerns were entirely theological. Even later in his life, when he was more prepared to attack the life and morals of the Catholic church, he insisted that moral reform was useless without reform of doctrine.[1] He had reached the inescapable conclusion that what some representatives of the church were teaching about the way to attain salvation was wrong. In order to understand why, it is necessary to understand how Christians regard sin, and what they mean by salvation. It will also be necessary to look in some detail at the way in which the medieval church dealt with sin and its consequences in order to understand why Luther's ideas met with such opposition.

### The medieval doctrine of salvation

For the Christian, sin is not an act: it is a state of being. The medieval church explained it with the Biblical story of Adam, Eve and the apple. The first humans lived in Paradise, but were forbidden to eat the fruit of the tree of knowledge of good and evil. The Devil tempted Eve, who gave the fruit to her husband Adam. Humans thus became aware of sin, and could not escape its consequence, which was damnation. The resulting fall from grace – the Fall – led to original sin, the state of sin from which individual sins flow.

The Jewish faith, in which Christianity was rooted, had a strong concept of sacrifice and atonement. However, no human sacrifice could really compensate for original sin, since humans were already flawed by original sin. The solution which Christianity offers for this problem is to postulate a human being, Jesus Christ, who is also God. He shares human nature and human temptations but is nevertheless perfect. He can therefore provide a sacrifice which is capable of paying for all human sin. This is what happens in the Biblical account of the Crucifixion. Through Christ's atonement, God and sinful humanity can be reconciled. Although humans are still sinful, they can as a result of Christ's sacrifice be saved. They are made righteous in God's sight and can thus engage in a right relationship with him. It is this process of being made righteous and entering into a right relationship with God which is summed up in the word "justification".

Where the Christian denominations differ (and where Christian doctrine has varied over time) is on the question of how humans can take advantage of that one atoning sacrifice – how they can be justified. The doctrine of the early church, exemplified in the letters of St Paul and the writings of Augustine of Hippo, was that human nature was too damaged by the Fall to be able to work towards salvation. Salvation could come only from God's free gift of grace. The alternative was the idea put forward by Pelagius, that fallen humanity could still deserve to be saved by its own acts. This was denounced by Augustine as heresy. However, Augustine's doctrine left the individual sinner with no guidance on how to live a Christian life. The consensus in the late medieval church, in practice if not in theory, was that fallible humans should do their best – *quod in se est* was the Latin phrase – and that God in his grace had promised that he would accept their efforts and make up their deficiencies.

There was still room for debate over how far God's initial grace was necessary in order to enable humans to do their best, and how far humans, sinful though they were, could cooperate in the process of salvation. The councils of the early church had failed to provide a theologically watertight definition of justification, the process of reconciliation following Christ's sacrifice. By the late medieval period, opinions were so diverse as to lead writers like Alister McGrath to talk of a crisis of authority on the subject.[2] The majority still adhered to the covenant theory: the view that God had promised to bestow grace on all those who did their best. But an increasing minority – many of them members of the Augustinian religious order which Luther himself joined – considered that humans were too depraved to be able to help themselves. For these theologians, God's grace was necessary *before* the sinner could be justified.

However, while the professional theologians developed their different schools of thought, most of them agreed that academic debate should not threaten the unity and authority of the Church. Furthermore, there was a tacit agreement that the Augustinian doctrine of justification only through God's grace was unhelpful in the pastoral context. Offering no guidance on right behaviour, it could lead to despair and the rejection of the moral codes which bound society together.

What the medieval church offered lay people was a framework within which the consequences of original sin were partly removed by the sacrament of baptism, the ritual washing of a young baby (or in unusual cases an adult) with consecrated water. The individual would nevertheless continue to sin. These sins were dealt with by the forgiveness which God channelled through the church. Sins were confessed before a priest who was then empowered to pronounce God's absolution. The sinner was required to be truly penitent; and penitence and the willingness to repent, in theory, required divine grace. However, authors of practical books of guidance on counselling and confession suggested that the sinner who did not experience perfect sorrow or contrition, but who nevertheless went to confession in accordance with God's commands, would then be helped to forgiveness by divine grace.

Absolution was only part of the process. The sinner was also required to make recompense for the sin. This might involve a practical remedy for the consequences of a sin which affected another person – restoring the stolen goods, mending the broken fences, marrying the pregnant girl. But sin was first and foremost an offence against God, so recompense was offered to God by penitential acts. These could range from the repetition of a sequence of prayers to a barefoot pilgrimage to the Holy Land. As it was reasonable to make financial recompense to the earthly victims of sin, so it seemed reasonable that recompense to God might be financial – by paying for candles in a church, for the repair of a church building, for the building of a new church.

Penance not done in the sinner's lifetime would have to be undergone after death, in a place of torment called Purgatory, a sort of little Hell but for a finite period of time. The Church claimed the right to remit time in Purgatory, offering "indulgences" which did not remove the need for confession and contrition but reduced the time which had to be spent in Purgatory making recompense for sin. Again, it seemed reasonable to allow the families of the deceased to buy indulgences on behalf of their dead relatives. Thus it was that, by steps each of which seemed logical and necessary, the medieval church reached the situation in which remission of the penalties of sin was up for sale to the highest bidder. From this it was only a short step to the sale of absolution itself: the distinction between remission of sins and remission of penalties was easy to blur and to misunderstand.

The idea of doing one's best, *quod in se est*, had its own inherent weaknesses. Orthodox medieval theologians like Gabriel Biel said quite explicitly that it was impossible for anyone to know that they had done enough to attain God's grace. The doctrine satisfied the majority of the laity but offered no reassurance to over-scrupulous penitents, over-whelmed with guilt and anxiety. This was the situation in which the Italian humanist Gasparo Contarini found himself when, in 1510, a number of his fellow-scholars from Padua entered the hermitage of Camaldoli in search of salvation through an ascetic monastic life. Contarini had no monastic vocation and despaired of finding salvation through his own efforts. It was a priest to whom he spoke on the evening before Easter Sunday in 1511 who convinced him that Christ's sacrifice had made satisfaction for all human sins. Contarini's description of his revelation sounds almost uncannily like Martin Luther's account of his own spiritual discovery later in the decade.

> Even if I did all the penances possible, and many more besides, they would not be enough to atone for my past sins, let alone to merit salvation . . . [Christ's] suffering is sufficient, and more than sufficient, as a satisfaction for sins committed . . . Through this thought, I changed from great fear and anguish to happiness. I began to turn with my whole heart to this greatest good which I saw, for love of me, on the cross, his arms open and his breast opened right up to his heart. . . . He was quick to accept me and to permit his Father to totally cancel the debt which I had contracted and which I was incapable of satisfying myself.[3]

The language with its emphasis on Christ's open wound is the language of medieval mysticism and even harks back to Bernard of Clairvaux's famous sermon on the Crucifix, but the basic thinking on salvation is that of the Reformation.[4]

Contarini was not the only intellectual to reach this conclusion in the years before Martin Luther did. In England, John Colet was empha-sizing the need for faith as a precondition for love of God and the overwhelming importance of Christ's part in the saving of sinners.[5] The French humanist Lefèvre d'Étaples, whose editions of the Psalms and the letters of St Paul were the basic texts for Luther's lectures, was clearly aware of Paul's teachings on the supreme importance of faith in the spiritual life. In Italy, the movement which has been called "Evangelism" stressed the importance of personal salvation. In retrospect, it seems as though the pendulum was beginning to swing back towards faith in Christ's sole sacrifice – as far as the intellectuals were concerned.

## Martin Luther's theological breakthrough

The future reformer Martin Luther was thus part of a growing trend when, as a young monk, he realized that he could find no assurance of salvation in the rigorous performance of the austerities of the monastic lifestyle. Historians of the Reformation are still divided over the precise path by which he came to his rediscovery of the doctrine of divine grace, or the exact time at which he reached it. Like many an academic, he seems to have reached a new understanding of his subject by explaining it to his students. As professor of biblical studies at the new university of Wittenberg, he lectured on a series of books of the Bible – the Psalms and the epistles to the Romans, Galatians and Hebrews. It was during the preparation of these lectures that he reached his theological breakthrough. From seeing the righteousness of God as a threat of condemnation and punishment, he came to interpret it as the righteousness which God gives to sinful humans.

Luther's famous account of his revelation in the preface to his first volume of Latin writings probably telescopes the chronology of the process: we are dealing with his recollections of a sequence of events some thirty years previously. However, the outline of his change of interpretation is clear.

> I hated that word "righteousness of God", which, according to the use and custom of all the teachers, I had been taught to understand philosophically, regarding the formal or active righteousness, as they called it, with which God is righteous and punishes the unrighteous sinner.
>
> Though I lived as a monk without reproach, I felt that I was a sinner before God with an extremely disturbed conscience. I could not believe that he was placated by my satisfaction. I did not love, yes, I hated the righteous God who punishes sinners . . .

At last, by the mercy of God, meditating day and night, I gave heed to the context of the words, namely "In it the righteousness of God is revealed, as it is written, 'He who through faith is righteous shall live'". There I began to understand that the righteousness of God is that by which the righteous lives by the gift of God, namely by faith. And this is the meaning: the righteousness of God is revealed by the gospel, namely the passive righteousness, with which the merciful God justifies us by faith, as it is written, "He who through faith is righteous, shall live". Here I felt that I was altogether born again and had entered Paradise itself through open gates ... and I extolled my sweetest word with a love as great as the hatred with which I had before hated the word "righteousness of God". Thus that place in Paul was for me truly the gate to Paradise.[6]

This, then, was one of the defining beliefs of the Protestant Reformation: that sinful humanity is totally unable to do anything about its sinfulness, but that God in his infinite mercy has wiped the slate clean. It is what the Protestant means by the crucial concept of justification. To be justified is to be (or to become) virtuous in God's eyes, in order to be able to enter into a right relationship with him. For Luther and those who came after him, it was not only wrong but blasphemous to suggest that any amount of human effort could make anyone virtuous in God's eyes. Only God himself could do that. All that humans had to do – all that humans could do – was to have faith in God's forgiveness.

Here it is necessary to say something about the specifically Christian meaning of the word "faith". Faith is not just belief. As Luther himself said, in his book on the basic statement of belief of the Church, the Apostles' Creed:

There are two ways of believing. First, our belief may be about God, as is the case when I accept what is said about him, in the same way as I accept what is said about the Turks, or the devil or hell. This kind of believing is not faith, so much as a sort of knowledge, or the taking note of something. In the other hand, we may believe in God. This is the case when I do not merely accept what is said about God, but I put my faith in him, I surrender myself to him, I venture to enter into association with him, believing without any hesitation that he will be to me and act towards me just as we are taught he will. This is not the form of my belief in regard to the Turks, or mankind in general, no matter how high their repute. It is easy for me to believe that a certain person is good: but I do not, on this account, build on him as my foundation. The kind of faith which dares to accept what is said of God, even if doing so means risking life or death, is the faith which alone makes a man a Christian; through it, all his desires are satisfied by God.[7]

There was nothing new about these ideas. As the above account makes clear, Luther had found his new interpretation of God's saving righteousness in the Bible, in the letters of St Paul. He found supporting arguments for it in the writings of St Augustine of Hippo, the saint credited with founding the religious order to which Luther belonged. Augustine's ideas were still current among academic theologians, particularly among those of the Augustinian order.[8] However, few scholars had access to Augustine's complete works. His ideas were known from the extracts from them which were found in collections of patristic texts. Furthermore, spurious texts had been added to these which claimed to be by Augustine but in fact ran counter to his thinking.

In October 1516, Luther chaired the disputation at which his pupil Bartholomäus Bernhardi defended his doctoral thesis. In outlining his thesis, Bernhardi attacked the idea that humans can fulfil God's commands by their own reason and strength. This idea derived from a treatise *De vera et falsa poenitentia* which was claimed to be by Augustine. Bernhardi and Luther disputed the attribution on the grounds that it ran counter to Augustine's authenticated writings. Andreas Bodenstein von Karlstadt, the dean of the faculty of theology at Wittenberg, was initially outraged by Bernhardi's claims. It was not until January of the following year that he was able to go to the Leipzig book fair and acquire a copy of the new humanist edition of Augustine's collected works (probably the Paris edition of 1515). Reading this book convinced Karlstadt of the validity of Luther and Bernhardi's arguments. From an opponent, he then became one of Luther's most stalwart supporters, eventually outstripping him in the radicalism of his ideas. In April of that year, 1517, he set out 151 theses defending the Augustinian doctrine of redemption and justification, and he subsequently lectured on the subject at Wittenberg.

Luther's breakthrough is thus best described as a rediscovery of Paul and Augustine's doctrine of justification. Luther further developed Augustine's ideas on God's righteousness. While Augustine suggested that sinful humans might nevertheless possess a righteousness which could assist and complement God's righteousness, Luther insisted that human righteousness was so flawed by sin that it was bound to be in contradiction to God's true righteousness. Nevertheless, Luther's basic doctrine was essentially that of St Augustine (and St Paul): true repentance was the product of God's justifying grace, and without that grace no repentance was possible.

What was different about Luther's revelation was the use he made of it. While his fellow-Augustinians had been prepared to treat the doctrine of justifying grace as a matter for academic debate, Luther saw it in terms of his pastoral responsibility to the parishioners of the Wittenberg churches in his care. For Luther, their reliance on prayers to the saints, pilgrimages and indulgences to save their souls was not only ineffectual, it was actively wrong. They were claiming for themselves a power which belonged only to God. His first challenge was in the form of a series of proposals for an academic debate on the doctrine of salvation and the inability of the individual to become good by his or her own efforts. He sent these proposals to the universities of Erfurt and Nuremberg but no notice was taken of them. Some weeks later, in October 1517, he drew up a further series of ninety-five proposals for a debate on the sale of indulgences. He may or may not have pinned these up on the church door at Wittenberg: it would have been a perfectly natural way to initiate a debate if he did. He had in any case preached on the subject on the Eve of All Saints in the previous year.

Luther's action was thus part of a long-term process of intellectual development. It was, however, triggered by a purely circumstantial situation. The Pope was offering an indulgence – an offer of time off from the pains of Purgatory – to raise money for the rebuilding of St Peter's Church in Rome. Luther discovered that his parishioners were buying indulgences and believing that this, rather than true faith, would save them. His feeling of responsibility for their spiritual welfare persuaded him to take the debate over salvation out of the academic environment and into the streets of Wittenberg.

As with his more general arguments on the doctrine of salvation, these ninety-five theses were initially ignored by the church. It was only when he published a German sermon on the same subject that his archbishop panicked and reported the matter to Rome, and it was a year before he was called to Augsburg to give an account of himself. He returned from Augsburg to his teaching post and took part in further debates on his ideas, backed by colleagues including Karlstadt. It was not until 1521 that the church took him seriously enough to make any serious attempt to silence him.

As Luther differed from his academic colleagues in the way he treated the doctrine of justifying grace as a matter of concern for ordinary people, so he differed from them in the way he dealt with disciplinary action from the church hierarchy. He refused to back down. Instead, he developed the implications of his basic ideas further and became more explicit in the way he expressed them. He was excommunicated in 1521 and spent much of the following year in hiding. By the mid-1520s he had published a series of books in German attacking the church for its perversion of the Gospel and calling on the German nobility to reform it. He translated the Bible into German and wrote catechisms for those who needed more basic instruction. His ideas on Biblical interpretation, the sacraments of the church and the relationship between the church and the secular state were fundamental to the development of Protestant belief and practice. However, for Luther, and thus for the early Reformers, their defining idea was the doctrine of justification by faith alone.

## Zwingli and the early Swiss reformers

The Zürich priest Huldrych Zwingli arrived at a similar conclusion about the primacy of faith in salvation but from a rather different starting-point. His first concern was with the multiplicity of observances which were imposed by the church in the name of salvation – prayers, rituals, restrictions on eating, restrictions on sexual activity. Zwingli's initial conclusion was that these observances might be useful but they were not necessary: they had to proceed from personal decision and commitment rather than compulsion. It was the faith which led to these actions which was important. He went on to develop this argument into a more systematic criticism of the rituals which the church imposed on believers. For Zwingli, the only binding observances were those which God asked for in the Bible. Anything else was a human invention, and to depend on human inventions was idolatry. "It is false religion or piety when trust is put in any other than God. They, then, who trust in any created thing whatsoever are not truly pious."[9] True religion "is that which clings to the one and only God".[10]

The trigger for Zwingli's declaration of faith was even more circumstantial than Luther's. Zwingli was a gifted humanist scholar who had studied Hebrew as well as Greek and corresponded with the great Erasmus. Like many scholars of the time, he maintained himself by working as a priest. He had already encountered the debate over indulgences and the commercialization of salvation. In 1517, he was parish priest at Einseideln, to the south of Zürich. The indulgence for the rebuilding of St Peter's in Rome was being sold around the diocese of Constance with the same high-pressure techniques that Luther had protested against in Wittenberg. Zwingli still accepted the theology of penance and the idea of Purgatory, but he was also aware of the importance of true contrition and confession as the precondition for absolution. He saw no need for a major debate on the subject, but he was probably one of those who simply excluded the indulgence-sellers from Einsiedeln.[11]

In 1519, Zwingli moved to become stipendiary priest at the Great Minster in the Swiss city of Zürich. He was appointed mainly because of his gifts as a preacher, and he spent his first few years there preaching on the Bible, working his way methodically through the Gospel accounts of the life of Christ, the history of the early church and the letters of St Paul and the other apostles, then back to the Old Testament. Zwingli's systematic approach to Bible study was not new: it derived from the earlier work of humanists such as Erasmus, but it was to become typical of the Reformation.

In the spring of 1522, Zwingli was working on a new edition of the Biblical letters of St Paul, which he wanted to publish in time for the Frankfurt book fair. This involved working in close collaboration with his printer, Christopher Froschauer. One evening, after a day's hard work on the printing press, he and Froschauer shared an evening meal with Froschauer's small workforce. The meal included a dish of sausages. The problem was that it was during Lent, the season of austerity just before Easter in the Christian calendar. They were reported to the city council and Froschauer was fined.

Under normal circumstances, that would have been the end of the matter. However, Zwingli decided to take it further. His study of the Bible had made him increasingly concerned about the multiplicity of restrictions which the Catholic church imposed on human behaviour, and the ease with which these restrictions could then be eased for a fee. Apparently, he did not eat the famous sausages himself. He did however go into print in defence of those who had, arguing that fasting should be a matter of personal choice. He had no disagreement with abstention as such: what he opposed was the action of the Church in enforcing abstention on everyone. In a short book, *Von Erkiesen und Freiheit der Speisen* ("Of Choice and Freedom in Food"),[12] he argued that there was no Biblical justification for imposing abstinence at particular seasons of the year. The restrictions of the Old Testament have been superseded by the new law of the Gospel, which is based not on human actions but on faith and love. The New Testament explicitly says that all the food which God has given is good (Zwingli was referring particularly to St Peter's dream in Acts 10:10–16 and to St Paul's letter to the Corinthians, 1 Cor. 6:12–14). While those who have decided to fast must be respected, the church should not impose fasts on those who do not feel called to abstain.

On a more practical level, Zwingli pointed out that many of the restrictions which the Church was imposing – such as abstention from eggs and dairy produce – were comparatively recent. And how could eating animal produce in Lent be inherently sinful when the church was so ready to allow it in return for money?

Zwingli based his arguments on the Bible, and when he was challenged by the Catholic church it was to the Bible that he appealed. "Nothing, therefore, of ours is to be added to the Word of God, and nothing taken from his Word by rashness of ours."[13] His insistence on the primacy of the Bible as the arbiter in matters of belief as well as conduct led him to challenge some of the other restrictions which the Church placed on human behaviour. Since the Gregorian reforms of the eleventh century, the western church had required all its clergy to be celibate. Members of religious orders had to obey even stricter rules which laid down every detail of their daily routine – rising in the night to pray, spending their days in singing church services, study and spiritual work, eating (in theory at least) an austere diet, owning nothing of their own. This austere lifestyle was thought to confer a special holiness on them. Their prayers were believed to be particularly effective, and they had particular access to divine grace.

Zwingli had already admitted publicly that he was completely unable to keep his priestly vows of celibacy.[14] He persuaded the city authorities to legalize clerical marriage in defiance of the Catholic church, and he himself married his current partner Anna Reinhart shortly before the birth of their child. He also insisted that the monastic lifestyle was a hypocritical sham which could not possibly confer special spiritual powers on its members. What mattered was not outward restrictions and a supposedly austere lifestyle but the faith of the individual Christian in Christ's sacrifice.

## Imparted and imputed righteousness

For some of the more radical reformers, Luther and Zwingli's doctrine of redemption was enough. Once saved by faith in God's sacrifice, they believed they were no longer sinners. God had given them his own righteousness. This idea is technically known as the doctrine of *imparted* righteousness: God imparts his righteousness to the sinner, who becomes holy.

For Luther and the "magisterial" reformers, however, justification did not remove the human tendency to sin. Justification, the renewal of a right relationship with God, was a process originating outside the

sinner. It was variously described as "extrinsic" and "alien". The righteousness it gave to the sinner was *imputed* righteousness. Christ's
redeeming sacrifice was credited or imputed to the sinner and removed
his or her own guilt. The individual's sinfulness was not removed, but
it was forgiven; no account would henceforth be taken of it. What
sinners could not do by their flawed and ineffectual attempts at goodness, by the righteousness of the world, God did by clothing the sinner
in his own true righteousness.

Luther's young colleague Philip Melanchthon described the process
of justification as a "forensic act", something akin to a legal process. As
a result, his theology of salvation has been termed *forensic justification*.
This interpretation of the process of justification in terms of a court of
law was vividly dramatized by the theologian Andreas Musculus:

> Christ steps into the courtroom, motions to the sinner to approach him,
> bends down, lifts him upon his shoulders and carries him pickaback to his
> father. First he turns to the sinner. "*Confide fili*", he says; " be of good
> cheer! I shall plead with our father on your behalf as earnestly and devot-
> edly as if your cause were my own". Next, he speaks to God. "Father",
> he says, "here is a poor sinner who has turned to me prayerfully, seeking
> counsel and succour. He has reminded me of the love I have shown the
> world by dying and rising again in obedience to your command. I beg you
> now to continue to help him, as you have assisted him in the past and,
> when the time comes, to perfect him with your righteousness". And to
> this God the Father replies: "My dearest son, I am well pleased with you.
> You have paid for this sinner with your own obedience, having fully satis-
> fied all my demands. I can refuse you nothing. Go, take him with you."[15]

Like Luther and his followers, Calvin saw the righteousness of the
world as totally alien to God's righteousness:

> They who seriously, and as in God's sight, will seek after the true rule of
> righteousness, will certainly find that all human works, if judged
> according to their own worth, are nothing but filth and defilement. And
> what is commonly reckoned righteousness is before God sheer iniquity;
> what is judged uprightness, pollution; what is accounted glory,
> ignominy.[16]

For Luther, Calvin and their co-believers, justification did lead to sanctification, but by a much slower process. Freed by God's gift of
righteousness from their terror of sin and its consequences, humans
were regenerated, born again into a new life. It was only after this that
they were able properly to repent their sins. Contrition was not the

means of justification: contrition followed grace and justification. Only then were Christians free to do willingly what they had been unable to do when the moral code of the church commanded it.[17] Sanctification was a gradual change, described by Calvin as the process by which God

> wipes out in his elect the corruptions of the flesh, cleanses them of guilt, consecrates them to himself as temples, renewing all their minds to true purity that they may practice repentance all their lives and know that this warfare will end only at death.[18]

The regenerate were then able to begin to follow God's law willingly, from the heart.

For most of the reformers, the process of regeneration was always partial and incomplete. They could not accept the radicals' claim that, once justified, humans had been saved once and for all and could no longer sin. This ran counter to Luther's own experience: he described himself as *always* a sinner – but always justified. Other reformers also insisted that in spite of their spiritual rebirth, humans remained sinful, unable to deserve God's approval or to do good by their own powers. The prayers which Cranmer wrote for the English Book of Common Prayer return again and again to this theme:

> Almighty God, who seest that we have no power of ourselves to help ourselves . . . (2nd Sunday in Lent);
> . . . because through the weakness of our mortal nature we can do no good thing without thee, grant us the help of thy grace, that in keeping thy commandments we may please thee; (1st Sunday after Trinity)
> O God, forasmuch as without thee, we are not able to please thee; Mercifully grant that thy Holy Spirit may in all things direct and rule our hearts. (19th Sunday after Trinity)

The Reformers insisted that the regenerate would want to do good, but not because they wanted to be saved. They would do good *because they were already saved*. It was this willingness to do good which reassured Protestants that they were in fact sure of salvation. The doctrine of justification by faith was reassuring to those who were confident of their faith, but faith is less tangible than the accumulation of penitential acts and indulgences.

There were weaknesses in Luther's position. On the one hand, it was vulnerable to the argument of the antinomian wing of the radical Reformation. If the regenerate want to do good because they have been saved by God's grace, then what the regenerate want must be good.

Against the arguments of the radicals, the more moderate reformers were able to appeal to the moral code enshrined in the Bible. However, Luther's insistence that we are saved only by God's righteousness and that our own actions are totally irrelevant nevertheless threatened the rules of conduct which underpinned society. Luther's colleague and follower Melanchthon was acutely aware of this, and constantly stressed the need for obedience to the moral code as well as faith. On the other hand, if the willingness to do good was a sign of salvation, there was a danger that Protestants would be encouraged to do good works simply to prove to themselves that they were saved. A Protestant doctrine of good works could thus emerge as a counterpart to the Catholic one.

Lutheran preachers and teachers had to steer a careful course along the narrow line which separated over-emphasis on humanity's helpless sinfulness and over-reliance on God's promise of salvation. Catechisms and prayers used regular repetition to hammer home the message of human depravity:

> *Question*: Tell me, what have you learned from the Ten Commandments?
> *Answer*: I have learned from them that we lead a damnable sinful life and that God cannot find a single good thing in us. For the Ten Commandments are the book of our vices and the record of our disgrace . . . [19]

> We acknowledge and bewail our manifold sins and wickedness, which we from time to time most grievously have committed, by thought, word and deed . . . The remembrance of them is grievous unto us, the burden of them is intolerable . . . [20]

but these were always followed by the assurance of God's forgiveness for all those who turned to him in faith.

## Predestination

There was always a danger that faith would become something which the Christian tried to achieve, and would be regarded as a "good work". Luther and Zwingli both stressed that faith came from God – "the pledge and seal with which God seals our hearts . . . the work of the Spirit in the believer". For Bucer, too, God "gives us this conviction and undoubting confidence". "Everything is to be attributed to divine goodness, and nothing to our merit".[21] But if faith comes from God, and if God's grace is irresistible, why does he not give the gift of faith to everyone? Why are all people not saved?

The answer which some of the Reformers were compelled to give to this question is one of the most difficult doctrines of the Reformation. If faith comes only from God, and if faith is not given to all, then God must have chosen to give faith to some and not to others. Thus, effectively, he has chosen to save some people and to damn others. This doctrine, known as *predestination*, is frequently attributed to Calvin but is inherent in the thinking of some of the earlier reformers. Luther and those who followed him most closely continued to emphasize the freedom of the human will and to argue that the doctrine of predestination effectively made God responsible for evil and human sin. However, as early as 1523, the Strasbourg reformer Martin Bucer was prepared to divide all humanity into the *elect*, those who God had already chosen for salvation, and the damned or *reprobate*. He later made clear that this separation took place before birth. It could have nothing to do with human actions or human goodness. Salvation was entirely dependent on God's free choice, made before the foundation of the world.[22]

The logic of predestination is inescapable but the conclusion is difficult to reconcile with the idea of an all-loving, merciful God. Like so much Protestant teaching on sin and salvation it derives ultimately from the thought of St Augustine. When Bucer and Calvin confronted this spiritual stumbling-block they were forced to fall back on the inscrutability of God's purposes:

> The judgements of God are a great abyss, they are inscrutable but just. For the Lord is just in all his ways, even where to our reason he seems otherwise.[23]

> But why one and not the other? This means much to me. It is an abyss, the depth of the cross. I can exclaim in wonder; I cannot demonstrate it through disputation.[24]

Calvin insisted that, though this state of affairs might seem unjust to humans, human reasoning had been perverted by the Fall and could not comprehend God's justice. Calvin repeatedly emphasized the infinite majesty of God, his incomprehensible greatness and purity. His justice was like his love, beyond human understanding. We cannot judge God by our earthly notions of justice. What God decrees *is* just, precisely because God has decreed it. After all, as Calvin reminded his readers, it was an expression of God's amazing mercy that some humans would be saved, since they were all totally depraved and deserved to be damned.[25]

Calvin's forbidding doctrine was the orthodoxy of many of the sixteenth-century Protestant churches. While Luther himself could not accept it, it was the inevitable corollary of his doctrine of grace and faith and was a fundamental part of the thinking of other early reformers in the Lutheran tradition like Bucer. This was yet another of the areas where they had left the liberal humanists behind; for Erasmus had always believed in the freedom of the human will. Even the Church of England was dominated by predestinarians in the sixteenth century, though by the early seventeenth century there were some Anglican theologians prepared to challenge the doctrine. Cranmer was in his mature years a predestinarian and tried hard to incorporate it into the doctrinal formulae of the 1540s. He was aware of the difficulties inherent in the doctrine and never made it explicit in his Prayer Books. However, it is enshrined in the Thirty-Nine Articles of 1562, which are still in theory the basic doctrinal statement of the Church of England. Article 17 states that

> Predestination to life is the everlasting purpose of God, whereby (before the foundations of the world were laid) he hath constantly decreed by his counsel secret to us, to deliver from curse and damnation those whom he hath chosen in Christ out of mankind and to bring them by Christ to everlasting salvation.[26]

This is predestination in its most extreme form, the idea that God knew before the Fall that Adam would sin and had already decided what to do about it and who to save. (The technical term is *prelapsarian* – "before the Fall".)

The Thirty-Nine Articles describe predestination as "full of sweet, pleasant and unspeakable comfort to godly people" while admitting that "for curious and carnal persons, lacking the spirit of Christ, to have continually before their eyes the sentence of God's Predestination, is a most dangerous downfall, whereby the Devil doth thrust them either into desperation, or into wretchlessness of most unclean living, no less perilous than desperation". This was the problem which Cranmer foresaw and which the Reformers had to contend with. The remorseless logic of predestination suggested that while some were chosen for heavenly bliss, others had already been rejected and destined for eternal torment. They had no incentive to live a Christian life, and every reason to reject the moral code of society.

The solution to this conundrum turned the medieval doctrine of salvation on its head. People were not saved because they were good; they were good because they had been chosen to be saved. This of course gave the believers a great incentive to be good and to try to convince themselves that they were good because they wanted to be – that (as the

39 Articles said) "they feel in themselves the working of the Spirit of Christ, mortifying the works of the flesh and their earthly members, and drawing up their mind to high and heavenly things".

A logical and satisfying solution: but it still left the problem of dealing with those who had not been chosen for salvation. For the radical reformers, this was easy. Their concept of the true church was of a community of saved believers, so those who were predestined to damnation could be excluded. For the magisterial reformers, whose churches had to cater for the needs of the whole community, it was not so simple. Their solution drew on the Biblical parable of the wheat and the tares. Jesus told a story about a farmer who sowed a field of wheat. The wheat grew mixed with weeds and the weeds could not be destroyed without destroying the growing wheat. But at harvest time the weeds could be pulled up and only the grain was taken into store. The magisterial reformers argued that it was impossible to tell who God had chosen for salvation. A man could sin all his life and still be saved at the last. Therefore the church would contain both the saved and the reprobate and had to be able to deal with both. It was the duty of the Christian magistrate to control the reprobate so that their behaviour did not give offence to the godly.

For Calvin, however, salvation was not the central doctrine of Christianity. When Cardinal Jacopo Sadoleto wrote to the Genevans urging them to return to the Catholic fold, the Genevans asked Calvin to reply. Sadoleto's letter was based on the assumption that our main objective in life is to achieve salvation. Calvin took issue with this, arguing that the primary function of any human being is not the saving of their soul but the glory of God.[27] An even simpler definition of the main aim of human life appeared in his 1545 catechism, a question-and-answer summary of the faith for basic teaching. The first question in the catechism is "What is the main aim in human life?" and the answer was "To know God".[28] For Calvin, therefore, salvation was not the logical beginning of the Christian experience. Elsewhere, though, he described justification, the process by which the sinner's guilt was set aside, as "the main hinge on which religion turns".[29]

The most extreme position on this doctrine was outlined at the Synod of Dort in the Netherlands in 1618–19. The Dutch pastor and academic Jacob Arminius had proposed a radical revision of the Calvinist doctrine of salvation. His argument was based on the belief that Christ had died for all, not only for the predestinate. Therefore, we must have some element of free choice in responding to God's offer of salvation. The necessary implication is that those who have been saved can fall from grace, and that God in his omniscience must be able to foretell who will respond to his call.

Arminius's overturning of traditional Calvinist teaching was discussed and rejected by the Synod at Dordrecht. Instead, the delegates to the Synod restated the doctrine of predestination in the most uncompromising terms, proposing the following five principles:

1. Total depravity: humans are completely corrupt and have no free will to accept or reject salvation
2. Unconditional election: God's choice is not based on human response
3. Limited atonement: Christ died only for the elect
4. Irresistible grace: once an individual has been chosen, they cannot resist
5. Perseverance of the saints: once they have been chosen, they cannot fall from grace.

(The initials TULIP provide a handy mnemonic in English.)

## Sin and salvation in the thinking of the radical reformers

Predestination was thus one of the basic doctrines of the Swiss or Calvinist Reformation, and was also accepted by most Lutherans. For many of the radical reformers, though, the doctrine of predestination was unacceptable because it ran counter to an even more fundamental Christian doctrine, that Christ died for all humankind. Andreas Karlstadt was convinced by Luther's arguments that salvation came through God's grace rather than human works. However, as early as 1520 he was uneasy about Luther's neglect of the moral aspects of reform. "Beware," he warned, "that you do not take a paper and loveless faith for the greatest work."[30] Karlstadt's complex spiritual journey involved an initial acceptance of the logic of predestination. He eventually rejected it in favour of a God who is fair and merciful in human as well as divine terms. Instead, he suggested that God offered his righteousness to all sinful humans, but that he also gave us the ability to choose. To believe otherwise, he argued, was to claim that God is the cause of evil.[31]

It is difficult to summarize the ideas on salvation of the radical reformers. There were many different groups, and in the absence of any central structure or guidance they were able to develop ideas which seem to us extreme and strange. For example, the Hutterites, a German group of spiritualist Anabaptists, described the process of salvation in terms reminiscent of late medieval mysticism. Salvation begins with the Light, which shines on all people but is rejected by most of them. Those who accept the Light also accept a personal cross, a willingness to suffer as Jesus suffered. This stage involves a personal descent into Hell and a sense of abandonment very similar to the "dark night of the soul" described by the Carmelite friar St John of the Cross.

Here as in other ways the spiritual Anabaptists are closer to Catholic mysticism than to the austerity of magisterial Protestantism. For the Hutterites, though, the consequence of their spiritual suffering and enlightenment was different. Physical and spiritual punishment, they believed, would bring them to a state of constant righteousness, in which they were no longer subject to temptation. Then they would receive the grace of the Holy Spirit, the "oil of gladness" of Psalm 45 and the Letter to the Hebrews. This would make them ready to endure torture and martyrdom and to enter into the heavenly Jerusalem.[32]

There are however some general themes which feature in the thinking of most of the radical reformers:

1. Christ died for the salvation of all human kind.
2. Salvation was a matter of personal choice.
3. Salvation entailed separation from the world.

Both Luther and Zwingli considered that the thinking of the radical reformers on salvation came dangerously close to the "works-right-eousness" of the Catholics. This was the idea that human actions could contribute to salvation, and as we have already seen, the idea that human actions cannot influence God was the one thing on which virtually all the magisterial reformers agreed. In his *Refutation of the Tricks of the Anabaptists* Zwingli argued that Anabaptism, by emphasizing the importance of the human decision to seek baptism, detracted from the significance of Christ's atoning sacrifice and was effectively as bad as the pride and hypocrisy of the monks of the Catholic church.[33] In one of his outbursts against his former colleague Karlstadt, Luther too accused the radicals of being little or no better than the Pope and his followers.

> Is not this to slander Christ? Is not this to deny Christ? Is not this to set oneself in Christ's place, and in Christ's name to murder souls, bind consciences, burden with sins, make laws, and in short, so to deal with

souls as if one were their God? . . . For this same reason, we have shown
the Pope to be the Antichrist, in that he infringes on such freedom with
laws, where Christ would have freedom. And my factious spirit [i.e.
Karlstadt] blunders up the same way. He would make captive what Christ
would have free.[34]

Whether or not they had been able to do anything to contribute to
their own salvation, some of the more extreme radical reformers
believed that once they had been saved they were no longer capable of
sin. According to their own fellow-believers, these *antinomians* (those
who believed that the moral law is not binding on Christians in a state
of grace)

have missed the truth and to their condemnation are given over to the
lasciviousness and self-indulgence of the flesh. They think faith and love
may do and permit everything, and that nothing will harm them or
condemn them, since they are believers.[35]

The Schleitheim Articles, the basic confession of faith of the Radical
Reformation, were in fact drawn up to deal with the ideas of this
extremist group.[36]

## Popular ideas on sin and salvation

So far, we have been considering how scholars and trained theologians
dealt with the complexities of the relationship between God and sinful
humanity. But if we are to assess the impact of the Reformation on
sixteenth-century society, it is necessary to consider how, and how far,
these new ideas were accepted by the majority of ordinary people. There
are practical problems in doing this. For the ideas of the theologians, we
have almost too much information; but for the ideas of ordinary people
we have very little. The professional theologians were also professional
communicators, their minds sharpened by the dialectic of medieval
scholasticism and the rhetoric of Renaissance humanism. The majority
of believers, however deep their piety, would have been much less articulate. We are talking about people who, even if they could read, were
rarely able to write – and who in many cases could not afford writing
materials. We are therefore obliged to deduce much of their response
from the often critical reports of church leaders.

The medieval doctrine of God's covenant and the promise of justification and salvation to all who did their best may have been difficult to

defend with reference to the Bible, but it was well adapted to pastoral use. It provided the average parishioner with a framework for both social and spiritual life. More, it was comprehensible and in accordance with everyday notions of justice and fairness. The doctrine of predestination may be logically watertight but its acceptance depends on human willingness to submit to God's inscrutability. For Luther, such faith was easy: as he says, it opened the gates of Paradise to him. Unfortunately, not all Christians found it that easy. There were those for whom it was impossible to know that one had the right kind of faith. The resulting anxiety produced a group of devout people who were constantly examining their consciences and actions to see whether they had the feelings appropriate to someone who had been saved.

The commonplace book of John Gwyn, a minor landowner in seventeenth-century South Wales, listed the seven marks of a justified man from 2 Corinthians 7:

1. Care to avoid sin
2. Clearing of your selves by plentiful accusation of your selves in a godly sorrow
3. Indignation with thy self that ever thou hast displeased god.
4. Fear of offending god
5. Vehement desire to please god with good works
6. Zeal and godly devotion in performing religious duties.
7. Revenge upon thy self by fasting watching etc.

and followed his seven points with a prayer:

> O most gracious and most blessed lord God vouchsafe to enlighten my soul by thy holy spirit so to try and search my ways by the glass of thy law that I beholding the mystery of my estate may humble my soul under thy mighty hand and turn my heart to keep thy Commandments for ever through Jesus Christ my lord and saviour
> Amen.[37]

It was the distinctively Protestant doctrine of good works which produced the typical "Puritan" lifestyle – a joyless austerity which ran directly counter to Luther's original inspiration.

Luther and his followers saw in the doctrine of predestination precisely those dangers which their academic predecessors had seen in the Augustinian doctrine of justification and redemption through grace: that ordinary people would misunderstand predestination and would be driven to despair and immorality. They were also concerned that the doctrine of predestination could be argued to imply that God was responsible for human sinfulness. Melanchthon's textbook of Biblical analysis, the *Loci Communes*, stressed the importance of human will (*voluntas*) in salvation and attempted to blur the issue of predestination. In a letter to Calvin in 1543, Melanchthon insisted that the Old Testament king, David, had sinned by his own fault and not God's, and that he retained the exercise of his will. He then attempted to defuse the conflict by deferring to Calvin's theological eminence and appealing to to his own pastoral concerns:

> I do not write these things as if handing down to you, a most erudite and skilful person in the exercise of piety, some dictates. Indeed, I know that these things harmonize with your ideas. However, mine are cruder, accommodated to use.

In 1551, two leading Genevans, Jerome Bolsec and Jean Trolliet, disagreed publicly with Calvin on the subject of predestination and appealed to Melanchthon's work in their defence. When forced to explain the discrepancy in their ideas, Calvin suggested that Melanchthon had been over-anxious about the pastoral problems which could arise out of the doctrine of predestination:

> Melanchthon, being a timid man and not wanting to give curious folk a reason for enquiring too deeply into the secrets of God, accommodated himself too much to people's common understanding. He has desired more to accommodate to people's common sense.

Calvin subsequently wrote to Melanchthon reiterating his own interpretation of the need for faith in order to benefit from God's promise of salvation. However, he praised Melanchthon for his moderation and appealed to him to avoid a public dispute.[38]

Luther had arrived at his theological breakthrough out of despair at the impossibility of satisfying God's demands by his own efforts. His understanding of salvation by faith in God's mercy brought him hope and consolation. Unfortunately, it did not bring the same comfort to the ordinary people of Protestant Europe. The Protestant emphasis on the priesthood of all believers and the importance of personal faith stripped away the helpful communal rituals of late medieval Catholicism and left people defenceless before an omnipotent God. The doctrine of predestination gave them no assurance of salvations. Some were themselves driven to despair and even to suicide. Emile Durkheim's classic study of suicide shows that suicide rates were higher in Protestant areas than Catholic ones. A detailed study of suicide in sixteenth- and seventeenth-century Zürich suggests that many of those who took their own lives were pious, God-fearing, Bible-reading men and women. A disproportionate number were from the local élite. Their piety had brought them no comfort.[39]

# 2

# *Sacrament and Ritual*

The doctrine of justification by faith, and the insistence that humans are powerless in the face of God's majesty, were fundamental to the movement we call the Protestant Reformation. For most medieval Christians, though, the church was less what it believed than what it did: the regular performance of prayer and worship and the sacraments. These were affected by the fundamental change in thinking about the significance of human actions and human behaviour towards God. In particular, the Reformers' ideas on salvation meant a complete change in the significance of the ritual acts called sacraments.

## The sacramental tradition

For a Christian, a sacrament is an encounter between the earthly and the sacred, a physical act or object which becomes charged with spiritual meaning and can thus convey or confer grace. The medieval Catholic church listed seven sacraments. Baptism was the ritual washing of a baby (or in exceptional cases an adult convert) with water which had been blessed by a sequence of prayers. The ritual was believed to wash away the guilt of original sin, and was accompanied by promises, usually made on the child's behalf by sponsors (the godparents). It was the only sacrament which could be administered by a lay person. Children who died unbaptized could not go to Heaven; at the best, their souls remained in a limbo, and their bodies could not be buried in consecrated ground. This was why, in an age of high neonatal mortality, midwives and other lay people were allowed to baptize any infant who might not survive long enough to be baptized in church.

Folk belief in some areas went so far as to refuse burial in consecrated ground to women who died in childbirth until the infant's body had been removed. This was never the official teaching of the church, though it does show the importance which traditional religion attached to ritual purity and the stigma associated with many of the natural functions of the female body. The harshness of folk custom was often moderated in practice, though, as when a woman who had died before the ritual post-childbirth purification called "churching" was churched by proxy, another woman standing in for her. Even the teaching of the official church on the necessity of baptism could be tempered: a compassionate midwife could declare the child alive for long enough to baptize it.

The sacrament of confirmation was usually taken in adolescence, though royal and aristocratic children were sometimes confirmed almost immediately after baptism. Confirmation normally involved the renewal of the baptismal promises in person before a bishop. The ritual admitted young adults to full participation in church and community life and allowed them to receive the Eucharist.

The Eucharist (also called the Mass, Holy Communion, and by the Reformers the Lord's Supper) was the ritual re-enactment of the meal which Jesus Christ shared with his closest followers on the evening before his sacrificial death – the meal generally referred to as the Last Supper. The Biblical account of the occasion describes how Jesus blessed the bread and shared it among his disciples, saying "This is my body which is given for you. Do this in remembrance of me." After the meal, he took a cup of wine, gave thanks and invited them all to drink it, saying "This is my blood which is shed for many for the remission of their sins." The Catholic church interpreted these words as meaning that, while the bread and wine retained their superficial appearance, they were changed in their essentials into the true flesh and blood of Christ. Their interpretation of exactly how this happened was based on Aristotle's philosophy of existence, which distinguished between superficial appearances, "accidents", and the inner reality, "substance". So, for example, we have sliced white bread, granary bread, *ciabatta*, tea bread – but they are all bread. The accidents are different but the substance is the same. Transubstantiation means that the accidents remain: what you see, touch and taste is still white bread, granary bread and so on. However, the substance, the essential reality of bread, has been transmuted into the reality of the flesh and blood of Christ.

The performance of Christ's command "do this in remembrance of me" became increasingly ritualized: from a shared meal, the Eucharist became a religious service with set prayers, music, incense and candles, and elaborate vessels – the chalice and paten – for the wine and the bread. Only ordained clergy could say the prayers which turned the substance of the bread and wine into the inner reality of flesh and blood. So great was the reverence owed to the consecrated bread and wine that lay people were not allowed to drink from the chalice in case God's blood was spilled by accident. Real bread was eventually replaced by little wafers which were less liable to shed crumbs of their sacred substance. It was necessary to be in a state of ritual purity before taking part in the Eucharist, so few lay people received communion more than once a year. The whole ritual was seen as being in some senses a renewal of Christ's original sacrifice on the Cross. Its repetition could therefore confer spiritual merit, and masses were said for the safety of travellers, for women in childbirth, and above all for the souls of the dead to secure their release from Purgatory. Priests who said Mass had to be paid; and so, as with the doctrine of indulgences, a logical progression from a theological interpretation of Christ's commands in the Bible produced an unacceptable situation in which salvation was for sale to the highest bidder.

The sacrament of penance has already been mentioned in connection with the medieval doctrine of sin. While baptism cleansed from the guilt of original sin, the effects of original sin remained and the individual was still prone to sinful acts. The guilt of these could be removed by the sacrament of penance. The contrite sinner confessed his or her sins to an ordained priest, who was empowered to absolve – to declare the sins had been forgiven. The sinner then made satisfaction to God for the sin by an act of penance. Linked with the sacrament of penance was the sacrament of extreme unction, the "last rites". After a final confession, the dying person was anointed with holy oil. This was in accordance with the instructions in the Biblical letter of St James:

> Is anyone sick among you? Let him call for the elders of the church, and let them pray over him, anointing him with oil in the name of the Lord; and the prayer of faith will save the sick man, and the Lord will raise him up, and if he has committed sins he will be forgiven.

However, the medieval church restricted this sacrament to the dying. Indeed, the popular belief was that those who recovered after receiving extreme unction were forever cut off from normal life.[1]

All Christians were expected to receive these sacraments – many times in the case of penance and the Eucharist. The final two sacraments were matters of choice. Marriage was seen as a sacrament because of Christ's blessing of the marriage at Cana in Galilee, at which he turned water into wine to provide for the festivities, and because of the analogy between marriage and the relationship of Christ to the church. And the sacrament of ordination, in which the bishop blessed entrants to the priesthood, set the priest apart and enabled him to perform the other sacraments.

## The Reformation of the Sacraments

Luther's initial challenge to Catholic orthodoxy concerned the doctrine of salvation by faith rather than human action. This led him fairly quickly to reconsider the part which the sacraments played in the process of salvation. For example, he soon became convinced that the Catholic view of the Eucharist as a repetition of Christ's sacrifice was wrong. It was in fact blasphemy, in the literal and technical meaning of the word: an attack on the honour due to God. For Luther and the Reformers, Christ's death on the cross was a once and for all sacrifice. Nothing more was needed. In particular, they saw the repetition of the Eucharist in order to persuade God to release souls from Purgatory as a perversion.

Luther's challenge to the central sacrament of the medieval church led the Reformers to reconsider the other sacraments as well, and even to doubt whether some of them were sacraments at all. Luther's central idea was that human action cannot wipe away the consequences of sin. It is perhaps surprising, therefore, that he continued for a while to treat penance as a sacrament. By the time he wrote *The Babylonian Captivity of the Church*, he was convinced that confirmation, marriage, ordination and extreme unction were not sacraments. There was no Biblical evidence that God had instituted them as channels of grace.[2]

Luther regarded as particularly pernicious the idea that the ordination of the clergy was a sacrament. The structure of an ordained priesthood, set apart and controlling access to all the other sacraments, underpinned the whole Catholic tradition and enabled the clergy to tyrannize over the laity and control access to the means of salvation. According to Luther, "if this sacrament [ordination] and this fiction ever fall to the ground, the papacy with its 'characters' will scarcely survive. Then our joyous liberty will be restored to us."[3] He was particularly concerned that the clergy elevated their ordination, which was a mechanical process, above the anointing by the Holy Spirit which came through faith. For Luther, it was not the laying on of hands and anointing with holy oil that made a priest, but his baptism and his relation with the Holy Spirit.

If they were forced to grant that all of us that have been baptized are equally priests, as indeed we are, and that only the ministry was committed to them, yet with our common consent, they would then know that they have no right to rule over us except insofar as we freely concede it . . . Let everyone, therefore, who knows himself to be a Christian, be assured of this, that we are all equally priests, that is to say, we have the same power in respect to the word and the sacraments.[4]

At the beginning of *The Babylonian Captivity*, Luther listed three sacraments, "baptism, penance and the bread" – "All three have been subjected to a miserable captivity by the Roman curia, and the church has been robbed of all her liberty."[5] By the end of the book, however, he had reduced the list to two, baptism and the Eucharist, since only they involved outward signs. Baptism uses water, the Eucharist uses bread and wine.

The remainder, not being bound to signs, are merely promises. Hence, there are strictly speaking but two sacraments in the church of God, baptism and the bread. For only in these two do we find both the divinely instituted sign and the promise of the forgiveness of sins.[6]

We cannot choose our own signs: they are chosen for us. The Reformers' main reason for rejecting five of the seven sacraments was that there was no evidence for them in the Bible. They could not therefore be pledges for God's promises. Luther, Melanchthon and Calvin were all particularly concerned about the corrupting effects of the rite of penance. The practice of confessing sins in detail and receiving absolution could be seen to diminish the significance of the sacrament of baptism. If baptism removes the guilt of sin, there is no need for a further ritual to cover every individual sin committed. The practice of performing penitential acts to make reparation to God for individual sins suggested that human action could wipe away the consequences of sin, which again contradicted the fundamental Reformation doctrine of salvation through faith. These concerns did not detract from the usefulness of confession of sins as a pastoral, counselling device. Luther described it as "useful, even necessary . . . a cure without equal for distressed consciences".[7] However, he wanted the emphasis to be placed on the need for full contrition and repentance rather than the completion of prescribed acts of penitence.

Confirmation and ordination were never mentioned in the Bible and could simply be regarded as human rituals. Calvin made fun of the Catholic argument for treating marriage as a sacrament since it was an analogy of the relationship between Christ and the church. On those grounds, he said, burglary could be a sacrament because "the day of the Lord comes like a thief in the night". Similarly, any of the other things to which the Gospel and the Kingdom of God were compared could be sacraments – a star, a mustard seed, a grain of salt, the yeast in the bread dough.[8] Extreme unction was defended by the Catholics by referring to the practice of the early church of praying over the sick and anointing them with oil. What the Reformers disagreed with here was the restriction of the ritual to the dying and the implication that God could be bound by it. This seems to have been what most concerned them about all the non-Biblical sacraments, the implication that humans could choose their own sacraments and that God could be bound by pledges of human invention.

Thus far, the Reformers were in agreement. However, divisions soon emerged over the significance of the sacraments. The other reformers followed Luther in his reduction of the number of sacraments, but differed in their interpretation of what the sacraments actually did. The medieval view had been that the sacraments actually acted as channels of divine grace – that irrespective of the personal qualities of the priest, the sacramental act or object could itself transmit something holy. For the reformers, only God's righteousness working through human faith could do this. What, therefore, was the purpose of the sacraments?

Luther's mature response to this problem was in its essentials surprisingly close to orthodox medieval Catholic thinking. In the *Book of Concord* he suggested that, while faith was all-important, God had given the sacraments so that faith could "have something to which it may cling and on which it may stand". While the sacraments could not save without faith, God's activity in the sacraments could precede faith, could call to faith and could establish faith.[9]

For Luther, the sacraments were similar to the Incarnation, the process by which God became human in the person of Jesus. The sacraments are just ordinary water, bread and wine: "but what a glorious majesty lies hidden beneath these things". Similarly,

> the glory of God is precisely that for our sake he comes down into the very depths, into human flesh, into the bread, into our mouth, our heart, our bosom.[10]

However, Luther argued that the sacraments were not necessary for faith. Faith was enough, without the sacraments, and faith could be given through the word of God without the sacraments. Luther sometimes spoke of God's word as "the one single sacrament", which was communicated through "three sacramental signs".[11] Above all, the sacraments had no merit as human actions and could not constrain God. "The sacrament was a sign of God giving something to man: it was not the Church giving something to its members to make them acceptable to God."[12]

For most of the reformers, the sacraments were a concession to human inadequacy. Philip Melanchthon, the gifted young classicist from Wittenberg who systematized much of Luther's thinking, suggested that God had given fallible humans the sacraments as a reminder of his promises. In an ideal world, we would be prepared to trust God on the basis of his word in the Bible. However, human sinfulness makes us mistrust God; we need some sort of concrete reassurance. "Signs are the means by which we may be both reminded and reassured of the word of faith."[13]

For the Zürich pastor Huldrych Zwingli, sacraments do not convey God's grace, but they remind us of it and confirm our faith. Zwingli followed Luther in his interpretation of the sacraments as pledges of God's love and forgiveness. Like Luther, he used imagery drawn from the experiences of his hearers. In this case, it was a story of a man who went on a long journey. Before he went, he gave his wife a ring with his portrait on it, as a pledge of his love and a reminder of him. So, said Zwingli, Christ has left his bride, the church, his own image in the sacrament of the Lord's Supper. It is as if Christ had said:

> I am wholly yours in all that I am. In witness of this I entrust to you a symbol of this my surrender and testament, to awaken in you the remembrance of me and of my goodness to you, that when you see this bread and this cup, held forth in this memorial supper, you may remember me as delivered up for you, just as if you saw me before you as you see me now, eating with you.[14]

However, Zwingli preferred to see the sacraments as public declarations of faith in that love and forgiveness. He drew on his experience as an army chaplain for an analogy:

> If someone sews on a white cross, he proclaims that he wishes to be a confederate [the reference is to the emblem of the Swiss Confederation]. And if he makes the pilgrimage to Nähenfels [where the Swiss defeated the Austrians in 1388] and gives God praise and thanksgiving for the victory vouchsafed to our forefathers, he testifies that he is a confederate indeed. Similarly, whoever receives the mark of baptism is the one who resolves to hear what God says to him, to learn of the divine precepts, and

to live his life in accordance with them. And whoever in the congregation gives thanks to God in the remembrance or supper testifies to the fact that he rejoices in the death of Christ from the depths of his heart, and thanks him for it.[15]

He rejected the idea that the sacraments convey the grace which they signify, "for by that argument restriction would have been placed on the liberty of the Holy Spirit, who distributes to every man as he will, that is, to whom and when and where he will".[16]

The articles of faith of the established Church of England attempted to steer a middle way between the Lutheran and Swiss standpoints. Article 25 describes the sacraments as "badges", "witnesses" and "signs" of grace, but goes on:

> by the which he doth work invisibly in us, and doth not only quicken but also strengthen and confirm our faith in him . . . in such only as worthily receive the same they have a wholesome effect or operation: but they that receive them unworthily purchase to themselves damnation, as St Paul saith.

For Calvin, faith and intellectual understanding were closely linked. He saw the sacraments as God's method of accommodating his way of communicating himself to suit human understanding. Like a teacher explaining (say) the Reformation to a class of young children, God uses simple language, stories and analogies. For those for whom the Bible is too difficult as a means of communication, God has provided these tangible signs. Calvin also saw the sacraments as providing a channel for the work of the Holy Spirit.[17]

There was a fundamental problem with all these attempts to explain what the sacraments were, and what they did. The earlier reformers believed that the sacraments initiate as well as nourishing faith. However, according to the logic of justification by faith, without faith we cannot receive the sacraments. Later reformers therefore moved towards the more logical standpoint that the sacraments were signs rather than causes of faith.

## Baptism

There were also disputes over the nature and practice of the two individual sacraments which the reformers accepted. For the group frequently termed the "magisterial" reformers, the medieval practice of baptizing infants (the technical term is *paedobaptism*) was still accept-able. However, the more radical reformers became increasingly uneasy about a practice for which they could find no Biblical precedent and no theological rationale. If baptism worked as a sacrament literally washing away the guilt of sin, it was obviously important to baptize children as young as possible. But if baptism was meant as a sign of redemption through faith, and a public demonstration of that faith, what was the purpose of baptizing babies who were too young to have any faith at all?

For Luther, the sacrament of baptism was ineffective without faith. He was nevertheless convinced that the baptism of babies was valid. In the first case, he argued, they were helped not by their own faith but by the faith of those who brought them for baptism. However, faith was a gift of God which could quite well be given to an infant who was too young to understand it. He quoted a number of Biblical and traditional texts to prove that very young children could have faith and could there-fore be saved. The traditional account of Herod's killing of the children of Bethlehem described them as "innocent", implying that they were holy, although they had neither speech nor reason. Christ himself had said, "Let the children come to me ... for the kingdom of heaven belongs to such as these."[18] And John the Baptist leaped for joy in his mother's womb when the pregnant Mary visited John's mother Elizabeth. Luther even argued that the faith of an infant could be more reliable than the faith of an adult who had been corrupted by the world. Infant baptism was in some ways the clearest example of Luther's doctrine of the relationship between faith and sacrament. In baptism, the baby is powerless; it is clear that the grace comes from God and the infant is the passive recipient.[19]

It is important to remember that the reformers did not see baptism as literally washing away sin. They believed rather that baptism signified the removal of the effects of sin: the technical term is the *imputation* of sin. For Luther, the gift of faith and the removal of imputed guilt could be channeled through the physical act of baptism: God had "desired that by [baptism] little children, who were incapable of greed and supersti-tion, might be initiated and sanctified in the simple faith of his word".[20] It was for this reason that Luther saw baptism as the more important of the two sacraments, "incomparably greater" because "the Eucharist is not so necessary that salvation depends on it".[21] For other reformers, though, the physical act was a symbol of the inner reality of spiritual regeneration. They had to find another reason for performing the ritual when the child was too young for this regeneration to have any meaning.

Some of the reformers argued by analogy with the Jewish ritual of circumcision, the ritual removal of a male infant's foreskin to demonstrate that he is a member of the chosen people of God. Baptism was a gentler ritual but for the magisterial reformers it performed the same function: a demonstration that both male and female infants were born into a believing community. Again, the inability of the child to understand what is being done is not a problem. Baptism is a covenant which publicly acknowledges the child to be a member of the Christian community, and the parents and godparents can enter into that covenant on the child's behalf as they would into a secular legal agreement. Children thus became members of a community of faith. Those who died in infancy had the faith which was necessary for salvation and those who grew to maturity would also grow in understanding of the meaning of their baptism. Calvin emphasized that the effect of baptism could not be wiped out by subsequent sin. Baptism was intended to reassure sinners that their sins could be forgiven: it was to be

> recalled to the memory of the sinner whenever he thinks of forgiveness of sins, so that from it he will gather himself, take courage and confirm his faith that he will obtain the forgiveness of sins, which has been promised to him in baptism.[22]

In spite of what he said about the importance of baptism as a sacrament, Luther did not in the last analysis regard it as vital for salvation. His thoughts on the subject are summarized in a little pamphlet, "Comfort for women who have had a miscarriage", which obviously derived from his own pastoral concerns. In this he suggested that the mother's love for the dead child would secure all that was necessary for its salvation, without the physical process of baptism:

> Because the mother is a believing Christian, it is to be hoped that her heartfelt cry and deep longing to bring her child to be baptized will be accepted by God as an effective prayer . . . Who can doubt that those Israelite children who died before they could be circumcised on the eighth day were yet saved by the prayers of their parents in view of the promise that God willed to be their God. God (they say) has not limited his power to the sacraments, but has made a covenant with us through his word.[23]

What Luther is saying here is not, of course, that the sacrament of baptism is meaningless. Rather, he suggests that in extreme cases that sacrament can be effective through prayer and faith, without the physical element of the pouring of water.

Like Luther, Calvin did not see baptism as necessary to salvation, though it was helpful. He too was prepared to trust in God's mercy for children who died unbaptized. Churches influenced by their ideas therefore placed no restriction on the burial of the unbaptized in consecrated ground. It is significant that the prayer books of the Church of England in the sixteenth and early seventeenth centuries placed no restrictions on the right of the unbaptized to burial. In practice, though, there was evidently a feeling that the unbaptized should not be buried with full ceremony. Some bishops instructed that unbaptized children should be buried quietly, without the burial service.[24] The decision in 1662 to include unbaptized children with excommunicates and suicides among the list of people who could not be buried in unconsecrated ground suggests the extent to which the post-Restoration Church of England had moved away from its Protestant origins.

For the radical reformers, it was not enough to claim that baptism was a public acknowledgement of a child's membership of a believing community. Their reading of the Bible led them to the conclusion that baptism was only valid if the person being baptized was an adult and capable of understanding the teaching of repentance and salvation. They considered infant baptism to be meaningless, and adult converts to the radical reformed groups were expected to be rebaptized. Hence they were described as *Anabaptists* from the Greek words meaning rebaptizers.

There was a wide range of theological standpoints among the radical reformers. However, the insistence on adult baptism was one of their defining doctrines. It formed the first of the articles of faith drawn up by a meeting of leaders of radical reformed groups at Schleitheim near Schaffhausen in Switzerland in 1527. The first of the Schleitheim Articles states:

> Baptism must be administered to those who have been taught repentance, and believe that their sins have been effaced by Jesus Christ, and who wish to walk in the way of the resurrection. Therefore it must be administered to those who ask for it themselves and not to infants, as is done in the Pope's kingdom.[25]

Thomas Müntzer opposed infant baptism but considered that children were ready for baptism at the age of 6 or 7. At that age, he suggested, the child could experience a kind of spiritual awakening or "wonderment". He even devised a ritual for the baptism of children. The children were still considered to need godparents but could take part in the ritual themselves. They were given salt, as a symbol of wisdom, and were summoned to "come to Christianity, that God may find you as ripe wheat".[26] However, the Austrian Anabaptist John Schlaffer suggested that thirty, the age at which Christ himself was baptized, was more appropriate. "The Christian life", he insisted, "is not child's play: but bitter earnestness, truth, courage and saintliness must be there."[27]

Zwingli was at one point influenced by the Biblical arguments of the Anabaptists but he was eventually convinced that adult baptism was a threat to his concept of the Christian community. In *Of Baptism* (1525), he suggested that baptism was a sign of God's covenant with humanity and thus belonged to the family and the community rather than the individual. Thus it could appropriately be offered to children born within the covenant.[28] Two years later, in the *Refutation of the Tricks of the Anabaptists*, he made the further point that rebaptism cast into doubt the validity of the baptism of generations of faithful Christian believers.[29] He was unwilling to split the true church for the sake of doctrinal reform; the radical reformers were unwilling to sacrifice doctrinal purity for the sake of unity.

## The Eucharist

The touchstone of Reformed sacramental theology, and the doctrine which caused most division among the reformers, was the doctrine of the Eucharist. Even the name given to the sacrament caused dissension. Catholics called it the Eucharist (from the Greek *eucharistia*, a thank-offering) or Mass (from the concluding words of the Latin liturgy, *Ite, missa est*). Luther continued to call it the Eucharist, but many of the other reformers preferred the phrase "the Lord's Supper". The semi-reformed established church of England tended to call it "the Holy Communion". This confusion of names stands as a proxy for much deeper divisions over the interpretation and significance of Christ's original command and the way in which it should be carried out.

For Luther, when Christ said "This is my body", that was precisely what he meant. The Biblical statement was clear and indisputable. However, Luther had been trained as a nominalist: that is, he belonged to the philosophical school which believed that the names for generic concepts such as "bread" were just that, names, and did not correspond to anything in reality. There was no substance of bread separate from the accidents of physical appearance, touch, taste and smell, and thus nothing which could be transmuted into the body and blood of Christ. There was nothing in Luther's ideas about the Eucharist which had not been said before by orthodox theologians and academics. Like his critique of the practice of indulgences, Luther's critique of transubstantiation was rooted in his academic environment – in this case, his studies in the nominalist epistemologies of William of Occam. Luther therefore rejected the complex Catholic doctrine of transubstantiation, not because he did not believe that Christ was really present in the bread and the wine, but because he thought the Catholic church had tied itself to an outmoded and unacceptable theory of existence in order to explain Christ's presence. Indeed, at one point he seems to argue that the doctrine of transubstantiation underestimates the extent to which the bread has become the body of Christ:

> For my part, if I cannot fathom how the bread is the body of Christ, yet I will take my reason captive to the obedience of Christ and, clinging simply to his words, firmly believe not only that the body of Christ is the bread, but that the bread is the body of Christ.[30]

Luther saw no need of complex philosophies to explain how bread could become suffused with the person of God in Christ. He preferred the homely analogy of a poker in the fire. If a piece of iron is placed in the fire, it glows. It now contains both iron and heat.[31] However, he did not see the doctrine of transubstantiation as a significant stumbling-block. "Of course, this error is not very important, if only the body of Christ together with the Word are not taken away."[32]

Where Luther really parted company with the Catholic church in his interpretation of the Eucharist was over the question of its purpose. As we have seen, the medieval church regarded the Eucharist as being in some senses a repetition of Christ's sacrifice. Its celebration could therefore be offered as a meritorious act. For Luther, this was unscriptural and profoundly wrong. Christ died on the cross once and for all. The Eucharist was a reminder of the promise of forgiveness which Christ had confirmed by his death; access to this forgiveness was by faith alone. The sacrament of the Eucharist could generate and encourage faith, but that was all.[33] Its repetition could not be offered as a fresh sacrifice. Ultimately, this is what unites all the Reformation doctrines of the sacraments and distinguishes them from the assumptions of the medieval Catholic church. Whether or not Christ is really present in the Eucharist, whether or not the sacraments can transmit faith, for the theologians of the Reformation the sacraments cannot be used to bind God to human intentions or to compel him to do what humans want.

Other reformers went further than Luther in their rejection of traditional Catholic doctrine. The Dutch lawyer and humanist Cornelius Hoen was much influenced by Erasmus in his approach to the text of the Bible and his attempts to recapture the original meaning of the words, stripped of their overlay of medieval interpretation. In a short study of the Eucharist which he circulated as an open letter, he proposed a different, more practical and everyday reading of the Biblical account of the Last Supper. He suggested that when Christ said "This is my body" we should read it as meaning "This signifies my body". In the same way, when Christ said "I am the true vine" (John 15:1), "I am the door" (John 10:9), "I am the good shepherd" (John 10:11, 14), what he meant was not that he had actually turned into these things but that they were metaphors to explain his mission. Thus, Hoen argued, in the Eucharist Christians do not receive God's body literally or physically but spiritually.[34] Hoen never considered himself to have separated from the Catholic church, but his ideas were immensely influential in the Reformation. In particular, they inspired Luther's colleague Andreas von Karlstadt to move away from Luther's doctrine of the Real Presence and to insist that Christ was present in the Eucharist in a spiritual sense which depended on the faith of the communicant.[35]

For the more literal reformers, Jesus could not be physically present in the Eucharist because he was elsewhere. The Swiss reformer Huldrych Zwingli argued forcefully that the Lutheran doctrine of the real presence was nonsense. In his pamphlet *On the Lord's Supper* (published in 1526),[36] he pointed out that the Creed, the basic statement of the Christian faith, which was recited during every celebration of the Eucharist, said Christ was in Heaven, at the right hand of God the Father. How then could his human body be on earth, wherever the Mass was being celebrated, to be torn by human teeth and digested in human stomachs, with all that that would entail? Zwingli then considered the account in chapter 6 of St John's Gospel, which tells of the miracle of the Feeding of the Five Thousand and Jesus' advice to his followers to seek spiritual rather than physical food. In the Biblical accounts of Jesus' last meal with his disciples, after saying of the bread "This is my body", he says "Do this in remembrance of me". For Zwingli, these words clearly indicated that the ritual re-enactment of the Last Supper commemorated someone who was not actually there. It followed that Jesus could not logically be present in the bread and the wine. They were there as reminders, as pledges, but not as the reality of his body. He suggested that Christ was actually referring to himself in a metaphor drawn from the Passover meal which he had just shared with his companions. Above all, Zwingli, argued, the Eucharist was a sacrament, which meant that it was a sign or symbol and not the thing itself.

> A sacrament is the sign of a holy thing . . . Now, the sign and the thing signified cannot be one and the same. Therefore the sacrament of the body of Christ cannot be the body itself.[37]

In Zwingli's *Exposition of the Faith*, written in 1531 and optimistically dedicated to the king of France,[38] he developed his case with the remorseless logic he had learned in his scholastic education:

> The body of Christ is truly and naturally seated at the right hand of the Father. It cannot therefore be present in this way in the Supper . . . For only that which is infinite can be omnipresent, and that which is infinite is eternal. The humanity of Christ is not eternal, therefore it is not infinite. If it is not infinite, then it is necessarily finite. And if it is finite, it is not omnipresent.[39]

It followed that the communicants at the Eucharist did not physically consume God's body. For Zwingli, however, what the communicants were doing was more than spiritual feeding. There was an added dimension which came from actually eating the bread and drinking the wine of the Eucharist; he called this "sacramental eating". In the same book he outlines the difference between spiritual and sacramental eating:

> To eat the body of Christ spiritually is equivalent to trusting with heart and soul upon the mercy and goodness of God through Christ . . . When you come to the Lord's supper to feed spiritually upon Christ, and when you thank the Lord for his great favour, for the redemption whereby you are delivered from despair, and for the pledge whereby you are assured of eternal salvation, when you join with your brethren in partaking of the bread and wine which are the tokens of the body of Christ, then in the true sense of the word you eat him sacramentally. You do inwardly that which you represent outwardly, your soul being strengthened by the faith which you attest in these tokens.[40]

Zwingli then turned to one of the touchstones of eucharistic theology, the question of what happened to those who ate the bread and wine without believing in Christ's sacrifice. If the consecrated elements really were (in whatever sense) the physical body and blood of Christ, even the unbelievers and those who ate while in a state of sin were still able to eat Christ's body. Whether it would do them any good was another matter. There were plenty of medieval stories about people who came to Mass as sceptics, saw the consecrated bread actually bleeding and were persuaded as a result. On the other hand, Luther agreed with the medieval Catholics that those who received the Eucharist while in a state of sin would be damned.

In the *Exposition of the Faith*, we can see Zwingli working his way towards the Calvinist standpoint. If Christ was only present spiritually in the consecrated bread and wine, then those who did not believe could not receive him. The more advanced reformers (like Calvin) considered that if the unbelievers did not actually receive Christ, it could do them no harm to participate in the Eucharist. Zwingli could not go that far. The unbelievers were not receiving Christ, but what they were doing was still wrong:

> But of those who publicly partake of the visible sacraments or signs, yet without faith, it cannot properly be said that they eat sacramentally. By partaking they call down judgement on themselves . . . for they do not honour the body of Christ.[41]

Zwingli went on to emphasize the importance of faith and witness. Without being sure of their faith and their willingness to testify to it, no-one should join in the Lord's Supper.

The Church of England steered a similar middle course. Article 28 of the Thirty-Nine Articles insisted that "The Body of Christ is given, taken and eaten in the Supper, only after an heavenly and spiritual manner" and (a little earlier in the same article), "to such as rightly, worthily, and with faith, receive the same, the Bread which we break is a partaking of the Body of Christ". Nevertheless, Article 25 stated clearly that "they who receive them [the sacraments] unworthily purchase to themselves damnation".[42]

If the Eucharist was a public profession of faith and of membership in a community of believers, it was meaningless unless it was shared. In the extract from Zwingli quoted above, it is participation which is necessary for sacramental eating. There was no purpose in a celebration of the Eucharist in which only the priest partook of the bread and wine. The prayer book of the Church of England insisted that, even when communion was taken to someone too ill to attend church, there should be "three, or two at the least" to share the Eucharist with the sick person. Sick people were not to be given the Eucharist alone; instead, the clergy were to reassure them that "if he do truly repent him of his sins . . . he doth eat and drink the Body and Blood of our Saviour Jesus Christ profitably to his soul's health, although he do not receive the Sacrament with his mouth". Only under the most exceptional circumstances, during outbreaks of serious infectious diseases when no-one was prepared to associate with the sick, was the minister allowed to share the Eucharist with a single sick person.

The communicants were to share fully in the Eucharist. One of the early touchstones of the Reformed faith was the insistence that lay people should receive the consecrated wine as well as the bread (the technical phrase is *communion in both kinds*). Luther rested his defence of this practice on the Biblical account of the Last Supper:

> What carries most weight with me, however . . . is that Christ says "This is my blood which is poured out for you and for many for the forgiveness of sins". Here you see very clearly that the blood is given to all those for whose sins it was poured out. But who will dare to say that Christ's blood was not poured out for the laity? And do you not see whom he addresses when he gives the cup? Does he not give it to all?[43]

With his habitual caution, Luther refused at first to insist that the lay members of the congregation be given the wine. His young colleague Melanchthon celebrated the Eucharist privately and offered wine to lay participants but was reluctant to go public. However, events in Wittenberg were running ahead of the theologians. The students were rioting in the streets and the Elector was getting agitated. It was Luther's superior, Karlstadt, who took the decision to celebrate the first public communion in both kinds. Not only did he allow the laity to share the wine, he allowed them to take the cup into their own hands.

The celebration could hardly have been more public. The service was in the castle chapel on Christmas Day, with a congregation of church and community leaders. Karlstadt went further. He conducted the service dressed as a layman, without the traditional vestments, and in the German language. The congregation had not made the customary preparations: they had neither fasted nor confessed and received absolution. In his excitement, Karlstadt dropped one of the consecrated wafers, which probably confirmed the misgivings of his opponents. The whole service was a public ceremony of considerable significance. By his actions, Karlstadt had declared his belief that the Eucharist was a communal celebration, only valid if it was shared. He had also made a powerful symbolic statement about the status of the clergy as servants of the people rather than a consecrated spiritual élite. It was, as Carter Lindberg says, "a hard act to follow", but he managed to follow it nevertheless. The next day he announced his betrothal to the daughter of a poverty-stricken local nobleman.[44]

As Luther later remarked, Karlstadt had swallowed the Holy Spirit "feathers and all". Having taken some time to be persuaded, he was headstrong in his devotion to Reformed ideals, and eager to act on his devotion. However, what was important about his actions was that he had made a powerful public statement of the central Reformed doctrine of the Eucharist: that it was a communal celebration of God's promise of salvation, not a private act which could earn spiritual merit.

There were thus some ideas about the Eucharist which were common to all reformers, but they tend to be negative definitions. That is to say, the reformers were agreed on what the Eucharist was not. It was not a repetition of Jesus' sacrifice on the cross. It was not a meritorious act which humans could offer to God, and it could certainly not be used to constrain God, to put him under an obligation to act in a certain way.

However, when the reformers had time to refine their definitions of what the Eucharist was, they found it impossible to agree. The ritual was so central to Christian worship and to the definition of the nature and purpose of that worship that slight shifts in eucharistic doctrine could produce irreconcilable splits between groups of reformers. By 1524, Luther and Zwingli had fallen out over their interpretation of Christ's words, "This is my body".[45]

The resulting highly public disagreement between Luther and Zwingli and their followers threatened the whole movement for reform of the Church. This was partly because disunity was seen as a sign of error. There were also more practical reasons. By the end of the 1520s the Emperor Charles V had made peace with France and the Pope and was free to deal with religious dissent. In 1529 the Landgrave Philip of Hesse arranged a meeting of all the leaders of the magisterial Reformation in his castle at Magdeburg. Representatives attended from Strasbourg and the south German cities as well as Luther from Wittenberg and Zwingli from Zürich. Agreement was reached on a range of issues from the nature of the Trinity to the authority of the Bible and the exact nature of justification by faith. On the Eucharist, however, the two groups were irreconcilable.

Less combative reformers like Melanchthon and the German-born Johannes Oecolampadius made increasingly desperate attempts to preserve a united front, on the sacraments as well as on the means of salvation. Calvin's *Little Treatise on the Lord's Supper*, published in Geneva in 1541, attempted an intellectual reconciliation of the two standpoints. He argued (not very tactfully) that Luther and Zwingli were both saying essentially the same thing but not very clearly. He had already outlined his own approach in the *Institution of the Christian*

*Religion*. He was not prepared to go as far as Zwingli did in distinguishing between the sign and what it signified. For Calvin, while the bread and wine were a sign of Christ's body and blood, they also communicated something of what they signified. But what they communicated was not the physical flesh and blood but a spiritual body which nourished the soul of the believer. So Calvin did believe in the Real Presence – that is, he believed that Christ was really present in the bread and wine of the Eucharist – but it was a spiritual presence, not a bodily presence.

By 1543 the cracks in the Protestant approach to the Eucharist were becoming apparent. In that year, a public disputation on the Eucharist between Luther and the Zürich theologians led by Zwingli's successor Bullinger brought about harsh condemnation of Zwingli by Luther and equally harsh comments by Bullinger. Calvin urged Melanchthon to restrain Luther but went on to attack Luther's attitude. Meanwhile, Melanchthon and Bucer of Strasburg were attempting to restore some measure of agreement, but Luther's "Shorter Confession" was an implicit attack on both men.[46] Calvin subsequently tried to provide a definition which would bring the two sides together. His suggested formula insisted on Christ's real presence in the Eucharist (so far in agreement with the sacramentology of Luther's Wittenberg Concord) but in words which were capable of a very different interpretation:

> In baptism the efficacious Spirit is present in order to wash and regenerate us. The Holy Supper is a spiritual banquet in which we truly feed upon the flesh and blood of Christ[47]

This is almost as ambiguous as the 1559 English prayer book with its merging of Cranmer's earlier translations:

> The Body of our Lord Jesus Christ, which was given for thee, preserve thy body and soul unto everlasting life. Take and eat this in remembrance that Christ died for thee, and feed on him in thy heart by faith with thanksgiving.

Christ's body is *really* there – but only in a *spiritual* sense. This was not enough for Luther. In 1549 Bullinger of Zürich and Calvin of Geneva drew up the Zürich Consensus (sometimes known by its Latin name, the *Consensus Tigurinus*), a formula which reconciled the ideas of Zürich and Geneva on the Eucharist. They hoped this would also be acceptable to the Lutherans – but it was not. Calvin's interpretation developed the argument outlined by Zwingli in his *Little Treatise on the*

*Lord's Supper* (above, pp. 53–4). For Calvin, the meaning of the Resurrection, as outlined in the Apostles' and Nicene Creeds, is that Christ ascended bodily into Heaven. A human body can only be in one place: so Christ's human body could not be both in Heaven and in bread and wine all over the place, whenever a properly appointed minister said the prayers of consecration. For Calvin, Christ was indeed present – but it was his divinity not his humanity which was present in the bread and wine, in a spiritual not a bodily sense.

Luther had developed a different interpretation of Christ's nature, geared to his insistence that, when Christ said "This is my body", that was precisely and literally what he meant. Luther therefore suggested that, while Christ had two natures, divine and human, the two were not totally separated. One nature could communicate qualities to the other. Christ's human nature could acquire the quality of ubiquity from his divine nature, and could thus be present both in Heaven and in the bread and wine of the Eucharist. Calvin and Bullinger, however, said that this was unscriptural nonsense.

The differences between the two groups went beyond their understanding of the Eucharist to affect their ideas of what constituted a true church. For those who agreed with Luther, the Body and Blood of Christ were there in the bread and wine. Anyone who took part in the Eucharist without believing in Christ did so to his own damnation. Those who agreed with Zwingli and Calvin insisted that Christ's body and blood could not possibly be there in the bread and wine since they were elsewhere. The bread and wine represented Christ's spiritual and sacramental presence. For those who took part in the Eucharist without believing in Christ, the sign would have no meaning. They would simply be taking part in an empty ritual, which could not hurt them but could not benefit them either. This was not the only difference between the two groups. There were differences in their church services, in the music they used, in church organization: but it was the crucial question of the Eucharist which became the touchstone by which Protestants were divided into Lutheran or Calvinist. Either Christ was physically present in the bread and wine or he was not: there was no way round it.

# 3

## "By this book": Authority and Interpretation

Luther's theological breakthrough derived from his detailed study of the Bible, as part of his academic duties. It was in the Bible that he found the doctrine of salvation which brought him so much spiritual comfort. It was the Bible which gave him the strength to challenge the authority of the Pope. Ultimately, for Luther, it was the Bible which constituted true religion:

> These are the true marks whereby one can really recognize the kingdom of the Lord Christ and the Christian Church: namely, wherever this sceptre is, that is, the office of the preaching of the gospel, borne by the apostles into the world and received from them by us. Where it is present and maintained, there the Christian Church and the kingdom of Christ surely exist, no matter how small or negligible the number of the flock.[1]

The medieval Catholic church fully accepted the primacy of the Bible as a source for Christian teaching. However, the problem with relying on the Bible for doctrine is that it is not a coherent or consistent text. It includes narrative history, mythology, prophecy, practical advice, spiritual meditation, liturgical song and some very erotic poetry (the "Song of Solomon"). Apart from the inherent differences between the ethical codes in the Old and New Testaments, there are numerous gaps and theological contradictions. There is, for example, no clear statement in the Bible of two fundamental Christian doctrines, the dual nature of Christ as God and man and the nature of the Trinity, the one God who nevertheless has a threefold nature. These doctrines had to be deduced out of the confusing and sometimes contradictory statements in different Biblical texts: and the medieval church claimed the authority to say which deductions were acceptable and which were not.

## Biblical authority and the Church

Most of the work of defining core teachings was done by the early Christian fathers. For the medieval church, therefore, the Bible was a crucial text but it had to be interpreted in the light of subsequent Christian teaching. Those who interpreted the Bible could claim as sanction for their decisions the third source of authority in the Church – divine revelation. To avoid the possibility of disputes over interpretation, the Church claimed that its collective decisions embodied the inspiration of the Holy Spirit. Christ had promised to leave the Holy Spirit to guide his followers: and the Holy Spirit spoke through the voice of the church, through councils and (increasingly) with the authoritative voice of the Pope. Acting on the inspiration of the Holy Spirit, the church also claimed the power to deduce doctrine from the Bible and even to add to it with the authority of tradition.

The layers of interpretation with which the medieval church approached the Bible were fundamentally unacceptable to the humanist viewpoint. Nevertheless, Luther was initially reluctant to dispute the authority of the church, and for several years the Reformers went on appealing to the authority of a church council. However, the argument soon moved on from an academic debate over doctrine and became a more far-reaching and fundamental disagreement over the right to decide what was true doctrine. In 1518, Luther was interviewed by the papal legate Cardinal Cajetan, who was in Augsburg to address the imperial assembly on the need for a new crusade against the Turks. Luther had understood that the meeting was to be a discussion of the theological issues. However, Cajetan stood on the authority of the Church and ordered Luther to repent and to refrain from teaching false doctrine. He had in fact come to Augsburg with confidential instructions to arrest Luther and send him to Rome, but Luther escaped in the nick of time.

At the Leipzig disputation in the summer of 1519, Luther was finally pushed into identifying Scripture as the sole source of authority. The context was still that of an àcademic debate. Dr Johann Eck of Ingoldstadt had been prepared to offer his friendship to Luther in 1517 but by 1519 he had turned against him. His initial attack was directed against Luther's senior colleague Andreas Bodenstein von Karlstadt, who he challenged to a public debate at Leipzig University. But Eck was an experienced public debater with an entertaining line in forensic savagery who could think quickly on his feet. Karlstadt, for all his intellectual abilities, was more of an academic, dependent on his notes and his reference books. There was no contest, until Luther was allowed to enter the debate.

Eck began by charging Luther with being a "Hussite" and a "Bohemian", members of fifteenth-century reforming religious groups which had already been declared to be heretics. This should have been a compelling point – rather like discovering that a moderate Labour cabinet minister had once been a member of the Revolutionary Socialist Party. Luther initially denied the charge; but then, like a good academic, he went to the library to find out more about Hus's teachings. (It is interesting that he does not appear to have known much about Hus before this point.) When he returned, he made the devastating claim that many Hussite doctrines were truly Christian and ought not to have been condemned by the church. There was uproar. Eck countered with the argument that the Hussites had been condemned by the Pope and the councils of the church. Luther was compelled to argue that both popes and councils could be wrong; the Bible was the ultimate authority.

In the short term, this was a debating triumph for Eck, who had pushed his opponents into making the most damaging admissions. In the longer term, and with hindsight, the Leipzig debate can be seen as the point at which differences between Luther and the Catholic church became irreconcilable. A theological argument can be settled by the appeal to reason and authority. A dispute over authority is a matter of fundamental principle and less subject to reasoned argument. The Leipzig debate thus forced Luther to consider the full implications of his arguments against indulgences. If the Pope rejected his arguments, on what basis could he say that the Pope was wrong? There is a logical progression from Luther's refusal to accept papal prohibitions in 1518 to his appeal to the authority of the Bible in 1519 and his stand at Worms in 1521. "I am bound by the Scriptures I have quoted and my conscience is captive to the word of God." By this time, he had been excommunicated; he had burned the Pope's letter declaring his excommunication; and he had published a series of attacks on the Pope.

There was still reluctance among moderates on both sides to regard the split as permanent. As late as 1541, Catholics and Reformers met at Regensburg to discuss the issues at variance between them. The sticking-point was again that question of authority. The Catholics insisted that the traditions of the Catholic Church and the doctrinal pronouncements of the Pope had the authority of divine inspiration. The Protestant delegates, headed by Luther's colleague Philip Melanchthon, insisted that only the Bible had that authority.[2] While Melanchthon and his fellow delegates were still anxious to reach a compromise, they could not contemplate any further concessions on the rôle and nature of the Church and the status of human authority within it.

## Humanism and the Bible

Luther was not of course the first scholar of his time to turn to detailed Biblical study: the Bible was part of the curriculum he was employed to teach. It was the impeccably orthodox Cardinal Ximenes, spiritual advisor to Ferdinand and Isabella of Spain, who instigated the multilingual edition of the Bible produced at the University of Alcala, the Complutensian Polyglot. This provided scholars with the text of the Old Testament in Hebrew, Greek and Aramaic and in three Latin versions, and the New Testament in Greek and in the Latin Vulgate translation.

The humanist scholar Erasmus of Rotterdam was regarded as an ally by the early reformers but firmly rejected their ideas as heresy. Nevertheless, in his influential *Enchiridion Militis Christi* (the "Handbook of the Christian Soldier"), first published in 1503, he attacked the unintelligible language of late medieval scholasticism and called for a return to the Bible and the writings of the early Christian fathers. The book received little attention at first, but between 1514 and 1520 it was reprinted twenty-four times in the original Latin and translated into several vernacular languages.

The *Enchiridion* was not in itself a radical book. Erasmus' call for a return to the original Biblical and patristic texts was in line with the general humanist desire to go back to classical sources and models. His dislike of late medieval scholasticism was on account of its obscurity of language and argument rather than its doctrinal teachings. However, his accurate and comprehensive editions of the writings of the early church fathers made their ideas accessible to a wider audience. His edition of the Greek New Testament, the *Novum Instrumentum omne*, published in 1516, provided both a full Greek text and a new Latin translation which differed at several crucial points from the traditional Vulgate translation.

The linguistic and critical skills for the study of the Old Testament were already in place thanks to the efforts of another group of humanist scholars. Konrad Pellikan had written a brief Hebrew grammar at the end of the fifteenth century. This was eventually published in 1504 as

*De modo legendi et intelligendi Hebraeum.* Within a couple of years, though, it was superseded by Johannes Reuchlin's more detailed *De rudimentis Hebraicis.* Luther bought a copy of Reuchlin's book shortly before he moved to Wittenberg, and seems to have worked his way steadily though it. He also used Lefèvre d'Étaples' Hebrew text of the Psalms from the *Psalterium Quincuplex* and his Greek text of the letters of St Paul from the *Epistola Divi Pauli,* as well as Erasmus's Greek New Testament. The steady improvement in his linguistic and textual skills can be traced in his lectures from 1513, when he first lectured on the Psalms, to the series of lectures on the Epistle to the Hebrews in 1517–18.[3]

Luther was rooted in the medieval scholastic tradition: his skills in Biblical analysis came later. His gifted young colleague Philip Melanchthon began his academic life as a classical scholar and became professor of Greek at Wittenberg in 1518. It was only then that, under Luther's influence, he developed an interest in theology. His early training gave him a particular emphasis on the authority of the Bible. His humanist perspective is reflected in his best-known work, the *Loci Communes* (the "Commonplaces"). This is a thematic analysis of the Bible, focused particularly on the doctrine of justification. Melanchthon's aim was to replace the medieval theological summaries with a book derived entirely from the Bible.

Zwingli, too, began his working life as a humanist and classical scholar. His initial ideas on reform were those of the humanists like Erasmus, who wanted to reform the church on Biblical lines but from within. Like Luther, he developed his ideas by lecturing about them. In Zwingli's case, it was a course of sermons which he preached on the Gospel of St Matthew which brought him to his conviction that virtually every aspect of traditional catholic religion – fasting, clerical celibacy, the cults of the saints and of the Virgin Mary – was fundamentally wrong.

## "Sola Scriptura"

Many of the early reformers had thus benefitted from a humanist education in the classics and the skills of textual analysis. These reformers were influenced by the ideas of leading humanists like Erasmus. Where they went beyond their humanist teachers was in their approach to the Bible. For the reformers, it was not enough to go back to the original text of the Bible for instruction and inspiration. For Zwingli and the more advanced reformers, both belief and worship must be based *only* on the word of God as found in the Bible.

Zwingli's initial challenge to orthodox teaching, on the eating of meat in Lent, was based on positive Biblical statements that all food had been created by God and that nothing was to be considered unclean. While these statements were originally aimed at the complex dietary restrictions of the Jewish faith, Zwingli pointed out their obvious relevance to the dietary restrictions of the medieval church. He was then faced with a dilemma. If the Bible said one thing and the church commanded another, which course should Christians follow? In his Sixty-Seven Articles and in successive publications over the next few years, Zwingli based his arguments on the Bible, challenging his opponents to correct him from the Bible if he was wrong.[4]

The Reformers had therefore to deal with the contradictions to be found in the Bible. Luther had particular difficulty with the conflict between St Paul's doctrine of salvation through faith and the ideas expressed by St James in his general letter to the church:

> The kind of religion which is without stain or fault in the sight of God our Father is this: to go to the help of orphans and widows in their distress and to keep oneself untarnished by the world ... You see then that a man is justified by deeds and not by faith in itself. (James 1: 27; 2: 24)

Luther was eventually driven to describing the Letter of St James as "a right strawy Epistle". He accepted that the Book of Revelation was an authentic part of the Bible but considered that it, too, contributed little to the essential message of salvation.[5]

Luther's colleague Andreas Karlstadt was also aware of these problems of interpretation. Karlstadt insisted on the authority of the Bible. The original Scripture, he said, "allows of no defect": it is the sword that judges all things and even secular rulers are subject to it. However, he was also aware that defects had crept into the text of the Bible as it had been handed down to his own day.

> Neither can I ignore the fact that many an error has grown in our codices, since on the same occasion one evangelist says more, they [the copyists] have added it to the other [gospel] because they consider it important. Actually, when one [manuscript] expresses the same idea differently, he who had read one of the four [gospels] first [would follow it] as an example for those that he considered to have been emended.

Karlstadt was also aware of the problems posed by obscure passages and the fact that some Old Testament teachings (such as the concept of the holy war) were outdated. On all such occasions he turned to the words of Christ in the Gospels as the final authority.[6]

Zwingli was not prepared to take such a ruthless approach. Like Luther, he had difficulties with the Book of Revelation. Nevertheless, for him, the contradictions were superficial. In his introduction to Bible study, *The Clarity and Certainty of the Word of God* (written in 1522 for the nuns of the Domincan convent in Zürich),[7] Zwingli claimed that the Holy Spirit would unfailingly reveal the meaning of the Bible to those who are genuinely seeking God's message. Through careful study, with faith and humility, and by God's grace, the reader would be able to reach full and coherent understanding.

> When the Word of God shines on the human understanding, it enlightens it in such a way that it understands and confesses the Word and knows the certainty of it.[8]

> Then you should reverently ask God for his grace, that he may give you his mind and spirit, so that you will not lay hold of your own opinion, but of his. And have a firm trust that he will teach you a right understanding, for all wisdom is of God the Lord. And then go to the written word of the Gospel.[9]

For the Reformers, the Old Testament was as fundamental to their ideas as the New. The doctrine of salvation was a basic concern for most of the early reformers, and the story of salvation began in the book of Genesis with the narrative of Adam, Eve and the apple. For Zwingli, the story of the Creation and the Fall had to be taken as literally true, something which happened in real, measurable time and exactly as described in the Book of Genesis.[10] Later reformers like Calvin took a more allegorical perspective. Literal interpretations of the Old Testament gave the Reformers many difficulties with its contradictions. For Zwingli, however, the Bible was not the product of human inspiration and had nothing to do with human reason. It could only be understood with God's gift of faith. No human interpretation could constrain it. "The Bible must be your master: you are not master of the Bible."[11]

For Luther, the conflicts over interpretation were ultimately irrelevant. He had found reassurance and a message of salvation in the Bible. For him, it was a source of joy and inspiration:

> One thing and one alone is necessary for life, justification and Christian liberty: and that is the most holy word of God, the Gospel of Christ, as he says, "I am the resurrection and the life: he that believeth in me shall not die eternally" (John 11:25); and also (John 8:36), "If the Son shall make

you free, you shall be free indeed"; and (Matt. 4:4) "Man shall not live by bread alone, but by every word that comes out of the mouth of God".

Let us therefore hold it for certain and firmly established, that the soul can do without everything except the word of God, without which none at all of its wants are provided for. But, having the word, it is rich and wants for nothing: since that is the word of life, of truth, of light, of peace, of justification, of salvation, of joy, of liberty, of wisdom, of virtue, of grace, of glory and of every good thing.[12]

Like many of the other reformers, Calvin began as a classical scholar. His first publication was not a theological work but an edition of Seneca's *De Clementia*. In Geneva, he has been credited with the complete reorganization of church government. However, his major activity was not administration but preaching and lecturing on the Bible. He also wrote commentaries on a number of books of the Bible. But like most of the other magisterial reformers, while he held to the idea of *sola scriptura* in principle, he qualified it in practice. For Calvin, Scripture had to be read in the light of the interpretations of the early Church fathers, especially St Augustine and St Bernard.

Nor was Calvin a fundamentalist in the modern sense. He believed in the fundamental authority of the Bible: but he most emphatically did not believe that every word of Scripture had to be taken literally. He pointed out that the Bible often describes God as if he were a physical human being with hands, feet, eyes, mouth and so on. This, Calvin argued, was God's way of dealing with our intellectual inadequacies – a sort of divine baby talk. The same was true, he insisted, of the Biblical account of the creation of the world in six successive days and the story of Adam and Eve, the first humans, who gave into the temptations of the Devil, ate the forbidden fruit of the Tree of Kowledge of Good and Evil and thus brought sin into the world. These, Calvin said, are stories designed to be told to simple people. They are simple stories, because God wants no intellectual barriers to be raised against faith.[13]

Calvin also made a subtle distinction between the Bible and the Word of God. Some of the reformers spoke as though the Bible *was* God's authentic voice. For Calvin, the Bible *embodied* the Word of God. God had spoken to the great leaders of the Old Testament and to the prophets. Finally, his word was written down in the Bible. The Word of God was infallible and the Bible contains the word of God: but Calvin was also able to allow for the stylistic peculiarities of individual Biblical writers.[14]

However, it was never going to be enough to say that the Bible was the ultimate authority, that the Bible should be available in the vernacular and that everyone who read it would derive true doctrine from it. As we have seen, even the leaders of the Reformation could not agree on their interpretation of Scripture. Most of them were professional theologians, but their theological and textual skills did not always lead them to the same conclusions. Furthermore, they were by definition strong-minded intellectuals, who had already shown that they were prepared to challenge established authority. It was even more likely that untrained lay people would find radically different readings in the text.

This was part of the problem with the Anabaptists and the radical reformers. They had a very straightforward and literal approach to the Bible. Few of them had the level of classical and humanist education of the leaders of the magisterial reformation. The magisterial reformers (educated theologians, most of them) regarded the Anabaptists as dangerously simplistic and selective in their approach. It was difficult, though, to counter their arguments. The Acts of the Apostles, for example, describe a communist society with itinerant spiritual leaders and baptism of adult converts. The Ten Commandments include the instruction "You shall not kill" (Exodus 20:13): and Christ ordered his followers not to take oaths (in the Sermon on the Mount: Matt. 5:34).

## The authority of the Spirit

Like the magisterial Reformation, the Radical Reformation was rooted in the authority of the Bible. Many of the early radical congregations originated in Bible study groups. However, some of the radicals went beyond the principle of *sola Scriptura* to claim authority from the direct inspiration of the Holy Spirit. For Caspar Schwenckfeld, the Bible could point the way to the truth but was not itself the ultimate truth. The Scriptures

> indicate, indeed, who and what the Word of God is, but do not pass themselves off for that Word. They always point beyond themselves to Christ ... who must preach and utter himself into the believing heart through the Holy Spirit, and who alone is the Word, Power and Wisdom of God.[15]

Thomas Müntzer and Niclas Storch in Zwickau both claimed that the Holy Spirit had revealed to them truths that were not in the Bible. Storch, indeed, said he was illiterate. His claim may have been true, but his Biblical knowledge was considerable. It is possible that he claimed to be illiterate in order to emphasize that he was not dependent on the written word for his authority.[16]

The Regensburg Anabaptist Umblauft was also worried about the problems of the illiterate believer. Like Schwenckfeld, he believed that Scripture was the witness and illumination for the inner word which God revealed to all.

> A man can be saved without preaching and the Scriptures: otherwise, illiterates or imbeciles could never be saved. God is understood as Redeemer not through the letter but through the indwelling Christ . . . Salvation should be ascribed alone to the inner Word of God.[17]

This was the main reason for Luther's opposition to the radicals. On the practical level, they threatened his strategy for the reform of the whole church because their ideas were unacceptable to the secular powers. But to Luther, on a theoretical level, their view of divine inspiration made them little better than the Catholics. When they used the authority of Scripture, they treated it as if it was the direct word of God, ignoring the way in which it had been mediated through the writing of fallible humans. Therefore, they refused to make use of human skills (textual criticism, the knowledge of Greek and Hebrew) in order to understand it. In rejecting the authority of the church, they had rejected human intellect as well.[18] Even more seriously, they presumed to claim direct contact with God, ignoring the framework of sacraments and Biblical texts which God had provided for their benefit.

## The vernacular Bible

If the Reformers believed that the Bible was the ultimate authority, and that all believers needed to understand as well as believe, they had to have access to the Bible – which meant that the Bible had to be translated into the languages spoken by ordinary people. Like so much of what the reformers did, this was not entirely new. There were a number of medieval vernacular translations of parts of the the Bible, into a whole range of European languages – German, French, English, even Welsh. However, the demand for a vernacular Bible was a fundamental part of many of the later medieval heresies. Wyclif and Hus had both insisted that ordinary people should have access to Scripture: and as a result the translation of the Bible had become suspect. Nevertheless, German printers were selling German Bibles in the 1480s, and by 1522 the New

Testament could be bought for the price of a supper. German mass books were also readily available.[19]

Luther wrote his German translation of the Bible while he was hiding in the Wartburg castle in 1521–2. The speed with which he accomplished this (while writing several other books) suggests that much of the work had been done earlier, but it was while he was in hiding that he had the time to put it together. His aim was to provide the people of Germany with a Bible in their own language, so that even those who could not read for themselves could have God's word read to them. The Bible translations of Luther and his fellow-reformers were very different from the earlier vernacular translations. Most pre-Reformation versions were translated from the Latin text known as the Vulgate, which was itself full of dubious translations and textual errors. The reformers used the textual skills of the humanists to rediscover the original Hebrew and Greek texts and translated directly from these.

However, the translation work of the reformers was not completely free from interpretation. For example, Luther translated chapter 3 verse 28 of Paul's letter to the Romans as "Man is justified by faith *alone*". The word *alone* was not in any authentic Greek text of the letter. Luther claimed he added it to put his translation into the contemporary German idiom, but also that it was in line with his interpretation of Paul's teaching on salvation.[20]

It was for this reason, the fact that translation can never be objective, that there were so many translations of the Bible in the sixteenth century. As well as Luther's German Bible, there were German translations from the Froschauer printing house in Zürich and from Strasbourg. While Luther concentrated on the translation of the New Testament and the Psalms, two of the radical reformers, Haetzer and Denck, beat him to the translation of the Old Testament prophets. Their work was published in Worms in 1527 and had gone through twelve editions by 1531. Luther published his translation of the Old Testament in 1532, possibly to provide an alternative to the theology of the "Worms Prophets".[21]

Nor was there agreement on which books should be included in the Bible. We have already seen that Luther and some of the other magisterial reformers were uneasy about the ideas on salvation in the Letter of James. Several of them also felt doubtful about the validity of the final book of the Bible, the Book of Revelation, the prophecy of the end of the world attributed to St John the Evangelist. More controversial, though, were the books of Jewish prophecy from the period shortly before the birth of Jesus. These are known as the *Apocrypha* (or writings of doubtful authority). The radical reformers derived many of their ideas from the Book of Revelation but they also found inspiration in these Jewish prophecies. They also included in their lists of authoritative texts several additional narratives of the life of Christ and the history of the early church, such as the Gospel of Nicodemus.

The insistence of the Protestant reformers that doctrine should be based on the sole authority of the Bible, and their wish to see the Bible translated so that ordinary Christians could read it, was one of the cornerstones of the Protestant Reformation. Nevertheless, as this chapter suggests, to say as William Chillingworth did that "The Bible is the sole religion of Protestants" begs as many questions as it answers.

# 4

# The True Church in the Protestant Tradition: Theory and Organization

None of the early reformers had any intention of founding a new church, or of splitting the one Catholic church in which they had been brought up. The existence of "one holy catholic and apostolic church" was a fundamental article of belief for Christians, enshrined in the Nicene Creed which was repeated whenever the Mass was celebrated. "That there is a universal church", Calvin said, "that there has been from the beginning of the world, and will be even to the end, we all acknowledge". But "the appearance by which it may be recognized is the question".[1]

Luther's early writings on the subject also make it clear that he wanted to reform the church, not to divide it. Early in 1519, for example, in the *Instruction on Sundry Articles*, he wrote:

> If, unfortunately, there are things in Rome which cannot be improved, there is not – nor can there be! – any reason for tearing oneself away from the church in schism. Rather, the worse things become, the more one should help her and stand by her, for by schism and contempt nothing can be mended.[2]

Later in that year, his famous debate with Johannes Eck at Leipzig did something to alter his views. As we have seen (above, pp. 61–2), this was the point at which issues of authority became crucial. If the Pope was the ultimate source of authority in the Catholic church, and if Luther had rejected the Pope's authority in favour of the ultimate authority of the Bible, he had effectively "torn himself away from the church".

The early Swiss reformers led by Zwingli were more ready to reject the authority of the Pope and the church in favour of that of the Bible. At the same time, they too insisted that they did not want to divide the church. In his first major statement of faith, the *Apologeticus Architeles* (the "Beginning and Final Defence"), Zwingli even claimed that he was trying "to restore the ancient unity of the Church". It was the opinions of his critics, he argued, which were breeding "anger, hatred, jealousy, ambition and the like". Nevertheless, he went on to reject the idea that the Bible implied the existence of a united church behind it. He pointed to periods of division in the early Church. Was not the Bible still there in the fourth and fifth centuries at the time of the Arian schism, when many in the Church denied that Christ was really God? Where was the Church when Matthew was writing his eye-witness account of the Resurrection? For Zwingli, the Bible came first, and the church received its authority from the Gospels. The Bible did not need the approval of the Church.[3]

As the authority of the Pope had become so fundamental to the identity of the late medieval Catholic church, rejection of his authority to determine true doctrine was inevitably going to mean rejection of the church he led. Still, the Reformers argued that they were not setting up a new church. Martin Bucer described the changes introduced by the Reformers as the restoration of *das recht, alt und ewig,* "the true and ancient church" which the Pope and his followers had perverted. He regarded his own church as the true church, and described the church of Rome as "a so-called church" and a "pseudo-church".

For Luther, issues of authority were initially unimportant. What was crucial was the understanding of the doctrine of justification and salvation. In comparison with the miraculous saving power of Christ's sacrifice, ecclesiastical structures and papal authority were not worth arguing about. In 1535, after all his attacks on Papal authority in books like *The Babylonian Captivity of the Church*, he was still prepared to acknowledge the Pope's power if the pope would in turn agree that remission of sins and everlasting life came only through Christ's death and resurrection and not through the observance of the traditions of the church.[4] Even as late as 1541, the discussions at Regensburg assumed that the split between the reformers and the catholic church was only temporary.

The failure of the Regensburg colloquy made it increasingly apparent that the split was likely to be permanent. Luther finally became convinced that the Catholic church of his day had lapsed into heresy – the heresy of Pelagianism which Augustine had done so much to combat. It was also becoming clear that the dispute was increasingly a dispute over authority: the authority to define true doctrine and to suppress false doctrine. It therefore became necessary for the Reformers to consider a definition of the True Church which would provide them with a valid identity and a valid reason for refusing to accept the authority of the Catholic church.

The Reformers also had to consider how their church would be organized. In rejecting the authority of the Catholic church, the Reformers had also rejected its structures – the hierarchy of Pope, cardinals, archbishops and bishops, archdeacons, parish priests, deacons and lesser orders. They were free to set up their own structures of church government, which could be modelled on the system they had left or could be redesigned from first principles.

However, the Reformers were still not prepared to contemplate the existence of more than one church. Toleration was impossible. Either a church was the true church or it was not. And if it was not the true church, it was a false church. There was no middle ground, no room for compromise, for live and let live. The Protestant definition of the true church necessarily excluded the Catholic one, and the definitions of the different groups of Protestants excluded each other. The leaders of the Reformation would have had no sympathy with the ideals of the modern ecumenical movement with its willingness to share the worship of different denominations and even different faiths. For them, compromise equated with cowardice.

Calvin was savage in his denunciation of those French protestants who continued to attend Catholic worship in order to avoid conflict and persecution. These Protestants were sometimes nicknamed the Nicodemites, after a Jewish priest called Nicodemus who visited Jesus at night so that his fellow-priests would not see him. They defended their behaviour by claiming that attendance at Catholic Mass could not harm them since they were themselves devoted to the true religion. Calvin's attitude was that false worship was always harmful, and that they should leave France (as he had done) or be prepared to endure persecution for their beliefs.[5]

Some urban trading communities like Strasbourg had a reputation for toleration, but it was a policy exercised by the city council in defiance of the wishes of the church leaders. Even in Strasbourg, "toleration" could mean that religious dissent was punished by beatings and confiscation of property rather than a gruesome death. The city council claimed to understand "the great difference between the meaning of the little word "tolerate" and the idea of taking something to be right" but it was a limited understanding and one that did not extend to the church hierarchy.[6]

## The Reformation doctrines of the True Church: theory and practice

The medieval church was defined by the Creed, the basic statement of Christian belief. The Nicene Creed proclaimed faith in "one holy catholic and apostolic church". The medieval church was united, holy and universal, and claimed continuity with the church established by Christ himself through the doctrine of the Apostolic Succession. According to this doctrine, Christ gave leadership in the church to his immediate followers. They passed that authority on to their successors by the physical act of placing their hands on them in blessing. The bishops and priests of the sixteenth-century church thus claimed to hold their authority by direct descent from Christ and his apostles through the sacrament of ordination. It was the authority thus given them which allowed them to administer the other sacraments and which made them and the church they represented the sole channel of God's grace.

Luther in his treatise *Concerning the Ministry* (1523) insisted that the true church could be recognized not by its customs or its continuity with the past but by the word of God:

> We are interested in the pure and true course, prescribed in holy Scripture, and are little concerned about usage or what the fathers have said or done in this matter . . . Herein we neither ought, should nor would be bound by human traditions, but clearly exercise our reason and Christian liberty.[7]

But this liberty was not the freedom to invent church structures: it was the liberty to follow the Bible rather than custom.

Luther went on to link his doctrine of the ministry with his doctrine of the sacraments and his theology of salvation. For Luther, the foundation of the true church was Christ and his sacrifice, "who alone and once for all by offering himself has taken away the sins of all men and accomplished their sanctification for all eternity". The church was itself part of the means of grace. According to Luther's Small Catechism, it was "in the Christian church" that God "daily and abundantly forgives all my sins".

The church here has to be seen as the fellowship of other Christians. For Luther, the witness and support of fellow Christians were indispensable.[8] For Bucer, too, the true church was emphatically a community. The title of his first published book, *That No-one Should Live for Himself*, stressed his belief that people were created not for themselves but for others. But the church was also defined by faith and by the fact that its members were chosen by God. Bucer had therefore to confront the problem that it was impossible to decide who in this world had been chosen by God. The church in the world was therefore an imperfect church: the saved and the damned were mixed. Only in Heaven could God's purpose for his church be fully realized.[9]

Bucer also believed that the true church should be an evangelical church in the modern sense, a church dedicated to preaching the Gospel. However, the early Protestant churches were not in any practical sense missionary churches. They were too much occupied with defending themselves against the Catholic church and winning over Catholics. The missions which took Christianity to South America and Asia were undertaken almost entirely by Catholics.

There were common Protestant traditions in the definition of the true church and the relationship between church and state. Nevertheless, the development of the Reformation doctrine of the true church and its organization on a practical level did not take place in a vacuum. The contrasts between Lutheran and Calvinist ideas on the nature of the church, in particular, were related to the different social and political contexts in which they evolved.

## The Lutheran state church[10]

Luther was not initially concerned to put forward a different doctrine of the true church from that of the Catholics. His concept of the true church was still close to the medieval idea. In 1539, in *On the Councils and the Church*, he listed as the seven marks of a true church:

1.  the word of God
2.  the sacraments of baptism and
3.  of the Eucharist rightly administered according to Christ's institution
4.  the offices of the keys and
5.  of the ministry
6.  public worship (prayer, praise and thanksgiving, including the

Lord's Prayer, the Apostles' Creed and the Ten Commandments) and

7.   the bearing of the Cross.[11]

The primacy Luther gave to the Bible was distinctive and crucial. Luther did not want to split the one holy catholic church but he did want to return it to what he considered to be the only foundation of a true church: Christ's redemptive sacrifice as explained in the Bible. But the other marks of a true church which he listed were near enough to the Roman doctrine. The Roman argument, of course, was that Luther and those who followed him were not just heretics but apostates – that their church was a false church. Luther's main concern was therefore to demonstrate that his reformed church was the true church, and that it was the Romans who had fallen away from the truth. In *Against Hanswurst* (1541) he again listed the identifying marks of the reformed church and argued that they were all to be found in the church of the New Testament, while the church of the Romans had fallen away from that early ideal.[12]

Luther had described himself as "always a sinner, always justified". It followed, therefore, that his church would be a church of sinners, and that the church itself would be full of faults.

> When you are indeed to pass judgement on the church, you must not look for a church in which there are no blemishes and flagrant faults, but for one where there are people who love the word and confess it before men.[13]

Luther's successors both developed his theory of the true church and gave more thought to the ways in which it should be organized. The 1530 Augsburg Confession was drafted by Luther's gifted young colleague Philip Melanchthon as a statement of faith for all the new Lutheran congregations. He defined the church as "the assembly of saints in which the gospel is taught purely and the sacraments administered rightly".[14] The phrase "the assembly of saints" has overtones of the gathered churches of the radical reformers (for which, see below pp. 84–6), but the definition of the church in terms of Gospel teaching and sacraments is pure Luther. The problem was, as Melanchthon eventually realized, that someone has to enforce the purity of the Gospel; someone has to supervise the appointment of priests who will administer the sacraments rightly; and ultimately someone has to take responsibility for dealing with those who defy the teaching of the true church.

Luther had no pressing desire to reorganize the administrative structures of the church, either. His attack on such traditional Catholic institutions as the sacramental priesthood and the monastic orders meant that he had to consider the practical task of providing new structures to take their place. However, he had no overarching theory of church organization. His pronouncements on the practical problems of church structures bear out Francis Higman's description of him as a "fireman": he responded to problems as he encountered them, without any clear theoretical overview.

For example: Luther had no objection in theory to bishops, if they would do what he considered to be their job – pastoral care and oversight. Nor had he any objection to a validly ordained priesthood. What he objected to was the idea that the doctrine of the Apostolic Succession and the sacrament of ordination could be used to defend clergy who were not doing their jobs. But when the existing bishops refused to co-operate, he was prepared to consider alternative models. A system of superintendents was set up in Saxony to oversee church discipline. They organized visitations of each parish, as the bishops had done (or should have done), enquiring into the beliefs, worship and behaviour of the congregations and the organization of church finances. The Lutheran church continued to appoint and ordain clergy, who continued to baptize, administer Communion and offer spiritual advice and counsel.

Nevertheless, there were profound differences in the way that the the clergy were appointed and in the understanding of their functions and powers. In 1523, Luther published a short treatise *That a Christian assembly or congregation has the right and power to judge all teaching and to call, appoint and depose teachers, established and proven by Scripture.*[15] His proposal was radical in the extreme, and if implemented would have brought the Lutheran church near to what we would now call Congregationalism. However, the pamphlet seems to have been purely speculative, an example of Luther working his ideas out while writing about them. It consists mainly of comments on the relevant Biblical texts. There is no guidance on how congregations could in practice institute and remove clergy.

Later in that year, Luther wrote a more detailed treatise, *Concerning the Ministry*, in response to the crisis in the Czech Hussite church.[16] For all their radical ideas on the sacraments and the vernacular Bible, the followers of John Hus were conservative in church organization. They believed in the Apostolic Succession and the need for priests to be ordained by a validly-consecrated and appointed bishop. However, by its very nature, the Hussite church could have no validly-appointed bishops. Czech priests were therefore forced to go abroad for ordination, and to promise to follow the Catholic faith – promises which they would have to renounce when they returned home. The Czechs were also forced to accept as priests men who had been ordained but had since fallen foul of the authorities.

To Luther, this was a recipe for chaos and "Babylonian confusion": the Czech church had become a church of beggars. Luther suggested that it would be better for the Hussites to do without an ordained ministry at all. The heads of households could read the Bible to their families and baptize infants, though they would have to do without the Eucharist. However, he also suggested another possible way out. Members of the church should meet and pray for the guidance of the Holy Spirit. Then they should choose suitable ministers, lay their hands on them, and appoint them as bishops, ministers or pastors. The new bishops, elected through what Luther describes as a "free and apostolic rite", could re-establish a legitimate ministry. If necessary, the bishops could be chosen from among those who had been ordained in the Catholic church, so that the tradition of the Apostolic Succession could be maintained.

Luther's suggestion was a strange mixture of episcopalian and congregational practice. The familiar structures of consecrated bishops and ordained priests were retained, but the spirit behind them was completely different. While accepting the pastoral value of continuity, Luther rejected the idea that the Apostolic Succession could guarantee the truth of the church. This, he said, made the ordination of priests an *execramentum* rather than a *sacramentum*. More fundamentally, he rejected the Catholic idea that the main function of the clergy was to offer the Mass as a regular repetition of Christ's sacrifice. For Luther, Christ's sacrifice on the Cross was unique, once and for all and unrepeatable. The claim of the Church to repeat that sacrifice daily was blasphemy. Further, the Catholic view of the clergy as a divinely ordained, sacrificing priesthood was at odds both with Christ's unique priesthood and with the priesthood of all believers.

Luther's doctrine of the priesthood of all believers did not mean that the church could be left without any structure for organization and supervision. Not all believers could act as if they were members of the clergy:

> However, no-one may make use of this power except by the consent of the community or by the power of a superior . . . therefore this "sacra-

ment" of ordination, if it is anything at all, is nothing else than a certain rite by which one is called to the ministry of the church.[17]

Luther's own ideas on ministry had both pragmatic and theoretical elements. On the one hand, he had a very exalted idea of the duties of the ministry. Inadequate clergy were to be removed as quickly as possible, and it was better to live without the sacraments than to receive them from unworthy ministers. This did not mean that the clergy were expected to be perfect. Humans were sinful and could never be perfect. Luther reassured the Czech Hussites that whatever they did as believers would be considered to be the work of Christ. Christ had promised that where two or three were gathered in his name, he would be there. His promise enabled Luther to make practical provision for the appointment of ministers by the community. Continuity in the church rested not in the transmission of ordination from priest to priest but in Christ's promises.

Luther was reluctant to consider the need for discipline in the true church. For him, what mattered was faith, the spirit which animated the administrative structures. Ideally, he hoped that, once Christians had been set free from the restrictions of traditional Catholic practice, they would be directed by the Gospel and would need no coercion. By 1527, he was forced to admit that he was wrong. For all his efforts, "the world goes its way like an untamed beast and follows not the word but its own desires".[18] It was Philip Melanchthon, though, who introduced the concept of discipline as part of the definition of the true church in the Lutheran tradition. By 1533 he was insisting on obedience to the ministry as well as the Gospel, and in 1555 he accepted that discipline and obedience should be enforced by excommunication.[19]

The development of church organization in Strasbourg was more complex. The city retained some of its Catholic churches and even a nominally Catholic cathedral, which was still technically the seat of the Bishop of Strasbourg. Meanwhile, the early reformers had encouraged the city council to take effective control of church discipline and administration as a way of fostering and defending the Reformation there. However, the council assumed powers over doctrine as well as organization and presumed to control and discipline the Protestant clergy. The church could only re-assert its independence by setting up its own administrative structures for training and disciplining the clergy. This was done through a Church Assembly, which began as an informal meeting of evangelical preachers and developed into a formal church council.

The sixteenth-century Church of England has been described as "Calvinist in its theology and Catholic in its organization". However, in its sixteenth-century structures, it is probably best considered as belonging to the Lutheran model. The church of Henry VIII, Edward and Elizabeth retained bishops in its organizational structure. Edward's bishops were appointed by a purely administrative process, very much like the church supervisors of the Lutheran German states. Henry and Elizabeth both nominated their own bishops but then had them consecrated by other bishops in the traditional manner and claimed that the apostolic succession had been preserved, though at times it hung by a thread. When Elizabeth's first Archbishop of Canterbury, Matthew Parker, was consecrated as a bishop in 1559, the only traditionally consecrated bishop who could be found to pass on the apostolic *charisma* to him was Bishop Barlow; and there were doubts even about the validity of Barlow's consecration. The difficulty probably originated in the poor record-keeping of his Welsh dioceses, but it enabled the Catholic church in the late nineteenth century to claim that Anglican orders were technically as well as spiritually invalid.[20]

## The True Church in the Calvinist tradition

According to Zwingli in the *Exposition* of his 67 Articles, the church was the community of all true believers in Christ, united through the spirit in one faith; and the head of the church was Christ, not the Pope. But the community of all believers was invisible and known only to God. Zwingli said that the church on earth, the visible church, should be modelled on the early church described in the Acts of the Apostles. Their church had no administrative structures, no canon law, no privileges. It consisted of groups of Christians living together locally as a community, and it was that which for Zwingli constituted the ideal church.[21] Such a church could not be ruled by councils or popes. It must be ruled by the word of God in the Bible. Zwingli went on to attack canon law, the legal system of the Catholic church, saying that it was only valid in so far as it agreed with God's word.

However, Zwingli's model of the church as a gathered community of Christian believers was impracticable in the circumstances in which Zwingli found himself. He wanted to bring all the Swiss cantons into his ideal of a reformed church. He was therefore forced to compromise over the extent and timing of some of his proposed reforms. The inevitable disputes over doctrine could not be settled by amicable debate: some structure of authority was needed. Zwingli was thus led towards a vision of the church in the world as a community of faith but under the authority of the secular government.

Calvin's doctrine of the true church was like Luther's in that it was centred on the preaching of the Gospel and the sacraments. He placed more emphasis than Luther had done on the need for control, and insisted that the civil authorities should have no control over the church in matters of religion. This led to a great deal of popular hostility in Geneva, and he was expelled from the town in the spring of 1538. One of his conditions for returning in 1541 was that he be allowed to impose proper discipline. He described discipline as the "sinews" of the church,

> like a bridle to restrain and tame those who rage against the doctrine of Christ; or like a spur to arouse those of little inclination; and also some-times like a father's rod, to chastize mildly and with the gentleness of Christ's Spirit those who have more seriously lapsed.[22]

The Institutes lay out a graduated series of disciplinary procedures, beginning with private warnings and ending with excommunication.

> If he [the disobedient church member] is not even subdued by this but perseveres in his wickedness, then Christ commands that, as a despiser of the church, he be removed from the believers' fellowship.[23]

A church which was prepared to excommunicate its members for persistent disobedience had moved some way away from the idea of a church which encompassed the whole community and towards the idea of a "gathered church", a community of the faithful from which unbe-lievers could be excluded. There are elements of the gathered church in Calvin's thinking. In Geneva in 1536 he and Farel proposed that each citizen should make a personal confession of faith, under oath. Their proposal contributed to the unpopularity which led to their expulsion in 1538.

Nevertheless, Calvin's idea of the true church remained inclusive. In a way, he wanted the whole of society to become a gathered church. This was just about feasible in a small city-state like Geneva. However, it did not work so well in larger states. The model of the exclusive, gathered church obviously worked particularly well when a group of Protestants was meeting in secret during periods of persecution or was forced into exile. During periods of persecution, Protestants left countries like England and the Netherlands and formed gathered churches in the countries which offered them refuge. The Dutch Protestants in particular tried to import a model of the nation as gathered church into the northern provinces of the Netherlands when they returned from exile in the 1570s. Unfortunately, what had worked in small exile communities was not practicable in larger and more mixed communities. There were problems, for example, over admission to the sacrament of baptism. The civil authorities in the Netherlands required the church pastors to baptize any child whose parents asked for it. The pastors were reluctant to baptize the children of those about whose beliefs they were doubtful. By the end of the sixteenth century, there was in the Netherlands a "two-tier" model of the church.[24] The Calvinist church was the official church and was broadly supported by an overwhelming majority of the population, but only a small minority became full members of the congregations.

Unlike Luther, Calvin considered the organization of the church to be an important priority: so much so that it was the first thing to which he turned his attention when he was persuaded to return to Geneva in 1541. The *Ecclesiastical Ordinances* which he drew up in the autumn of that year laid down quite detailed prescriptions for church government. He envisaged four orders: pastors, doctors, elders and deacons. The pastors were responsible for preaching and administering the sacraments and for overseeing spiritual discipline. The doctors were responsible for the teaching of scripture and had oversight of preliminary education. The elders were laymen, chosen from the governing councils of the city, and had charge of discipline in conjunction with the pastors. Deacons were also laymen. They cared for the sick and the poor and managed the finances which the church had designated for those groups.

The consistory, the governing body of the church, was made up of the city pastors and the twelve elders. At the head of the Consistory was one of the Syndics, the heads of the city's government. The elders and deacons were all lay people: Calvin thus envisaged a high level of lay vocation and lay involvement. The Consistory was responsible for moral as well as religious discipline. Church and State were thus expected to collaborate in the enforcement of morality as well as justice. The Consistory was expected to encourage rather than to punish, but it had the ultimate sanction of excommunication, exclusion from the celebration of the Eucharist. This section of the *Ordinances* was the most contentious: the city council insisted on several re-drafts and it was not for some years that Calvin was able to persuade them to accept that excommunication was a spiritual matter and should be the responsibility of the church authorities.

The consistory was powerful, but the power base of the Genevan Reformation was the Company of Pastors. Calvin's 1541 ordinances mention five pastors and three assistants. By the time of his death there were about nine pastors in the city and seven in the outlying villages. The pastors were expected to meet once a week for Bible study. It was not always possible for the village pastors to attend, but the regular meetings facilitated communication as well as improving standards. Calvin's personal influence in Geneva was limited – it was not until 1559 that he became a *bourgeois* of the town and was given voting rights. Nevertheless, as effective leader of the Company of Pastors, his power was considerable.

## The Gathered Church in the doctrine of the Radical reformers

It was the radical reformers who developed the idea of the church as a community of the faithful to its logical conclusion. In Zürich in 1524, when Zwingli was moderating some of his proposals for reform in order to try to extend the Reformation to the whole Swiss confederation, the radicals refused to compromise. Zwingli and the radicals had fundamentally different priorities. For Zwingli, the church had to include the whole community, and compromise was justified in order to do this. For the radicals, the church had to be pure in membership and doctrine, and it was worth excluding the majority in order to achieve purity.[25]

Most of the radical reformers were Anabaptists: that is, their reading of the Bible had led them to the conclusion that baptism was only valid if administered to adults who could understand the doctrine of repentance. New converts were rebaptized in order to become members of the church. This implied that membership of the church was a matter of choice. Furthermore, it was possible to tell who had been saved, because they had made a public profession of their beliefs and received adult baptism. The church of the radical reformers was thus very different from the community-based churches of the magisterial reformers, in which it was assumed that all members of a state or community would be members of one church, and that it was impossible to tell who had truly been saved. The radical reformers understood the church as a visible community of the faithful, people who had chosen to separate themselves from the world. They still believed in the "communion of saints" of the Creed, the basic statement of belief of the Christian church. But where the Catholic communion of saints was a vast body, visible and invisible, the Radical communion could be a very small group indeed. At one point, Luther's former colleague Karlstadt limited the size of the true church to "the brethren in Orlamünde, a few brethren in Zürich and Rothenburg, and a Swabian furrier whom Karlstadt met at the Black Cloister in Wittenberg".[26] (The Swabian furrier was in fact the early Anabaptist preacher Melchior Hoffmann.)

Excommunication, "the ban", was as important as baptism to the Radical doctrine of the true church. Membership of the church came not from birth but from a deliberate choice resulting in a profession of faith and leading to baptism. But if you could choose to join the church, you could also be expelled from it, for misbehaviour or unorthodox belief. Menno Simons described the ban as the command of God, to be exercised against "all who openly lead a shameful, carnal life, and those who are corrupted by a heretical, unclean doctrine". The ban was part of the process by which the congregation cared for each other, for it was "instituted to make ashamed unto reformation". It was not intended to cut the excommunicated person off from spiritual help and advice:

> The ban is also a work of divine love and not of perverse, unmerciful, heathenish cruelty. A true Christian will serve, aid and commiserate with everybody; yea, even with his most bitter enemies ... we should not practise the ban to the destruction of mankind (as the Pharisees did their Sabbath) but to its improvement; and thus we desire to serve the bodies of the fallen, in love, reasonableness and humility ...

However, excommunication was also designed to preserve the purity of the congregation, "that we should not be sullied by the leaven of false doctrine or unclean-living flesh, by apostates". It was taken so seriously that it could separate husband and wife, parents and children. "What use is there in the ban", Simons rhetorically asked, "when the shunning and avoiding are not connected with it?"[27]

The radical reformers saw the true church as a cohesive comunity, separated from an evil world. Many (though not all) of them believed in the common, shared ownership of property as a logical consequence of the sharing of the Lord's Supper. Early radical congregations in the countryside outside Zürich marked their community of goods by breaking the locks off their doors and cellars.[28]

> In this community, everything must proceed equally, all things be one and communal, alike in the bodily gifts of their Father in heaven, which he daily gives to be used by his own, according to his will ... In brief, a brother should serve, live and work for the other, none for himself;

indeed, one house for another, one community for another in some other settlement in the land, wherever the Lord grants it that we gather together, one communion, as a body of the Lord and members one to another.[29]

They derived their ideas from the descriptions of the early church in the Acts of the Apostles:

This we see in all the writings of the holy apostles, namely, how one brother, one congregation, serves the other, extends assistance, and supplies to the other in the Lord.[30]

Like their ideas on adult baptism, their view of the church as a sharing community with common ownership of property meant they had to separate themselves from the rest of society. Their challenge to the power structures of a society based on property-ownership was one of the reasons why they were so generally persecuted and reviled. Tens of thousands of them were executed in the sixteenth century. Persecution led them to place considerable emphasis on another identifying feature of the true church – that it suffered and was persecuted.

The seventh ordinance is that all Christians must suffer and be persecuted, as Christ has promised them and said thus (John 16:33): The world shall have joy, but ye shall have tribulation: but be of good cheer, for your sorrow shall be turned into joy . . . [31]

## The clergy: priests or ministers?

The medieval doctrine of the true church meant that only validly-ordained clergy could administer the sacraments. The moral shortcomings of individual clergy were excused because of their status as ordained priests and their control of access to the means of grace. The Reformation cut away their exclusive status. As a result, the shortcomings of the clergy now much more of an obvious problem. The senior clergy in particular were vulnerable to criticism because of their wealth and secular power. It was easy for the Reformers to contrast these with the poverty of Christ and his apostles.

Zwingli's attack on clerical power in the *Schlussreden*, the discussion of his sixty-seven propositions, was directed mainly at the abuse of their power, the way in which the bishops had become swaggering aristo-crats, warmongers, cheats and traitors. However, he also initiated an attack on the basis of clerical power, the spurious Donation of Constantine, by which the Emperor Constantine was supposed to have given power in the Roman Empire to the Pope and the church. Luther's principle of the priesthood of all believers also cut away at the temporal as well as the spiritual power of the church.

Nor were the clergy of the Protestant tradition a separate caste, set aside by their ritual purity and abstention from sexual activity. The Catholic church had insisted on celibacy for parish priests as well as senior members of the hierarchy since the Hildebrandine reforms of the eleventh century. Complete clerical celibacy had proved impracticable in practice. In many parts of Europe unofficial clerical marriages were tolerated and the sons of priests became priests in their turn. However, this was obviously an unsatisfactory compromise and left young priests in particular to struggle with their sexual feelings. Zwingli had been forced to admit to the Zürich town council that he was unable to keep his vows of celibacy in spite of his personal determination to do so.

> Some three years ago I firmly resolved not to touch any woman . . . I succeeded poorly in this, however. In Glarus I kept my resolution about six months, in Einsiedeln about a year . . . [32]

By 1522 he had convinced himself that there was no Biblical foundation for the demand that all clergy should be celibate. In that year he married Anna Reinhart, the widow of a local landowner. The marriage was secret, but he obviously regarded it as a marriage rather than an unofficial relationship. Shortly afterwards, he and ten other Zürich priests published a petition to the bishop of Constance and the Swiss Confederation in defence of the married priesthood. It was an eloquent and moderate appeal, based on Biblical evidence and pastoral experience. The petitioners pointed out that a young priest who was required to hear intimate confessions and to be in close contact with girls and young married women could be dangerous; but given a wife, children and a home his passions would be cooled. They stressed that they were not asking for special privileges for clerical wives and children, only that they be allowed to live openly and that they should not be debarred from the craft gilds.[33]

However, support for clerical marriages was bound to be more than a matter of practical pastoral organization. It challenged the identity of the priesthood as a ritually separate group, set apart by the sacrament of ordination and by their sexual purity. It was nevertheless an attractive idea for the many clergy who were struggling with the demand that they be celibate when they had no vocation to be so. The possibility of clerical marriage may even help to explain the acceptance of the Reformation in otherwise conservative areas like Wales. Here the clergy had continued to marry openly. Senior diocesan clergy and even monks and abbots had wives, and their children were openly acknowledged and even included in family pedigrees.

The Reformation was not initially an anti-clerical movement – how could it be, when so many of its leaders were themselves clergymen? The popular image of the uneducated layman preaching a simple understanding of the Gospel evaporates when we look at the evangelical preachers of sixteenth-century Germany. The majority in the early years of the Reformation were former clergy of the Catholic church and were men of mature years when they embarked on careers of evangelical preaching. They were usually graduates, often with higher degrees, and a surprisingly high proportion were drawn from the urban élite. These were the men who by their preaching took the ideas of the Reformation to local communities across Germany. The Reformation was thus in its origins essentially a clerical movement. Even the radical extremist Thomas Müntzer was an ordained priest who had had a conventional university education and clerical career.[34]

Nevertheless, as it spread through lay society, the Reformation tapped into a vein of anticlericalism which was always present in medieval attitudes. This was probably no more than the hostility of any society towards the staff of large organizations. They may perform a necessary service and individuals may well be respected but it is too easy to blame them for the deficiencies of the organization. Modern equivalents might include the hostility of some western societies towards public sector employees like teachers and social workers. The medieval church was wealthy and set standards of conduct which many of its clergy were unable to live up to. Tithes, the tenth of all agricultural and craft produce due to the church, were resented, particularly when the money went to priests who were already perceived to be wealthy.

Historians are currently reassessing the evidence for anticlericalism in the early sixteenth century and its influence on the Reformation. It is easy to find instances of resistance to the payment of tithes, but hard to estimate how widespread resistance was or how far it stemmed from genuine anti-clerical feeling. The potential for resentment was obviously there and some of the early reformers were ready to exploit it. Zwingli's first comprehensive statement of his beliefs, the *Apologeticus Architeles*, contrasted the easy lives of the clergy with the hard labour of ordinary people.[35] However, anticlericalism did not always equate with

Protestant beliefs. The English Pilgrimage of Grace was essentially a protest against the religious changes which Cromwell and Cranmer were introducing in the wake of Henry VIII's divorce. Nevertheless, it was associated with anticlericalism. The Pilgrims expressed their resentment of tithes, the tenth of the produce of their land which they had to give to the church. There was also criticism of the clergy for laziness and absenteeism. Anticlericalism could mean dislike of the new Protestant clergy as well as of the old Catholic priesthood.[36]

Luther's attack on the power and status of the clergy was more fundamental. It was directed against their claim that the ordained clergy were indispensable to the church – that they were, indeed, the institutional church – and that they controlled access to the sacraments and to the means of salvation. Their claim stemmed from the fact that they were ordained by a ritual which was regarded as a sacrament. As a result, they had what Luther called "despotic power" over lay people. Luther regarded this as a perversion of the true rôle of the clergy, which was to be ministers to the people.

Although they no longer considered ordination as a sacrament, the mainstream churches in the Reformed tradition retained the idea of the clergy as a separate group, trained and formally appointed and expected to exercise some form of leadership and discipline. Most of the early reformers were already ordained in the Catholic church. For the second generation of Reformers, though, it was necessary to devise procedures for the appointment and training of ministers.

Luther saw the appointment of the clergy as a twofold process. The individual pastor had to be called by God to the ministry. This concept of vocation is fundamental to the Protestant concept of the clergy. Then the pastor had to be called to the community he would serve. Luther seems at first to have envisaged individual congregations electing their own pastors. He eventually decided that congregational control was leading to disorder, and reverted to a more organized system. Clergy were appointed by the church councils, which were in effect in most Lutheran countries departments of the state government. However, he continued to insist on the need for a process of ordination, by which senior clergy consecrated new recruits.

The appointment of the early pastors in the Swiss reformed churches was more haphazard, possibly because there was less state control. Guillaume Farel, who brought Calvin to Geneva, was never formally ordained. He believed himself to have been called to the pastorate by God. He was himself invited to serve by the Basle reformer Johannes Oecolampadius, who was one of the early reformers who had been ordained in the Catholic church. Farel himself invited Calvin to serve as a minister in Geneva, so the Reformers could continue to claim something approaching the apostolic succession of the Catholic church. However, there was obviously a need for more formal procedures. Calvin's *Ecclesiastical Ordinances* made detailed provision for the selection and appointment of pastors. There was no specific training course for the ministry, but aspiring candidates were subjected to a thorough process of assessment lasting several days. They were expected to deliver sermons and Bible commentaries and were questioned carefully by the existing pastors. It was the Company of Pastors who decided on suitable candidates and presented them first to the city authorities for approval and then to the congregation they were to serve.[37]

There were thus two obvious differences in the status of the clergy in the Protestant tradition. First, they no longer controlled the means of grace. They were not priests but ministers, servants of the people, there to teach and discipline. This did not mean, though, that they were controlled by the people they served. In the early years of the Reformation, evangelical preaching was popular. Preachers travelled from village to village spreading new ideas. When they could not get permission to preach in church, they used barns or preached in the open air. Congregations also wanted resident preachers to minister to them, men of good ability and moral standards. Initially, local communities were able to take the initiative in seeking out such men, but by the mid-sixteenth century most Lutheran states had church councils and superintendents who appointed and controlled the clergy. The same framework was adopted in the Calvinist territories in Germany. In some of the Swiss city states the city council appointed the clergy, but this was still control by an élite minority. Only in the gathered churches of the radical reformers was there any real community involvement in the selection and appointment of the clergy.

The second crucial difference was that the Protestant clergy were officially allowed and even encouraged to marry. In theory, this meant that they should have been more clearly "of the people", sharing their everyday concerns. Oddly, the opposite seems to have happened. In most Protestant countries, the Reformation created a new social group, the clerical family, drawn mainly from the middle ranks of society. A detailed study of the clergy in sixteenth-century Württemberg found that, of the pastors whose family background could be traced, no less than 63 per cent were the sons of pastors. A similar picture has been described in Strasbourg, where the Church Assembly obviously provided a framework for social life as well as professional discipline.[38]

The clerical dynasty was nothing new: the term "nepotism" was coined to describe it. Even clerical succession from father to son had survived all attempts to enforce clerical celibacy. What seems to have been new about the Protestant clerical class was its openness and self-awareness. While the Protestant clergy rarely had complete control of church appointments, they were often able to act as a group to oversee the admission of new members to clerical status and to train existing members. As university teachers they also had charge of the training of the next generation of clergy. Their control of admission and training contributed to a new sense of professionalization among the Protestant clergy.

A sense of group unity was also fostered by the flattening of the clerical hierarchy. Bishops were no longer remote, wealthy and powerful figures. At the other end of the scale, the Protestant churches did not have a clerical underclass of chantry priests living on short-term appointments to say Mass and other prayers for the dead. Instead, church superintendents were paid as state servants, and it was assumed that each pastor would have a permanent post with a congregation to care for.

The new rôle of the clergy as teachers and preachers demanded higher educational standards. The same study of the Württemberg clergy found that virtually all of them had been to the local university, Tübingen. Some were paid for by their families, but there were scholarships provided by the state government for gifted young men from poor families. Providing university education for all prospective clergy was a challenge for poorer and more remote areas and for countries with no university of their own. Young men from Wales, for example, had to go to the English universities of Oxford and Cambridge. There they spoke English and were taught in Latin, before returning home to minister to exclusively Welsh-speaking congregations. Little wonder, therefore, that the Welsh dioceses did not set too high a priority on sending their future clergy to university. In 1563, the Welsh diocese of St Asaph had only fourteen resident graduates in nearly 120 parishes.[39]

Providing a university education for prospective clergy was made more difficult by the fact that clerical incomes generally remained low. Parents of limited means who invested money in providing an education for their sons needed some return on their investments. Most of the Württemberg clergy had state stipends which were the equivalent of the average income of a small-scale craftsman. Many were obliged to farm or work as teachers in order to make ends meet.

The parish clergy of the medieval Catholic church had been drawn from the same social background as their parishioners. This caused tensions but ultimately the church was probably strengthened rather than weakened by the resulting community of interest and outlook. However, few peasant families could afford to send their children to university if they were to become poorly-paid clerics. Again, the clergy of Württemberg provide a useful case study. Of those who did not come from clerical families, most in the sixteenth century were the sons of artisans. By the eighteenth century, though, the vast majority were from the families of the state bureaucracy. Ironically, although it had ostensibly set out to diminish the prestige and mystique of the clergy, the Protestant tradition increasingly emphasized the separation between minister and congregation. The clergy were to be an intellectual élite, providing instruction and patriarchal discipline rather than the comfort of the sacraments. They were discouraged from attending and sharing in the entertainments of their parishioners. They tended to remain a group apart, seldom settling their families in the areas where they worked. German society at this period was still overwhelmingly rural and agricultural, its culture tied to the rhythms of the farming year. By the seventeenth century, however, virtually all the Lutheran states had clergy drawn from urban society, men who had been brought up and trained in the cities. Hsia describes them as "mediators between peasant beliefs and an urban culture and religion" but also emphasizes the ambiguity of their rôle as both insiders and outsiders, bringers of spiritual consolation and enforcers of the edicts of an alien state culture.[40]

There was some disagreement among the radical reformers about the rôle of the ministry in the true church. Some of their ideas were constrained by practical realities: most of the radical churches were poor and could not afford to pay for a full-time stipendiary ministry. However, they were also influenced by their reading of the Bible, in particular the Acts of the Apostles, which described a church with itinerant pastors for spiritual leadership. Some of the Anabaptists eventually decided that a proper church must have a pastor, but the itinerant ministry remained an option for others. The Schleitheim Confession, which embodies mainstream opinion among the Radical reformers, suggests that the main duty of the pastor is to read the Scriptures and to teach, warn and admonish in the light of what the Bible says. He (always *he*) leads the prayers and breaks the bread for Communion. He is also responsible for taking the lead in disciplining the congregation and exercising the ban "in the name of the congregation". However, he is appointed by the congregation and can be disciplined by them.[41]

The more extreme radicals rejected the idea of any ordained ministry. Karlstadt, for example, although he was himself an ordained priest of considerable seniority, became violently anti-clerical in his later years. He would only accept the title "brother" from the congregation which he served at Orlamünde. He attacked the pretensions of the clergy in the crudest language. Referring to the ritual by which the priest lifted up the consecrated bread in the Eucharist, he said "Woe to you, for you shall be lifted up, like a tail above an arsehole (you who have been placed above all the nations of the earth) because you smear and desert the Saviour." Eventually, he came to the viewpoint that any lay person could break the bread and pour the wine for the Eucharist just as well as an officially-ordained pastor. He also rejected the intellectual superiority of the clergy and encouraged his congregation to challenge his ideas and even to interrupt his sermons and to preach themselves in church.[42]

One thing which virtually all the reformed churches rejected, along with the idea of clerical celibacy, was the idea of the religious orders, a spiritual élite vowed to live a particularly holy life and having special spiritual powers as a result. Luther had tried the religious life and found it wanting. The austerity and dedication of his monastery had brought him no assurance of salvation. If the individual human is saved by faith, then choosing a particular lifestyle can make no difference. Indeed, the monastic life can be a dangerous distraction, since it gives monks the illusion that they are doing something which will save them.

> It does not help the soul if the body is adorned with the sacred robes of priests or dwells in sacred places, or is occupied with sacred duties or prays, fasts, abstains from certain kinds of food, or does any work that can be done by the body and in the body. The righteousness and the freedom of the soul require something far different, since the things which have been mentioned could be done by any wicked person. Such works produce nothing but hypocrites. On the other hand, it will not harm the soul if the body is clothed in secular dress, dwells in unconsecrated places, eats and drinks as others do, does not pray aloud, and neglects to do all the above-mentioned things which hypocrites do.[43]

The logical conclusion was that the monastic life was a waste of time, and that the land and other endowments which had been given to support monasteries should be confiscated and put to a more useful purpose.

Luther's decision was in line with the fundamental Protestant belief that vicarious prayer and sacrifice were meaningless. In practical terms, though, it left the Protestant churches without those groups of men and women who were to serve as the shock-troops of the Catholic Reformation. Without the Jesuits, the new orders of friars and the teaching and nursing sisterhoods, the Catholic church of the sixteenth and seventeenth centuries would have been much weaker. It was the religious orders which provided the missionaries who took Christianity to South America, Africa and Asia; and the Christianity they took was Catholic Christianity.

The decision to abolish religious orders also left the Protestant churches without the organizations which had undertaken so much educational and welfare work. Luther repeatedly suggested that the property of dissolved religious houses should be converted to socially useful purposes. Some was, but much simply came into the hands of the local rulers. The Protestant churches had therefore to make alternative provision for those socially-useful tasks which the religious orders had undertaken. The means they chose to accomplish this tell us much about the relations they wanted to see established between church and state.

## 5

# Church and State: The Protestant Churches and Secular Authority

There had of course been splits and break-away movements within the Catholic church in the centuries before Luther. What made the schism of the early sixteenth century irreversible was the strength of the break-away group. Their strength was largely the result of the support which Luther and the Swiss reformers had obtained from secular rulers. This uncoupling of religious reform from political radicalism was one of the great strengths of the sixteenth-century Reformation and probably explains why it succeeded where previous reform movements had failed. Wycliffe and Hus, and the Cathars and Waldensians before them, had been defeated not by theological argument but by the force of secular authority. Luther, by contrast, was defended by the Elector of Saxony, and the doctrines of the Swiss reformers were protected by the increasing independence of their cities and cantons.

The dependence of the early reformed churches on secular power and authority thus necessitated a fundamental redefinition of the relationship between church and state. The power and jurisdiction of the medieval church was based on its reading of the "two swords" mentioned in Luke 22:38. These were interpreted as referring to spiritual and secular jurisdiction. The view of the medieval church was that spiritual jurisdiction took precedence. The Church hierarchy exercised spiritual jurisdiction and permitted the lay authorities to exercise secular jurisdiction. The church had in fact acquired extensive secular powers as well. Bishops ruled principalities in Germany, and the Pope had what was virtually a kingdom of his own in Italy. As a result, spiritual leaders spent much of their time on the concerns of secular rule – concerns which included making war in defence of their political interests.

The reformers challenged the medieval interpretation of the doctrine of the two swords, arguing that the ecclesiastical hierarchy should lay aside all secular powers. Instead, the clergy (including the Pope) should be subject to properly-constituted civil authority. The duty of the magistrates to keep good order extended to the order of the Church. For this, they were entitled to be paid – and the money must be found by taxation. Zwingli reminded his readers that Christ had accepted the principle of lawful taxation and had instructed his followers to "render to Caesar what is Caesar's". The claims which the medieval clergy made for exemption from taxation, Zwingli therefore considered to be unjustified.

## Church and State in the Lutheran tradition

Luther's *Address to the Christian Nobility of the German Nation* (1520)[1] made an obvious appeal to patriotism. Although Luther was still prepared to be reconciled with the spiritual authority of the Pope in 1535, in this early work he was already attacking the Pope's control over the organization of the German church. Interestingly, Luther claimed that France had resisted the power of the Pope, and used this as an argument to urge the German rulers to do the same. The political status of the Papacy meant that any attack on the authority of the church in Rome had immense political implications. Having put behind them the troubles of their exile in Avignon, the schism and the brief revival of church councils, the Popes were powerful secular rulers and their authority was seen as a challenge to the independence of other rulers. The theological ideas of the early reformers could be manipulated to provide a justification for an attack on the Pope's political status. This made Protestantism attractive to rulers who were not worried about their own salvation but who were worried about territorial independence. They were thus prepared to offer their protection to the Reformers.

However, reliance on secular authority brought problems with it. The German peasants were suffering from the results of rising population: land shortage, and in particular the loss of much of their common land. There was a series of peasant uprisings in the early sixteenth century. In 1524 the peasants of southern Germany rose in rebellion and asked Luther for support. Luther, however, saw the peasants as forces of anarchy who could threaten his purely religious aims. He was also concerned about the involvement of more radical reformers like Thomas Müntzer in the rebellion. Luther therefore wrote one of his most violent books denouncing the rebels. Its title, *Against the murderous and thieving hordes of peasants*, gives a fair idea of the contents and tone.[2] The book was written early in 1525, when there were successful uprisings all over central and southern Germany. Unfortunately, by the time it was printed, the peasants' main army had been slaughtered and their leaders captured and tortured.

Luther's attack on the peasants was perhaps inevitable, given his priorities, but it remains one of the most unpalatable episodes in his career. He had followed the implications of his initial stand against indulgences to their conclusion, that the Pope was not the ultimate authority in matters of religion. However, in seeking another source of power which could defend his reforms from the worldly power of the Catholic church, he was forced to accept the protection of sympathetic secular powers. He had to concern himself with politics and organization. From a movement which stressed the primacy of the individual's relationship with God, his had become one which stressed social and institutional order. In the aftermath of the Peasants' War, Luther took part in a visitation of the parishes in Ernestine Saxony in 1529. The experience strengthened his belief in the importance of the secular power as a force for religious reform and discipline.

By the end of the sixteenth century, in virtually all the Lutheran territories, the church had been completely integrated into the running of the state. The clergy were appointed, paid and disciplined as if they were state officials. In turn, they were expected to act as outposts of the state, supplementing the work of local officials and enforcing government policies. Many of the Lutheran states had a *Kirchenrat*, a Church Council, as one of the departments of state. Church Superintendents were appointed as state officials with the duty of visiting local churches and questioning clergy and congregation alike. It was the machinery of the state which attempted to impose moral discipline on peasant society and enforce Lutheran orthodoxy in the face of residual Catholicism, the challenge of more radical reformed ideas and the traditional beliefs and rituals of agrarian society.

Lutheran theologians were prepared to criticize the secular authorities, but always acknowledged the ultimate power of the magistrate. As the legal theorist Veit Ludwig von Seckendorff asserted in 1685:

> The authorities should be more than the executors of spiritual power; they must also take upon themselves the furtherance of Christian teachings and the creation of good church laws. The authorities have the might to reform the inadequacies of the Church and the clerical estate.[3]

The development of doctrines of church–state relations was inevitably constrained by the different forms of state organization with which the Reformers had to deal. In northern Germany, Luther and his colleagues were dependent on the support of individual rulers, men who had autocratic power within their own dominions. They were thus forced to allow secular rulers a considerable measure of responsibility for the functioning of the church. In cities like Zwickau, too, the city council took control of religious affairs, appointing preachers, controlling Anabaptists and other radicals. For them, the Lutheran Reformation offered them a convenient excuse to attack the powers of the institutional Catholic church and to take fuller control of civic affairs.[4]

The pattern of church–state relations which this produced reached its most extreme form in England, where Henry VIII proclaimed himself "Supreme Head of the Church" and ordered that his coat of arms be painted in all churches to replace the medieval wall paintings of Christ and the saints. The appeal to the godly prince and the godly magistrate remained as a commonplace of English political thought in the early seventeenth century. James I and VI was praised as a model Protestant leader. However, his son Charles I tried to introduce a more sacramental approach to worship into the services of the state church. Eventually, and reluctantly, the convinced Protestants among his subjects opposed him, and when civil war broke out they were virtually all to be found among his opponents.

The situation in the city-states of southern Germany was more complex. They were located in the vortex of the international power politics of the mid-sixteenth century as France and the Empire used northern Italy as a battleground. In Strasbourg, for instance, Martin Bucer had to fight to establish his vision of the true church in a city where a number of other interests had to be conciliated, and he was criticized by some for the compromises which his political situation forced on him.

The early evangelical preachers in Strasbourg had been obliged to appeal to the ruling council of the city to support their doctrines against the authority of the local bishop. In effect, what the early evangelicals had done was to use popular support to force the council to accept religious change. The Strasbourg authorities did not like having their hands forced. However, the reformers were prepared to flatter the council and to argue that the secular authorities could regulate many of the externals of religious life. The councillors were thus given the opportunity to claim control of church doctrine and discipline as well as organization.

When the city's Protestant statement of belief, the *Tetrapolitana* (so called because it was subscribed to by the four cities of Strasbourg, Constance, Lindau and Memmingen), was presented to the Emperor at Augsburg in 1530, it was presented not as the opinion of the reformers but of the city council.[5]

The revival of Catholic military power in 1547 meant that many of these southern cities were reconquered (for a while at least) by the Catholic Emperor Charles V. Lutheranism thus became a way of articulating resistance to the political power of the Empire. In Strasbourg, the city fathers reluctantly accepted a compromise settlement that left the city Catholic but free of direct imperial control. However, the Lutheran townspeople continued to harass the Catholic clergy and were tacitly supported in their actions by the city magistrates, who simply failed to take action against them. Eventually, in 1560, the city returned openly to the Lutheran faith.

Regensburg had only declared itself Lutheran in 1542. Here again, the city magistrates were obliged to accept nominal Catholicism to protect themselves against invasion. However, they expressed their continuing loyalty to the Reformation in visual terms. The record books of the city were re-bound with covers decorated with emblems of Protestantism including pictures of the early reformer John Hus and of Luther himself. The Reformation was thus embedded in the identity and memory of the city.[6]

External pressures continued to affect the progress of the "long Reformation" in cities like Strasbourg. Most of its immediate neighbours were Catholic, and the (Catholic) bishop of Strasbourg retained considerable power in the region. He presided over the *Landtag*, in which deputies from upper and lower Alsace met to deal with a range of economic and social problems as well as military threats. The communities represented there had to set aside their religious differences and work together to deal with things which threatened them all, from poverty and bad harvests to the threat of foreign invasion. The Strasburghers had to balance the conflicting demands of the other German Lutherans and their Swiss Calvinist trading contacts and of the Catholic superpowers, France, Spain and the Hapsburg Empire. The civic authorities also had to consider the best interests of their internal manufacturing and trading communities and extend a measure of practical tolerance to refugees from different religious groups. Their awareness of these competing interests set the city council against the clergy, some of whom wanted a much more hard-line approach.[7]

## Church and State in the Swiss Calvinist tradition

Like the Lutherans of the southern German cities, the Swiss reformers developed their ideas in city states and semi-independent cantons, dependent on the support of local magistrates rather than individual rulers. In Zwingli's Zürich, as in the German Lutheran cities, the city council was well organized and in a position to lead the demand for change. It was to the city council that Zwingli appealed in 1522 for an opportunity to prove the truth of his principles "according to the truth of Holy Writ".[8] The council arranged a public debate in which Zwingli would attempt to prove his propositions by reasoned argument. It was like a traditional academic disputation, with the crucial difference that proceedings were to be in German and that the laymen of the council should decide who had the better arguments. Potter likens it to a modern public enquiry, "arranged by a government whose duty it was to ensure that proper preaching and teaching was available for its subjects".[9]

At the disputation, Zwingli succeeded in defending his approach to the preaching of the Bible as the only authority in matters of religion. The council agreed that his sermons should continue and that all the clergy of Zürich should adopt his evangelical stance in their own preaching. Zwingli had thus enabled the council to claim the right to oversee religious belief and to control public worship and preaching within its boundaries. The same model of a disputation arranged by the secular authorities was followed at Basle, Berne, Lausanne and Geneva, with the additional rule that arguments had to be based on Scripture.

Zwingli's model of the true church was based on the early church of the apostles, with groups of Christians living together in community. In such a church, if there was a conflict over true doctrine, "the people" had to decide, guided by the Bible. In Zürich, however, and in most of the churches of the Swiss reformed tradition, "the people" meant in practice the people's spokesmen, the organized government of city and canton. It was the city council which had to arbitrate doctrinal disputes and enforce church laws. The authority of the Pope and the councils of the church was thus in effect transferred to the secular power. In the Lutheran states of Germany, the secular power was the godly prince; in the city-states of southern Germany and Switzerland it was the godly magistrate.

The Zürich council had always had extensive powers over the church. In Geneva, by complete contrast, much of the running of the secular life of the city had been the responsibility of the Bishop's administrators.

When the city decided for the Reformation, all these clerical bureaucrats left, taking with them the administrative, legal and financial skills on which the city had depended. The city council still inclined towards the Zürich model of a religious rôle for secular government. However, Calvin and his mentor Guillaume Farel were determined that the church should not be controlled by the civil authority in matters of religion.

In Reformation Zürich, the city council even had the power to excommunicate – to declare that serious offenders were excluded from the church and the community of the faithful. Calvin, however, considered that church and state should cooperate, but that there were some matters on which the church should have supreme authority. It took him some years to enforce his views on the city council, but eventually it was agreed that in Geneva excommunication should be the responsibility of the church assembly, the Consistory. The Consistory had a majority of lay members (the elders and the syndic) but they were there as part of the fourfold ministry of the church. The compromise – control by the laity, but incorporating the laity in the structure of the church – worked in a close-knit community like Geneva (though even in Geneva there were tensions) but was less well suited to large countries like England and the Netherlands where the leaders of lay society were more likely to have divergent ideas.

## Church and State in Calvinist Germany

Calvinist ideas on the relationship between church and state thus evolved in the very specific context of the oligarchic city-state. However, Calvinism also proved attractive to the rulers of a number of territorial German states. In some cases, they were clearly motivated by purely religious conviction. For others, though, there were compelling political reasons for change. Calvin had taken the doctrine of salvation by faith to its logical extreme and Calvinist doctrine had a more rigorous and coherent approach. It was thus able to offer a more intellectually hard-edged response to the challenge of the Counter-Reformation. Many of the German princes had Calvinist family connections. They were attracted by the internationalism of the Calvinist church, which could be used as an effective counterweight against the international power of Spain and the Holy Roman Empire.

The Calvinism of the German states was in most cases imposed from above, by princes and a small academic and official élite. It was generally resisted by local aristocracies and ordinary people alike. In the

German states, Calvinism thus changed its political complexion and became an instrument of centralizing state power. It could be used by reforming princes to overrule regionalism and the established privileges of local landowners and urban corporations. The relationship between church and state also changed. Authority moved from the clergy and the local congregations to the state bureaucracy. As in the Lutheran states, secular officials dominated the church councils. It was they who controlled the appointment and supervision of the clergy and the visitation of individual congregations. The church consistories continued to meet but they had no powers to appoint clergy or excommunicate recalcitrant laypeople.

The high point of German Calvinism came in 1619, when Frederick, the Calvinist ruler of the Palatinate of the Rhine, accepted the crown of Bohemia. For one brief moment, Calvinists could indulge visions of a united front against the Hapsburg Empire. It was even possible to dream of a Calvinist Emperor and the crushing of the Counter-Reformation. But this was also the beginning of the end for Calvinism in the Holy Roman Empire. The revived power of Counter-Reformation Catholicism, backed by the financial and military might of the Empire, was too strong. Within a couple of years, the Emperor had reconquered Bohemia. His Spanish allies had occupied the Palatinate and Frederick was driven into exile. The war continued until 1648, by which time virtually all the participants had forgotten what they were fighting about. The peace settlement which was eventually reached in 1648 guaranteed the rights of individual Calvinist communities, but Calvinism was destroyed as a political force in Germany.

The established church of England has been described as Calvinist in its theology and Catholic in its organization. The Thirty-Nine Articles, the basic statement of faith hammered out in 1571, were broadly predestinarian in tone, though with a great deal of creative ambiguity.[10] However, the organization of the church was perhaps closer to that of the German Lutheran and Calvinist principalities. True, there were still bishops, and they claimed to hold their offices by the apostolic authority passed on from Christ himself through St Peter. But in fact they were state officials, appointed by the monarch. They could not in theory be removed, but Elizabeth came pretty close to it with some of her more stubborn bishops.

It was the bishops in turn who appointed some of the parish clergy. However, many of them – perhaps a majority – were appointed not by the bishop, not by the congregation, but by the local landowner. The right to appoint the parish priest (the technical term is the right of *advowson*) was in many cases part of the property of the local manor. Control of the church at local level was thus in the hands of the local gentry. As they also provided the leadership of local society and administered law and order as justices of the peace, the integration of church and state at local level was considerable.

## The radical reformers: the separation of church and state

The magisterial reformers had a vision of the true church as inclusive of the whole community. They were thus forced to cooperate with existing systems of secular authority. The radical reformers had more freedom of manoeuvre. Their vision of the church as a gathered community of the saved made it easier for them to separate from and even to attack secular power. Thomas Müntzer, the early Zwickau reformer, reviled the rich and the secular authorities in his sermons – and was forced to depart from Zwickau as a result.

Having declared themselves independent of existing authority, the radical reformers were also more ready to attack the established social and economic order. Their Biblical literalism led them to advocate the almost Communist society of the early Christian church as described in the Acts of the Apostles. Here they found an idealistic vision of a community in which "not one of them claimed any of his possessions as his own, but everything was held in common". As we have seen (above, pp. 85–6), this was part of their definition of the true church, but it also made some of them more critical of the organization of secular society.

The links between religious and political radicalism in the sixteenth century are not straightforward. In theory, while political radicals like the leaders of the German Peasants' Revolt wanted to change society, the leaders of the Protestant radicals wanted to separate themselves entirely from society. Nevertheless, radicals like Karlstadt supported the German peasants in their uprising in 1524. There were radical preachers who wanted not so much to separate themselves from the world as to impose their own religious ideas on it.

The politically radical tendency found its most violent expression in the events at the episcopal city of Münster near the border between Germany and Holland. Here a group of radical preachers took over the town council in 1534, expelled those who would not be rebaptized and instituted a communist regime. In accordance with Anabaptist social

principles, all property was held in common, house doors were to be left
open and the use of money was outlawed. The Anabaptists' leader Jan
of Leiden also introduced polygamy in emulation of the Old Testament
patriarchs. The city was besieged by the bishop's army and was eventually betrayed by two of the inhabitants. In the ensuing battle, many of
the inhabitants were killed; their leaders were captured and publicly
tortured to death.[11]

Whatever their ideas on participation in secular government, the
radical reformers had insisted from the beginning that church discipline
was a matter for the church community. The second of the Schleitheim
articles stated:

> The practice of excommunication must be exercised among all those who
> profess themselves Christian, having been baptized, but who nevertheless
> fall into some fault inadvertently and not deliberately. These must be
> exhorted and admonished secretly twice; on a third occasion they must
> be publicly banished from the whole congregation, so that we may break
> bread together and drink from the cup with a shared zeal.

However, the Schleitheim Articles went much further than Calvin's
Institutes in their complete separation of the worshipping community
from the power of the state. Article 4 was one of the most threatening
to secular authority:

> A man must separate himself from all the pollutions of this world and be
> joined to God . . . any use of arms is diabolical.

Article 6 took this standpoint further:

> We agree that the use of the sword is commanded by God, outside the
> perfection of Christ. Princes and the authorities of the world are thus
> ordered to punish and kill the wicked. But within the perfection of Christ,
> excommunication is the ultimate sanction, without bodily death.

The refusal of the radical reformers to swear oaths meant they had opted
out of the whole legal system:

> We have reached this agreement on oaths, that they are an affirmation to
> be made only in the name of God, and truly, not lying, according to the
> commandment of the law. But to Christians all oaths are forbidden by our
> Lord Jesus Christ.

The Schleitheim Articles thus describe a church which has withdrawn from the world and from the control of all secular authority. It was therefore a threat to civil society. The pacifism of the radical reformers was a particular problem in Switzerland, where so much of the revenue of the poorer cantons came from the money paid to their mercenary soldiers. However, in a society in which military service was one of the obligations of citizenhood, the description of the bearing of arms as "one of the pollutions of the world" was a threat to the security of any state. Ultimately, the refusal of the radical reformers to participate in civil society on religious grounds was tantamount to accusing those who did participate of being unchristian. Like their egalitarianism, their separatism contributed to the general hostility against them.

Many secular authorities were prepared to tolerate and even to promote the ideas of the magisterial reformers because they could be used to increase their own powers. The radical reformers had nothing to offer secular authority: indeed, they were more likely to challenge the existing social and economic order. The city council in Zwickau was happy to appoint Lutheran preachers – and to use Lutheran ideas to increase its own powers – but was never prepared to tolerate the radicals who threatened council control of secular as well as religious life.[12]

## The One Catholic Church and the nation-church

There were even more fundamental theoretical issues in the relationship between church and state after the Reformation. The Apostles' Creed was still the basic statement of faith for most of the reformed churches. Like the more detailed Nicene Creed quoted above, it proclaimed a belief in "the holy catholic church". The medieval church had served the whole community: indeed, in a way, it *was* the whole community in its religious aspect. Was the post-Reformation church still a church for the whole community (as both Lutherans and Calvinists believed) or was it a church only for the faithful, those who were known to have been saved (as some of the radical reformers argued)? And if the church was to be a state church, a church for the whole community, what would happen to those who could not accept the confessional stance of the church in their own state? Where could they be married, where could their children be baptized and their dead buried? Could their beliefs be tolerated or would they have to move? And who could dictate the confessional stance of a state church – the wishes of the majority or the beliefs of the ruler?

One partial solution was suggested at the Imperial Assembly at

Speyer in 1529. The proposal accepted the existence of Lutheran states but proposed different treatment for Lutheran and Catholic territories. Lutheran minorities in Catholic territories were not to be tolerated and would have to move. Catholic minorities in Lutheran territories, however, would have to be tolerated. The Lutheran princes protested against such discrimination, and it was this which led to their being called the Protestants. However, an even more obvious flaw in the Speyer solution soon became apparent. It made no provision for the increasing number of states in Germany which had adopted the confessional stance of Strasbourg and Zürich and could not be called Lutheran.

A series of meetings failed to resolve the problem. There was no formula which could reunite even the Catholic and Lutheran churches; divisions between the reformed churches were becoming more obvious; and there was no possibility of a framework for co-existence. Europe was divided on confessional lines and for ten years from 1545 to 1555 the Catholic Empire fought the Lutheran Schmalkaldic League. Eventually, in 1555, a peace of sorts was reached, though like the Speyer formula it ignored the non-Lutheran Protestants. The basis of the Peace of Augsburg was that, in each of the German states, the religion of the ruler would determine the religion of the people: the Latin phrase *cuius regio, eius religio* sums it up. Technically, there were only two choices available to the rulers: Catholicism or the strict Lutheranism of the First Augsburg Confession. However, a number of German rulers did decide to go Calvinist in spite of the risk that the others would simply ally against them.

After the Peace of Augsburg in 1555, therefore, the doctrine of the unity of the church was reduced to a doctrine of unity within one kingdom. Nevertheless, the importance of the central doctrine of Christian unity, even when it was obvious to all that the church had been split, is still essential to our understanding of political developments in the late sixteenth and seventeenth centuries. The British civil wars of the mid-seventeenth century are an excellent example of the strains placed on the body politic when one king rules over three nations of radically different religious persuasions. The majority of the Scots were Calvinistic Presbyterians (though a substantial minority in the Highlands remained Catholic); the English and Welsh were moderate Calvinist episcopalians; the majority of the Irish were Roman Catholic. It was impossible for Charles I to force them to agree, and equally impossible for him to allow them to differ. Even in England, where one tendency in the established church wanted further reform and another tendency wanted a return to something nearer the Catholic church, it was impossible for both tendencies to co-exist. Nor could they form two independent churches. They had to fight it out like two wild animals in a sack: and while the dispute over religion was not the only cause of the British civil wars, it certainly gave them much of their savagery.

## The Revolution of the Saints?

One school of thought among historians of the British civil wars of the seventeenth century has identified the extreme Protestant tendency in the Church of England, the group known as the Puritans, as one of the sources of the revolutionary spirit of the seventeenth century. Books with titles like *The Puritan Revolution* and *The Revolution of the Saints* testify to the popularity of this perspective on the political dynamics of Protestantism. In recent years, the identification of Puritanism with political radicalism has been questioned, and historians have pointed to the ways in which Protestantism was used to uphold the authority of the state. It is nevertheless tempting to see the Protestant Reformation as a defiance of the established order in secular as well as ecclesiastical matters.

Martin Luther began by opposing all forms of resistance to the emperor. By 1531, however, he was prepared to argue that the sovereign had a duty to protect and maintain true religion. If the emperor failed to do this, and if he tried to impose false religion, the lesser princes of the empire were entitled to resist him. Nevertheless, the right of resistance was limited to the lesser lay authorities: ordinary citizens had no right to act of their own accord. Only as a last resort did they have the right of self-defence in a war which had clearly been started by an enemy acting out of malice and a desire to exterminate the truth.[13] While Luther's ideas attacked the authority of the emperor, they thus enhanced the powers of those princes who had been supporting him.

Luther's deference to established authority was in part pragmatic: he needed the protection which the princes of the Empire could give, and he could not afford to make them hostile. Zwingli was similarly deferential to secular authority. In his *Schlussreden* he pointed out that Christ had submitted to being enrolled and taxed by the Imperial government and had ordered his followers to "give to Caesar the things that are Caesar's". The only permissible exception to the rule of obedience to the civil power was if a Government order was contrary to God's word. Zwingli was evidently aware of the difficulties of resisting evil authority. He spent some twenty pages of the *Schlussreden* discussing the problem, though without reaching any satisfactory conclusion. Tyrants might not be killed; rebellion was ungodly. Ultimately, all he could suggest was mass disobedience, a sort of general strike. Had he developed these ideas further, they might have made him the father of the twentieth-century doctrines of passive resistance and non-violent action, but he did not. His concerns with the problem of tyrants were largely speculative. He was really writing for his own community of Zürich, which was a civic oligarchy and prepared to support the Reformation.

The pietist movement in later seventeenth-century Lutheran Germany could have provided the focus for resistance to the authority of the state over the church. The pietists can in many ways be compared to the English Methodists of a century later. Pietism was essentially a return to a more reflective, spiritual approach to religion as a counter-weight to the dogmatic, doctrinally-based teaching of the official Lutheran state churches. Its roots were in the devotional literature of the English Puritans and, even earlier, in the Catholic tradition of the *devotio moderna.*

However, pietism was itself subverted. In the hands of the Hohenzollerns, the ferociously efficient rulers of Brandenburg-Prussia, it became a bourgeois ideology tailored to the needs of an absolutist, militarist state. Johan Sigismund, Elector of Brandenburg, had converted to Calvinism in 1613 and he and his successors tried to run Brandenburg as a Calvinist-absolutist bureaucracy. The political testament of Friedrich Wilhelm, the Great Elector (1640–88) suggests that he saw Calvinist austerity as God's way to the creation of the perfectly-run state. However, the majority of the people remained Lutheran, and Lutheranism was used to express resistance to the absolute control of the Electors. By the end of the seventeenth century, Pietism was becoming stronger in Brandenburg. The Electors encouraged its spread as a way of reducing the power of orthodox Lutheranism. The emphasis which the Pietists placed on social action and moral discipline was ideal for the Electors' programme of administrative efficiency. In turn, the Pietists supported the Electors because the Electors were prepared to defend the Pietists against the orthodox Lutherans.

There was an element of social egalitarianism in Pietism. Its emphasis on sprituality cut across social divisions. The Lutheran church in Brandenburg reflected the social hierarchy. Churches were full of the tombstones and coats of arms of the local nobility. Landowners controlled the local clergy and used them to enforce deference to the social order. In the towns, urban leaders expected to take the best seats in church and to receive communion before ordinary people. Pietism was fundamentally opposed to all this, but in Brandenburg its egalitarianism was used to reduce the power of the aristocracy and their ability to resist the authority of the Electors.[14]

Nor was the Calvinist tradition initially favourable to those who wanted to overturn established authority. The framework of the relationship between church and state laid down in Calvin's *Ecclesiastical Ordinances* envisaged co-operation and even a measure of identification between church and secular authority. In Geneva, the supreme governing body of the church was dominated by the elders, laymen who were selected from the governing councils of the city. It has even been suggested that the popularity of Calvinism with some German rulers may owe something to the formidable disciplinary structures which made it such an effective instrument for social control.

On the other hand, Calvin's structure of pastors, elders and deacons and his insistence on the autonomy of the church could be translated to allow the church to deal with a hostile environment. If the elders were chosen from among the leading lay members of the congregation, this gave the Calvinist church a social stature and cohesiveness which enabled it to survive without the support of the state. Such a church government was not, however, democracy or popular control. In an emphatically hierarchical society, it was the wealthiest and most powerful members of the lay community who became elders. The ordinary people were controlled and disciplined far more effectively by their local superiors that the would be by a distant monarch.

Calvin's own teachings were far from encouraging revolution. In the *Institution of the Christian Religion,* he explicitly taught that individual Christians should obey the secular government. He expressed no preference for any particular form of government: he was not prepared to express a preference for republicanism over monarchy, for example. The Christian had a duty to obey the ruler, even if the ruler was evil: Calvin quotes numerous Old Testament stories to support his point. If the ruler is wicked, it is the responsibility of the lesser state officials to deal with the situation. Individual members of society cannot take action on their own account. They can only pray to God for deliverance. God may choose to help them, by sending in a deliverer with a special vocation or by using one evil power to oppose another. However, if God does not act, humans must submit to their earthly rulers.

The only exception to this rule is if the head of state orders the subject to do something contrary to Biblical teaching – commiting immoral or idolatrous acts, for example. Under these circumstances, Christians are allowed to defy the orders of the ruler. However, they are still not allowed to rebel. Using as his models the Old Testament heroes like Daniel, who refused to obey the evil commands of evil kings but offered them no resistance, Calvin argued that Christians must refuse to do evil but must then accept the punishments imposed on them by the evil ruler.

Calvin's teaching on these difficult questions derives partly from his own attempt to provide a coherent framework for political action based on the Bible. It was also constrained by the political realities of his situation. He could not afford to recommend a policy of defiance of legitimate secular authority. Nevertheless, the doctrine of limited and non-violent resistance made Calvinism an unpromising creed for the potential revolutionary. The Catholics developed a far more radical doctrine of armed resistance. The potential for using Catholic traditionalism to bolster social protest had been explored as far back as the 1530s. The English Pilgrimage of Grace was ostensibly a popular religious movement which protested against Protestant changes in the English church. However, it became associated with protest against a number of social and economic issues such as high rents, entry fines for peasant holdings, and the enclosure of common land. Some historians have even regarded the Pilgrimage as essentially a movement of social protest which used the language of religion to articulate and legitimize political radicalism. Whichever of these interpretations is nearer to the truth, it was the language of *Catholic* religion which the protesters were using, and for some at least of them the restoration of traditional religion seems to have been their main concern.[15] In 1570 the Papal bull *Regnans in Excelsis* excommunicated Elizabeth I and announced that it was the duty of good Catholics to assassinate her. The Pope's actions firmly linked Catholicism with the doctrine of armed resistance to established authority.

So far from being political radicals, many of the more fervent Protestants in the Church of England pinned their hopes on the leadership of a godly monarch. Elizabeth I was compared to Deborah, the prophetess who judged the people of Israel in the Old Testament (Judges 4–5). James I and VI was praised for his theological skill. It was only when Charles I seemed to be returning the Church of England nearer to Catholicism that some of the Puritans were prepared to oppose him; and even then, they did so with great reluctance.

The same political conservatism extended to the organization of the church and its discipline at a local level. The local church in England and Wales was no more democratic than that of Calvin's Geneva. Along with their cult of the godly monarch, the Puritans promoted a cult of the godly magistrate, the English equivalent of Geneva's lay elders. These magistrates were the landowners who enforced law and order and implemented government commands at county level. By virtue of the church property they had acquired after the break-up of monastic estates, it was often they who collected in the income of the parish, the tenth of all produce that was due to the church. They also nominated the incumbents of many parishes. And in individual parishes it was the more prosperous farmers and craftsmen who served as constables, churchwardens and overseers of the poor and administered ecclesiastical as well as social discipline. A detailed study of the Essex village of Terling describes the emergence of an élite of wealthy yeoman farmers and lesser gentry. It was these men (and very occasionally women) who served as churchwardens, overseers of the poor and parish constables. Educated, literate and Puritan, they used their religious beliefs for the social and moral control of the labourers and smallholders, prosecuting them for sexual immorality, drunkenness and riotous behaviour.[16]

In Scotland, the political situation was initially different from England and Wales. In the early sixteenth century, Scotland was fighting to retain its independence from England and was being forced into closer and closer alliance with France. In 1542 James V of Scotland was killed fighting the English. His daughter Mary, later known as Mary Queen of Scots, was still a baby. Her mother was French, and Mary was sent to France in 1548 to be betrothed to the heir to the French throne. Scotland was thus very much under the control of the Catholic French monarchy, but was also open to Calvinist influences.

While the Reformation in England was initiated by the state, in Scotland it was very much a popular movement, and it was from Scotland that some of the most politically radical Calvinists came. Their leader was John Knox. He had spent nineteen months as a French galley slave as punishment for his involvement in a Protestant revolt in 1547 and was ready to embark on political action against a child-queen in whose name idolatry was being forced on the Scottish people. However, when he approached Calvin for support, Calvin insisted that it was never lawful for subjects to rise in rebellion against an idolatrous ruler. The most they could do was emigrate or refuse to obey and accept the consequences.

The Reformed church in France was not at the outset politically radical. In the 1530s, it must have seemed quite possible that France would have a Reformation led from the top, like England and some of the German Lutheran states. Francis I, king of France, had founded the

*Collège des Lecteurs Royaux* in Paris, an institution on humanist lines dedicated to the study and teaching of Greek and Hebrew. The king's own sister, Marguerite of Navarre, had written a book inspired by reformed thought, the *Mirror of a Sinful Soul*, and she had an evangelical preacher for her own household. Calvin dedicated a number of his works to the French king and other leading Frenchmen. The printing industry in Geneva expanded in the 1540s and 1550s largely to produce works for the French market.

There was a period of persecution in France in the mid-1530s as a result of the activities of a group of extreme Protestants inspired by the early Swiss reformers. On the night of 16 October 1534 this group put up posters in Paris and a number of other French cities denouncing the Catholic Mass as idolatrous. Posters even appeared on the door of the king's own bedchamber in the palace of Amboise. The attack, known as the *affaire des placards* ("the business of the posters"), seems to have been the work of Protestants for whom the limited reform of the church in France did not go far enough but who were concerned that it would satisfy the majority of people. Their attempt to provoke conflict certainly succeeded: a number of them were executed, books were burned, and for a while Francis attempted to ban the printing of all books in France.

It has been suggested that the incident of the posters marks the point at which Francis I began to turn against Protestantism, and that as a result the development of the Reformation in France was permanently crippled. However, even after the episode of the *placards*, Francis I continued to take an interest in Reformed ideas. His extreme reaction to the posters was probably the result of his fear of sedition. Those responsible for distributing the posters obviously had a highly efficient organization which even extended to the King's private apartments. If they could distribute posters with such efficiency, they could do more damaging things as well.

Francis's support for reform was probably as much political as intellectual and linked with his attempts to ally with France with some of the Lutheran German rulers. The construction of a moderate Protestant axis to oppose the power of the German and Spanish power bloc ruled by Charles V would have put France in a leading position and finally relegated England to a subordinate rôle. This seems to have been in Francis's mind as late as 1546 when his envoy was in England discussing both political alliance and religious reform with Henry VIII and his archbishop Thomas Cranmer. Cranmer subsequently claimed that discussions had covered the abolition of statues in churches and the ringing of church bells and had even gone as far as the reform of the liturgy of the Eucharist in line with Protestant thinking.[17] It was not until the political crisis after the deaths in quick succession of Francis's son and grandson, and the series of regencies which followed, that the French monarchy became securely Catholic again.

Calvin's aim was always a Reformation in France. By this he did not mean the establishment of a breakaway French Reformed church: schism in the one church was still to be deplored. What he wanted was the reform of the church in France. To that end he initially discouraged attempts to establish an institutional Reformed church in France, though he kept in constant touch with the house-groups in which people with Reformed sympathies gathered for prayer and Bible study. It was in the immediate aftermath of the incident of the posters that he published the first edition of his *Institution of the Christian Religion* and dedicated it to Francis I. In the introduction, he attempted to convince the king that he was simply presenting the Gospel of Christ and that the ideas he was putting forward had nothing in common with the dangerous radicalism of the Anabaptists.[18]

For all Calvin's cultivation of the French king and nobility, Protestant worship remained illegal in France and was punishable by prison, banishment or burning. Martyrs make converts; the Protestant movement spread rapidly, mainly in the towns and among intellectuals. In 1555 the Paris house-group decided to overrule Calvin and establish an organized church with a pastor and elders. This opened the floodgates: by 1559, when the first French National Synod met in Paris, 72 churches were represented. By 1562 there were over 2,000 Protestant churches with about 2 million adherents.

Calvin was forced to accept that a Reformed church had been established in schism from the Catholic church. The 1559 Synod approached Calvin and asked him to devise a Confession of Faith for them. He suggested they use his existing confession but was eventually persuaded to write something more specific. The French church then redrafted the text: having established themselves in defiance of Geneva, they were deliberately distancing themselves to some extent from Genevan influence. The reasons for their attitude may well have been political. Calvin's argument to the French king had been founded on French patriotism, and it was obviously in the interests of the Reformed church to present itself as thoroughly French.

The Reformed church in France may have begun as a movement of urban artisans and intellectuals, but by 1560 numbers of the nobility were joining the movement. By 1562 as many as half the French nobility may have been Calvinist. This shifted the political balance of the movement and made it more of a threat to the French crown. The French nobility were still the military leaders of the country, and only they were allowed to wear swords. The Reformed church in France is now so small that it is hard to realize that for a brief period in the mid-sixteenth century it actually seemed likely that France would become Protestant. After all, France's traditional ally, Scotland, became Calvinist under similar circumstances and facing similar opposition. But in France the government's decision in 1562 to recognize the legitimacy of the Reformed church (in France called the Huguenot church: the derivation of the name is uncertain[19]) led to a civil war which involved repeated atrocities on both sides and the eventual defeat of the Protestants.

Calvin remained reluctant to consider any resistance to established authority in France. After his death, however, and after the massacre of thousands of Protestants on and after St Bartholomew's Eve in 1572, Calvin's successor Theodore Béza decided that resistance was justified. It was widely believed that the French king, Charles IX, had ordered the massacre. Even in terms of Calvin's doctrine of passive resistance, this would constitute something so evil that subjects could refuse to obey, though they still could not rebel or resist punishment. Béza and Hotman, the Professor of Law at Geneva, took Calvin's doctrine of limited resistance further and reverted to a medieval view of government as a contract between ruler and ruled, with duties and responsibilities on both sides. If the monarch failed to meet his obligations, the subjects were released from theirs. However, when Louis XIV finally declared Protestantism illegal in 1672, the majority of Huguenots left the country rather than defy him.

In the Netherlands, the Reformation became associated with the desire for independence from the (Catholic) Spanish Empire. The early development of several varieties of Reformed Christianity was met with increasingly savage persecution from Charles V and his son Philip II. Calvin advised the Reformed churches that armed resistance was not justified, but an increasing number defied his instructions. There were outbreaks of rioting and church meetings were held openly in defiance of government prohibition. Eventually, Philip's governor in the Netherlands, his half-sister Margaret of Parma, compromised by allowing limited freedom for the reformers. Refugees who had left the Netherlands to practise their religious beliefs returned, bringing with them much more radical ideas. There were outbreaks of iconoclasm, and Philip II reimposed the policy of persecution. Savage fighting followed, from 1568 until 1648, when the Netherlands were eventually divided between the independent, Protestant north and the Spanish, Catholic south.

The Netherlands appear therefore as a classic example of Protestantism being used to justify the defiance of established authority. It is worth remembering, too, that the Calvinists were in the minority in the northern provinces as late as the early seventeenth century. It was the efficient organization of the Calvinist church that enabled it to spearhead the struggle for independence. Even in the Netherlands, though, it is hard to define the reformed church as radical. The fight for independence was dominated by the nobility, who found in Protestantism a vehicle for articulating their desire for freedom from foreign control. If the rule of Philip II could be stigmatized as ungodly it was easier to oppose it. The Dutch Calvinist church of the twentieth century is a good example of the way reformed Protestantism lends itself to political parties of both right and left. In South Africa, different tendencies in the Reformed church were among the staunchest defendants and the fiercest opponents of apartheid.

The Calvinist doctrine of limited resistance to established authority was a necessary consequence of the Calvinist doctrine of the true church. For the Calvinists, the church was to encompass the whole of a society. It was difficult to see how such a church could be established without the co-operation of those who were in authority in that society. For pragmatic and political reasons, therefore, churches in the Calvinist tradition tended to support the authority of the state wherever possible. The different ideas which the radical reformers had on the nature of the true church gave them more freedom to challenge established authority. If the true church was a small group of the elect, and the majority of society was corrupt and heading for damnation, it behoved the true Christian to challenge the authority of those who were in control in that society.

Nevertheless, we are still not certain about the exact nature of the links between political and religious radicalism in the sixteenth century. The German peasants of the *Bundschuh* (the league which took its name from the laced boots worn by the peasants) had a programme with a number of elements in common with the reformers. They wanted an end to clerical pluralism, reductions in payments to ecclesiastical authorities and limitations on the powers of the ecclesiastical courts. In some areas they also wanted to end auricular confession. And they justified all their demands by reference to the law of God, as evidenced in the Bible. In 1517, responding to the beginning of Luther's campaign for reform, they extended their demands to include the abolition of tithes and the free election of pastors by their congregations.

The peasant uprising of 1524 was supported by a number of the early radical reformers, including Karlstadt and Balthasar Hubmaier, though Karlstadt did try to influence the peasants towards non-violence. Much of the disturbance early in 1524 was the result of revolutionary preaching by Thomas Müntzer, a priest and academic from Thuringia. He insisted on the right of ordinary people to use violence both to resist oppresison and to bring in the kingdom of God on earth. Nevertheless, Müntzer did not create the peasants' unrest: he used it. He helped to channel it and may have given it a religious dimension which it would otherwise have lacked. It was Müntzer, for example, who gave the peasants their banner, a rainbow on a white background with the words "May the word of God last eternally". But the unrest was there already, long before Müntzer came on the scene.

## Social discipline and the reformation of manners

Theories of the relationship between church and state also affected the Reformers' ideas on the rôle of the church in enforcing social discipline. On the one hand, there was the Genevan model of discipline as the third mark of the true church, with control exercised by the church consistory. On the other, there was the Zürich model with social discipline left to the civil magistrate because the church consistory cannot police a whole society. There was thus a tension between the Reformed desire for social discipline as the third mark of the true church and the awareness that the church cannot control the whole of civil society.

If this was true in a small and cohesive city state like Zürich, it was even more true in countries like England and the Dutch Netherlands and in the German Protestant territorial states. As princes and magistrates took more and more control over the running of the church, so they also had to take responsibility for controlling the morals of their people. Attempts to enforce social order were one of the ways in which these rulers set about building up the identities of their states. The anonymous treatise *On the Office of the Christian Magistrate* (published in 1586) sums up the ideal of the Protestant ruler:

> a person whom God has appointed to preside over his people on earth, to oversee the execution of just laws, and in order that piety, justice and peace are upheld among them.

Both the prince and the magistrate thus had the duty of acting as God's representative as well as God's servant. In both Lutheran and Calvinist states it was the secular authorities who issued laws regulating morality and behaviour. Lutheran rulers worked through the church councils, consistory courts and parish visitations. Their authority was backed by the individual confession of sins which all members of Lutheran churches were expected to make before they could be allowed to receive communion. Lutherans, like Catholics, were supposed to treat the confessional as absolutely confidential. However, under pressure from visitation committees, the principle could be set aside.[20] Even when the privacy of the confessional was treated as sacrosanct, the framework of confession still gave the local pastor considerable powers in the enforcement of social discipline. Calvinist rulers were sometimes obliged to use the church hierarchy of synods and provincial meetings, but the result was the same. The authority of the church, and its power to exclude dissidents from the sacraments, was used to bolster the state's moral code.

The church was also used to reinforce more general instructions on social rôles and responsibilities. Luther's Shorter Catechism emphasized civic morality and social discipline as well as the understanding of Christian doctrine. His explanations of the fifth and seventh commandments – "Honour your father and mother" and "You shall not commit adultery" – were particularly geared to inculcating these rules of moral and social behaviour. In turn, the state backed the Lutheran reformation by enforcing regular study of the Catechism in schools as well as churches.[21]

Luther's doctrine of justification by faith and Calvin's insistence on its corollary, predestination, could easily have diminished rather than reinforced the power of secular authority. For the radical reformers, the state could have no power over those who had been saved. However, the Lutheran and Calvinist traditions still held to the idea that God would punish sin in this world. Individual sinners might be punished, but the whole of a sinful society could also be punished by the infliction of natural disasters like epidemics and violent storms. Such a doctrine gave secular governments all the defence they needed for their attempts to control human behaviour.

One of the greatest concerns of these secular guardians of morality was the control of sexual activity, which had obvious economic implications. Contraceptive techniques were primitive, and premarital sexual activity almost always resulted in extramarital pregnancy. Premarital sex was (as far as we can see from the available records) so common as to be the norm, and marriage usually followed when the young woman became pregnant. However, in times of economic difficulty, if the young man was unable to earn enough to keep a family, he might refuse to accept his responsibilities, and the mother and child would have to be maintained by the community. Both prostitutes and their clients were punished by state authority, as were male householders and employers who sexually exploited their female servants. The language of religion and the Seventh Commandment, "Thou shalt not commit adultery", could be used to enforce what was essentially a social prohibition.

Secular authority could regulate other social relationships as well. The idealization of celibacy as the highest human state was anathema to the Protestant reformers. Instead, they idealized the married state and saw the patriarchal household as the model for social as well as spiritual order. The domestic authority of fathers and male heads of household was protected by the legal system. State-controlled church courts intervened in matrimonial and domestic disputes and sometimes attempted to protect women from violence, but the authority of the husband was generally paramount.

There was a negative side to the theologians' arguments for patriarchal power. Following St Augustine, most Reformers saw human nature as inherently depraved and corrupt. Even babies were regarded as having an innate tendency to evil. Fatherly authority was necessary to break the child's will and turn it towards virtue. Women were regarded as too gentle and too liable to indulge their children.

The secular courts in Protestant states also strengthened the powers of parents over their children. The Catholic church had recognized the right of young people to choose their own marriage partners, but virtually all the Protestant churches insisted on parental consent. An emphasis on parental authority suited the interests of the state. Left to their own devices, young people would marry before they were financially independent and their households would be poor. Marriages arranged by parents might not be as affectionate but they would be better funded. The secular authorities needed stable, prosperous households which would pay taxes and defend the existing order. The increased number of prosecutions of women for infanticide can be seen as part of the buttressing of patriarchal authority: women were to be given no alternative to a life of bearing and rearing children. Male homosexuality was seen as a threat to the familial household. Sentences for sodomy became more severe in the course of the sixteenth century and sometimes included the death penalty.

Other social prohibitions were also dressed up in a religious guise. The expensive celebration rituals which accompanied christenings, weddings and funerals had Catholic and even pagan undertones. They were also a social problem, as families who could not afford such conspicuous display were forced into debt in order to maintain their local status. Secular rulers condemned excessive spending on these celebrations and justified their prohibitions in religious terms, but their priorities were social as much as moral.

The enforcement of morality was most effective in the small and cohesive Calvinist city-states. Here, there was a high level of community support for the enforcement of moral codes, and offenders were often reported by their neighbours rather than by the officials of church or state. There was more resistance in the territorial states of Germany and in Britain and the Netherlands.[22] As the example of the English village of Terling demonstrates, even with the co-operation of the local élite, moral policing was an uphill task.[23] Ultimately, the power of the state could only enforce a moral code if it had both the approval of the local élite and the acquiescence of the rest of the population.

## The common weal: poverty and social welfare

The medieval system of social welfare was organized through the church and underpinned by ideas on the spiritual value of poverty. Members of religious orders took vows of poverty as well as chastity and obedience. Even for those who had no choice in the matter, poverty was seen as conferring spiritual benefits. The prayers of the poor were considered to be particularly effective. All kinds of poor relief, from almshouses and hospitals to the distribution of food and clothes at funerals, were based on the assumption that the poor would pray for the souls of the dead and that their prayers would be answered.

Changes in these ideas predate the Reformation. In Zwickau, for example, the rationalization of welfare provision dates back to before 1480, with the establishment of the *Reiche Almosen*, a centrally-administered voluntary fund for poor relief.[24] In the expanding towns of the late fifteenth century, private provision was no longer enough to deal with the growing problem of poverty. At the same time, a distinction was beginning to be drawn between the "deserving poor" (invalids, the elderly) and the "undeserving poor" (those who could work but would not – and they were seen as undeserving if they were physically able to work, even if there was no work available). The more prosperous people were increasingly reluctant to make charitable provision for the "undeserving poor", those who were felt to be partly to blame for their own poverty.

What happened in the early sixteenth century was that the Reformers picked up on these ideas, developed them and gave them a moral and theological justification. It was no longer just harsh but commercially necessary to refuse to give to beggars on the street; it was *right*. Protestant thinking about intercessory prayer meant that the prayers of the poor were no longer considered useful. As a result, the poor were no longer thought to have anything to offer to society just because they were poor. Better to put them to work: and if they could not work, they should receive some kind of organized provision and be suitably grateful for it. The establishment of the Zwickau common chest predated the Reformation, but it was not until the ideas of the Reformers had gained acceptance that begging was actually forbidden. The poor were now to be solely dependent on the common chest for relief.

Luther's ideas on salvation led him to reject the whole medieval ideal of the spiritual value of poverty. Discussing the Biblical account of the Sermon on the Mount, he insisted that Christ was speaking not about physical poverty but about humility, poverty of spirit:

> nothing is accomplished when someone is physically poor and has no money or goods ... There is many a beggar getting bread at our door more arrogant and wicked than any rich man.[25]

Luther was thus able to attack the way in which the religious orders sanctified begging more effectively, since he was arguing from a theological perspective. He also attacked begging on practical grounds, claiming that religious begging encouraged others, the "vagabonds and evil rogues", to take advantage of the Christian charity of ordinary people.

The Reformers' attack on monasteries and religious orders was based on their belief that prayer and sacrifice on behalf of others was useless and that there was nothing particularly virtuous about the monastic lifestyle. The main purpose of the monasteries was to lead lives of prayer and austerity. However, religious orders had also taken on socially useful rôles such as education, poor relief and nursing. Historians are still arguing about how effectively the religious orders were doing these things by the sixteenth century. At best, their provision was patchy, and it was almost always regarded as a by-product of their main duties of prayer and meditation.

Nevertheless, the dissolution of religious orders in virtually every

Protestant country meant that alternative frameworks had to be provided for the care of the poor and the sick. What many of the Reformers hoped was that the property which had been taken from the monasteries could be used for socially useful purposes. The new frameworks were to be more effective and more comprehensive than the patchy monastic provision had been. In particular, the Reformers wanted to do away with the idea that poverty and begging were spiritually valuable. Instead of charitable relief, the poor were to be set to work wherever possible; those who would not work were to be punished.

Many late medieval cities already made provision for the care of the poor and sick. Luther suggested that this system should become universal. The detailed arrangements he suggested to the people of Leisnig in Saxony in 1523 give an insight into his ideas on the funding of poor relief. He suggested detailed procedures for closing down the local religious houses. Their property was to be taken into the hands of the secular authorities. Monasteries in the towns could be converted into schools or poor-houses. The estates of the monasteries would provide a common chest, "out of which gifts and loans could be made in Christian love to the needy of every land".[26]

The same ideals were put forward by the "Commonwealth men" in England – and with about as much effect.[27] The great fear which Luther expressed in *The Ordinance of a Common Chest* was that monastic property would be seized for private profit, and that landowners would "grab these ecclesiastical possessions and claim as an excuse that I was the one who put them up to it". He wanted socially-useful foundations to be set up "to forestall such a catastrophe while there is still time . . . lest there be a mad scramble and everyone makes off with whatever they can lay their hands on".[28] In England and Wales as in Germany, this was exactly what happened. In both cases, some monastic estates were used for founding schools and hospitals, but the overwhelming bulk of the property ended up in private hands.

The dispersal of monastic property left Protestant countries with the continuing problem of making alternative provision for poor relief. Meanwhile, the problem of poverty (and particularly urban poverty) was becoming worse in the course of the sixteenth century. This had nothing to do with the Reformation. Rising population levels and increasingly commercialized farming meant that large numbers of people were leaving their peasant holdings, wandering in search of work and ending up in the large towns. There, they were desperately vulnerable to low wages and economic fluctuations. In his *Address to the*

*Christian Nobility*, Luther encouraged civic authorities to take responsibility for their own poor. He suggested appointing wardens who would know the resident poor and could notify the city councils of their needs. However, he also suggested that the secular authorities should prevent begging by outsiders. His failure to recognize the changing nature of poverty fatally undermined his strategies for poor relief.

The same underlying problem is found in virtually every Protestant country. Many of the reformers had hoped that, once the offerings of the devout were not being diverted to maintaining unnecessary monks and nuns and providing candles and other decorations for the church, the money would become available to help the poor. Unfortunately, in most cases, this did not happen. Much of the casual provision of help for the poor also dried up, since the poor could no longer be paid for their prayers. In Zwickau, for example, donations to the *Reiche Almosen*, the voluntary fund for poor relief, declined considerably after the advent of Lutheranism.[29] In Strasbourg, Martin Bucer encouraged churches to ask their congregations for offerings at every Communion service:

> The claim to belong to the church of God is an empty boast when men who enjoy God's blessings and are able to give fail to offer to Christ's members (and indeed in them to Christ himself) all the things which they need to live in Christ... It was from this teaching that the earliest churches adopted the practice whereby at every celebration of the Holy Communion each of the faithful, according as the Lord had blessed him and as far as he enjoyed the things which belong to this present life, of his love for Christ and his members, gave something to the use of Christ in his least ones, the hungry, the thirsty, the exiles, the naked, the sick, the prisoners.

Bucer coupled his exhortation with an insistence that no-one should beg unless they were unable to work:

> It will make it easier for any church to display this charity if care is taken to excommunicate any who refuse to work and eat their own bread (2 Thess: 3) when they are able to do so.[30]

In Bucer's Strasbourg, the senate and the Council of XXI had replaced the church as the organizers of poor relief. A lay board, the *Almosenherren*, was set up to administer the system. Their funds were derived from the property they had taken over from Catholic church corporations. However, the reorganization was not directly linked to the Reformation: it paralleled simlar developments all over Europe. The distinction between deserving and undeserving poor ran right through sixteenth-century European society, Catholic as well as Protestant.[31]

Calvin's church organization as outlined in the *Institutes* made provision for social welfare and the relief of poverty. In discussing the various kinds of ministry as outlined in the Bible, he said:

> Scripture specifically designates as deacons those whom the church has appointed to distribute alms and take care of the poor, and serve as stewards of the common chest of the poor... Here, then, is the kind of deacons the apostolic church had, and which we, after their example, should have.[32]

Calvin thus saw the care of the poor as an aspect of the work of the church, to be performed by members of the official ministry.

In England and Wales, poor relief was organized at parish level but by laymen. Officials called overseers of the poor collected money from local landholders according to the value of their holdings. The money was distributed in regular payments to those unable to maintain themselves, and in casual grants to individuals in need of specific help – clothes for a young person going into service, medical payments, funeral expenses. The poor were expected to return to their parish of origin for help, making mobility of labour impossible. There was no provision to help the homeless or people who were travelling in search of work. Instead, "vagabonds" and "sturdy beggars" were savagely punished by whipping and mutilation.

In eighteenth-century Brandenburg, the Electors encouraged Pietism for political reasons, as a counterweight to orthodox Lutheranism. The emphasis which Pietism placed on social action and moral discipline was ideal for the creation of an efficiently-run bureaucratic state. Instead of offering charitable relief to the destitute, the Pietists established workshops to employ them. They taught the poor to read and write, and used the Christian moral code to encourage them to become disciplined workers and obedient subjects.

# 6

## *Literacy, Education and the Popular Response to the Reformation*

The Reformation may eventually have become a popular movement, but it had its origins in the intellectual developments associated with Humanism and the Renaissance. The early reformers were virtually all of them university-educated men. Most of them were trained theologians, but they had also had a solid grounding in classical scholarship and in the techniques of logic and rhetoric: the ability to construct a good argument and to put it over convincingly. The rediscovery of classical texts – Greek as well as Latin – and the revival of classical standards of eloquence were the two pillars of the intellectual movement we now call the Renaissance.

Protestant Christianity was always going to have an intellectual element in it because of its emphasis on the authority of a written text (the Bible) and its insistence on the right and the duty of every Christian to take responsibility for their own spiritual lives. As a result, the Protestant churches had to place a premium on education for the mass of the people as well as intellectual development for the élite.

## Print and Protestantism

Intellectual developments could now affect a wider spectrum of the population because of a recent technological innovation – printing. After the middle of the fifteenth century it was no longer necessary for books to be copied one at a time by scribes, an expensive process which inevitably introduced accidental variations and sometimes deliberate amendments. Instead, text could be set in metal type and reproduced in (theoretically) identical multiple copies.

This was a revolution in communications which can only be compared with the invention of the Internet in the late twentieth century. Like the Internet, it made mass communication available for a small capital investment. Early printing presses were small and simple, and needed no more than four people to operate them. The technique spread rapidly from Germany through northern Italy, France and the Netherlands. Printing had no necessary intellectual or ideological implications. It could be used by intellectuals, who could now compare and collate different variants of a text and could attempt to provide a definitive version. However, printing made books much cheaper and thus meant that far more people could afford them. Printing was essentially a commercial undertaking, and printers had to produce what the public wanted to buy.

Like the Internet, printing could be used to spread official propaganda and confirm existing ideas. Many of the earliest printed books were conventional devotional manuals and collections of prayers. These, it seems, were what the market wanted. However, again like the Internet, the cheapness and comparative flexibility of a small printing press meant that it was an ideal instrument of subversion. Martin Luther's initial announcement of his arguments against the sale of indulgences was ignored by the authorities. It was when bootleg printed versions were published in university towns all over Germany that the authorities hit the panic button. Much of the subsequent debate was conducted in print. The official responses of the Catholic church were undoubtedly subsidized, but there was evidently enough of a market for Luther's polemical writings to make their publication commercially viable.

The new technology also added to the excitement of new ideas. The Zürich printers who ate those famous sausages in the Lent of 1522 were working on a new edition of the letters of St Paul. They had worked until they were exhausted and ravenous, and claimed that the sausages were needed to enable them to continue. The atmosphere must have been similar to one of the dot.com companies of the late 1990s, with a major new project and work continuing all night fuelled by coffee and pizza.

Nevertheless, we should not assume that the Reformation was the only influence on the development of lay education. The spread of literacy meant there was a mass market for secular as well as religious books. Where the contents of private libraries can be studied,[1] they were dominated by pious works including Bibles, sermons, prayer books and catechisms, but they also included books on history and medicine, classical texts and guide books on a range of practical subjects.

## Oral culture and the spread of the Reformation

Nor should we assume that printing was the only means by which the ideas of the Reformation were transmitted. Sixteenth-century culture was still largely oral, and most people were unable to read. Even in the towns, where the Reformation first took hold, it is unlikely that the majority of the population could read anything as complex as a theological treatise. Books were still expensive, beyond the means of most ordinary people. Furthermore, the written word was more public than speech and thus easier to censor. The communication of ideas still depended to a considerable extent on traditional oral means, though these were now backed up by printed books and pamphlets.[2]

Literacy was not even essential for access to the Bible. Luther himself emphasized the importance of preaching, oral communication of the Bible message:

> We are speaking of the external word, preached orally ... for this is what Christ left behind as an external sign by which his Church or his Christian people in the world should be recognized.[3]

In a society in which much learning was based on listening and repeating, there were many who encountered the Bible by hearing it read aloud, and who relied on their own memories to retain the text. The Welsh fisherman Rawlins White heard the Bible read (probably in English, though there were Welsh translations available in manuscript) in Cardiff. He wanted to hear more but felt that he was too old to learn to read himself: so he sent his son to school instead. The boy read to his father, who learned enough of the text to be able to expound it to his fellows.

The story of Rawlins White is an excellent example of the patterns of oral transmission which the Reformers could use. One man hears the Bible read, has more read to him, and transmits what he has learned to others, also orally. Rawlins White was one of the few Welsh martyrs during the reign of Mary Tudor. The story of his death in Foxe's *Acts and Monuments* suggests that he was the leader of a group of extreme Protestants, though none of the others was executed.

Preaching was immensely important as a means of communicating new ideas. The new preaching was often informed by printed works as well as by the increased availability of the Bible. Woodcuts of sixteenth-century Protestant sermons often show the audience with books in their hands, following the argument and even taking part in discussion. But preaching could also communicate effectively to the totally illiterate, and they could in turn pass on what they had heard to a wider audience. In a culture based on oral communication and memory, hearers were able to retain and transmit a surprising amount of what they had heard. Niclas Storch, the Zwickau radical, claimed to be illiterate, though he may have been trying to identify himself with the humble labourers of Zwickau.[4]

There were also more informal ways of communicating ideas orally. Discussions in inns, at markets and family gatherings or in the workplace all feature in accounts of the spread of the Reformation from region to region. Long-distance trade links facilitated the spread of ideas by word of mouth as well as the diffusion of printed material. Itinerant workers could also take ideas with them. It is probably significant that in England as in Germany weavers, who were both itinerant and connected with international trade, were often in the forefront of Reformation activity.

Groups of interested people might meet in each other's houses for discussion. Like the sermons, these informal discussions might be triggered by the fact that one of the group could read and had managed to acquire a Bible or a pamphlet putting forward evangelical ideas. Reading aloud seems to have been the most usual form of reading in the sixteenth century and one literate individual could communicate the contents of a book to a wide circle of acquaintances. Some Protestant pamphlets were specifically written to encourage reading aloud.

Reformed ideas could be transmitted orally in the most memorable form by singing. From hymns to scurrilous ballads, songs could communicate both ideas and events. Like preaching and discussion, a traditional method of communication was now backed up by the printed word. A new song might be printed and sold, then passed from person to person. The market for printed material was also a market for ideas. Sellers of pamphlets and ballads advertised their wares by reading and singing them, and their ideas were thus transmitted from the printed word to those who could not read.

## Faith and reason

The sixteenth century is generally seen as a time of respect for intellectual learning and the "Renaissance man". Running in parallel with intellectual development, though, was a growing anti-intellectualism. It was partly a result of the crude materialism which was also responsible for much of the anti-clerical feeling of the period. However, Luther was himself aware that he had helped to promote the new anti-intellectualism by his attacks on monastic schools and universities. Luther's own superior Karlstadt sided with the anti-intellectuals, renouncing his own academic degrees and dissuading students from studying at the university. Luther warned them that they were going too far. The Reformation needed learning as well as the inspiration of the Spirit.[5]

But the demand for education had to extend beyond the universities to the whole of society. Knowledge was not enough to secure salvation, but it was an essential precondition. Luther's early works were designed to defend and promote his theological breakthrough and to explain his dispute with Rome. However, he soon turned his attention to explaining the basics of the faith to ordinary people. The visitation returns for Saxony in the winter of 1528–9 had revealed appalling levels of ignorance about the basics of the faith. Luther hoped to deal with the problem by means of a formal catechism – a series of questions and answers which covered all the crucial points of doctrine. He had great confidence in this technique. In 1528, shortly before the publication of his first Catechisms, he declared:

> By the grace of God, I have brought about such a change that nowadays a girl or boy of fifteen knows more about Christian doctrine than all the theologians of the great universities used to know in the old days. For among us the catechism has come back into use: I mean the Lord's Prayer, the Apostles' Creed, the Ten Commandments, and all that one should know about penance, baptism, prayer, the cross, how to live and how to die, the sacrament of the altar, also about marriage, civil obedience, the duties of father and mother, wife and children, father and son, master and servant. In short, I have established the right order for all estates in society and have brought them all to a good conscience so that each will know how to live and serve God in his appointed rôle.[6]

His Greater Catechism, published in April 1529, was actually a series of sermons designed to show pastors how to teach the basics of the faith. The Shorter Catechism, published in May, gave the pastors a framework which they could use to drill their congregations in what they had to learn. Luther had moved away from his idealistic belief in spiritual independence and now embarked on a programme of compulsory instruction and examination.

Other reformers placed greater stress on the need for understanding of the basic principles of the faith rather than rote learning. Martin Bucer insisted that the basis of faith was not blind trust but informed belief. Even the authority of the Bible was not enough without understanding.

> And since it is universally acknowledged that nothing else is required of us except that a man serve his neighbour to the glory of God, let him always be able to give a reason for what he thinks must be done or avoided, other than "Scripture says so".[7]

Calvin, too, stressed the need for knowledge and understanding:

> Faith rests not upon ignorance but on knowledge . . . [St Paul] suggests that it is not enough for a man to believe implicitly what he does not understand or examine. But he requires explicit recognition of the divine goodness upon which our righteousness rests.[8]

In his letter to the citizens of Geneva in 1539, Cardinal Sadoleto insisted that the proper attitude for lay people was to accept with humility the teachings of Mother Church. Calvin replied that all Christians were responsible for being able to give a reason for their faith: not only theologians, not just the average man, but even "the rudest clown".[9] It was this insistence on the importance of individual responsibility and understanding which was eventually to make the Reformation an influence on democracy – but in the sixteenth century it still had a long way to go.

## Literacy and education

The question-and-answer format of the catechism made it suitable for learning by people who could not read. However, for ordinary people to have full and independent access to the Bible, they did ultimately have to learn to read it. Luther appealed to the German rulers to establish schools in their territories. These schools were to teach both boys and girls the basics of Christian doctrine and to instil discipline, piety and morality. First of all, though, they were to teach them to read, so that books could be used to teach them the other things. The emphasis which

Luther and his followers placed on education for women is particularly significant. Admittedly, much of it was geared towards inculcating the Protestant feminine ideals of humility, obedience and devotion to houswifery. However, for almost the first time, a structured and state-funded system of schools was available to teach girls as well as boys. The 1593 ordinance for the girls' school in Göttingen sums up the objectives of a Lutheran education for women:

> to initiate and hold girls in propriety and the fear of God. To fear God, they must learn their catechism, beautiful psalms, sayings and other fine Christian and holy songs and little prayers, so that they can both read and recite them. For propriety they must learn to love God's Word, to honour their parents, to guard themselves against disobedience, improper talk and gestures, the temptation to steal and lie, and to turn indolence into work, reading, writing, sewing, in order that they are kept busy and forget thereby other frivolities . . . [10]

It is difficult for us now to understand how radical a programme Luther's was. For most children before the sixteenth century, education meant training in craft skills. Reading, and more particularly writing, was a craft skill for clerks: it was not necessary for most people. While we should not underestimate the extent of literacy in the later medieval period, it was not expected that ordinary people should be taught to read and write. Literacy was certainly not seen as the means to moral advancement. For reading and writing to be set alongside sewing as suitable work for young women was particularly radical. On the other hand, female education was set firmly in the context of domestic duties and domestic piety. Young women were expected to return from school to the home. They were being educated to make them better wives and mothers. There was no longer the possibility of going further, of the advanced spiritual education of a formal religious community or the charitable work and collective piety of an informal sisterhood.

Luther was acutely aware of the important contribution which the religious orders had made to education. If anything, he overestimated it, as he believed it had been one of the original functions of monasteries. In his critique of the monastic life, he complained that the "free Christian education" which monasteries had once offered had been perverted, and proposed that they should be restored to their original function. "Monasteries would then have the character God intended for them and nothing else. They would simply be Christian schools for youth . . . "[11]

The initial enthusiasm of the Lutheran Reformation soon gave way to a renewed insistence on social control, discipline and authority. The education which these Protestant children were to receive did not encourage flexibility, independence of thought and a critical mind. Instead, they were trained to be passive, trusting and obedient to authority. Teaching methods involved little more than memorizing by endless repetition of basic facts and concepts. Fear and shame were seen as the basis of virtue. The ordinances of the Württemberg school in 1559 stated that children were to learn "the fear of God, right doctrine and decent conduct". The difference was that these were now taught and imposed using the written word.[12]

Education was thus an instrument of social control: but mass education was also potentially an agent for social change and manipulation. The intention of the Lutherans was that all children should attend school. They were to be removed to some extent from the control and influence of their families and they were to be socialized into different norms of thought and behaviour. Ultimately, though, as it worked out in Lutheran Germany, there was nothing subversive about education. Pupils were removed from the influence of their families with the intention of making them docile and obedient subjects of the state. The control of doctrine remained even more powerfully in the hands of the pastors. The educational advances of the Reformation did little or nothing to empower ordinary lay people.

The Reformation meant changes in higher education as well. The syllabus in universities which had accepted the Reformation was modified. Scholasticism was abandoned. Instead, classes in Greek and Hebrew prepared students for the study of the Bible and the theologians of the early church. New universities were founded. Some were at the heart of Europe's trade and communications, like Leiden and Utrecht in the Netherlands and Calvin's own Geneva. Many were founded in nations on the periphery of Europe: Debrecen in Hungary; Trinity College, Dublin; Aberdeen and Edinburgh in Scotland. There was even a scheme for a Welsh university at Tintern, though it collapsed with the death of its originator William Herbert. Some of the other new universities were short-lived. The Lutheran university of Leignitz, in Poland, was founded in 1526 but only survived until 1530. But the majority survived and changed the educational map of Europe.

For these universities were not just training schools for pastors and theologians. They offered the solid grounding in classical culture which was considered essential for any educated man. Luther wanted higher education to train men for the service of the government as well as the church. In a way, he argued, the government needed well-educated persons even more than the church did.[13] By the late sixteenth century, however, the state universities of Lutheran Germany were in decline. They came increasingly under the control of the confessional territorial states and lost their autonomy and international, humanist perspective. State control of appointments and syllabus turned them into institutions for the training of clerics, schoolteachers and bureaucrats. Staff and students were recruited locally or from other Lutheran states. Speculation and exploration were discouraged. The theology they taught was rigidly controlled, orthodox Lutheran theology and their publications were rigidly censored. The Calvinist universities remained more international in outlook, though even here the universities of the German Calvinist states were increasingly geared to instruction rather than learning.[14]

The essential paradox is that, for all the stress the Reformers placed on education, the destruction of the frameworks of medieval Catholicism led in many areas to a decline in knowledge of the basics of the faith. Particularly damaging were the repeated changes in religion imposed by heads of state in countries like England and some of the German principalities. The Palatinate went from Catholic to Lutheran to Calvinist, back to Lutheran then back again to Calvinist in just over 20 years. The confusion eventually led to indifference; it was impossible to teach doctrine without a clear idea of what the official doctrine would be by the end of the week.

A survey in the university town of Heidelberg at the end of the sixteenth century discovered that a majority of heads of households could not recite the Creed, the Lord's Prayer or the Ten Commandments. Similar complaints can be found in the parish registers of Strasbourg.[15] For all the failings of the medieval church, the basic programme had been widely taught and well known. In the English diocese of Carlisle in the early seventeenth century, an old man who was questioned about his beliefs was forced to admit that he knew nothing of Jesus but what he remembered seeing in a play when he was young, "a man on a tree and the blood ran down". He was obviously remembering one of the Kendal mystery plays, organized by the town guilds and offering an annual re-enactment of the Biblical story of sin and redemption from the Creation and the Fall through the life and death of Christ to the Last Judgement. Much of their detail was apocryphal but they provided a sound and accessible grounding in Scriptural narrative. They were briefly abolished in the middle of the sixteenth century, revived in Mary's reign and survived for some years under Elizabeth but were performed with less frequency after the 1560s. Had the medieval tradition been preserved, the old man would at least have known who Jesus was. However, as the reformers would argue, the mystery plays would not have taught him much about the meaning of Jesus' sacrifice and how it fitted into his own life.[16]

## Visual culture, visual literacy and iconoclasm

It is misleading to assume that the average member of a medieval congregation was ignorant of the basics of the faith. They may have been illiterate in terms of the written word, but they had a wealth of visual imagery in their churches to reinforce and amplify what they were taught orally. Some of this imagery made theological statements of considerable complexity.

There were two problems with medieval visual literacy. One is that visual language relies on statement and assertion rather than reasoned argument. A medieval depiction of the Crucifixion might have great depth of spirituality and might embody complex ideas about Christ's nature and the implications of his sacrifice. Nevertheless, these ideas were presented for devout contemplation rather than discussion. They are in that sense rather like a Buddhist meditative painting, in which a number of ideas are simultaneously present, to be viewed in all their complexity and richness. The contemplation of spiritual mysteries left the medieval viewer ill-prepared for the approach the Reformers wanted, which was that worshippers should be able to give a *reason* for their faith.

The other problem was that contemplation of visual images could easily slide into image-worship. Popular religious literature encouraged the contemplation of images and provided prayers to be said while contemplating. Popular religious literature also encouraged prayers for the help of the saints, and gave stories of miracles worked by saints in response to such prayers. The relics of the saints were generally believed to be able to work miracles, and it was an easy transition from this to believing that images of the saints also had supernatural powers.

There were technical safeguards against such assumptions. Every priest was expected to teach his parishioners that worship was due to God alone and that saints were to be venerated, not worshipped. However, the distinction between worship and veneration was not obvious to the untrained mind. Both Luther and Zwingli had been brought up in environments where it was common to see people praying to images of the saints. Zwingli had himself been closely connected with the miracle-working shrine of the Virgin Mary at Einsiedeln. They were thus aware that the contemplation of visual images could direct the worshippers' attention back to the material world and could lead them to worship the things which God had created rather than worshipping the Creator.

For the Reformers, it was no longer enough to reform the abuse of traditional practices. It was necessary to distinguish between human customs and divine ordinances. As Zwingli said during the First Zürich Disputation:

> We desire to speak of the truth, whether a man is bound by divine ordinance to keep that which on account of long usage has been set up as law by men. For we of course think that custom should yield to truth.[17]

And the injunctions of the Bible were clear. "You shall not make a carved image for yourself, nor the likeness of anything in the heavens above, or on the earth below, or in the waters under the earth. You shall not bow down to them or worship them . . . " (Exodus 20:4–5).

For the Reformers, the Commandment was conclusive. Not only were images a misleading distraction, they were actually forbidden in the Bible. The problem was how to proceed against them. The money and the devotion offered at shrines which claimed miraculous images suggested they were popular. However, there was also in late medieval society a vein of crude materialism which could turn into an attack on many of the doctrines of the church. Once the reformers had challenged the veneration of images, this materialism could produce outbreaks of iconoclasm – the deliberate destruction of images. Such outbreaks sometimes occurred in association with seasonal carnivals, those celebrations in which the established order of society could briefly be mocked or reversed.

It is difficult to distinguish traditional carnival rituals, which paradoxically confirm authority by the licence they are given to invert it, from true iconoclasm. Mocking an image of the local bishop could be licensed parody: but the ritualized humiliation and debasement of crucifixes and relics of the saints which are recorded in some German cities from the 1520s go too far for traditional inversion rituals. Such iconoclasm, though, was rooted in crude materialism and traditional anti-clericalism rather than in any doctrinal consideration of the theological dangers of venerating images. It had, too, undertones of the medieval rite of the humiliation of images, in which a saint who was believed to have failed in his or her duty to the community (protecting

the crops, averting plague, bringing rain in a dry season) was symbolically punished by beating or otherwise abusing their image or
reliquary.[18]

It was Luther's colleague Andreas von Karlstadt who began the theological attack on "idolatry". His main attack was directed against what
he called the "idolatry" of the Catholic sacraments, in which consecrated bread, salt and water were worshipped as if they were themselves
holy. However, his criticisms of the externalization of worship were
also extended to the denunciation of images. Like religious rituals, religious images were of human manufacture. For Karlstadt, this meant that
both had to be destroyed. In a pamphlet published in 1522, *On the
Abolition of Images*, he argued that images in churches are contrary to
the second commandment; that they are dangerous because they are
bound to the physical world and they distract viewers from spiritual
worship; and that it is therefore necessary and praiseworthy to destroy
them.[19] In particular, Karlstadt rejected the argument that visual images
were the books of the poor. As far as he was concerned, visual images
were a poor substitute for literacy, and their dangers far outweighed
their benefits. It would be better to teach the poor and provide them
with the Bible.

In the explosive situation in the town, Karlstadt's outspoken criticism
unleashed an outbreak of iconoclasm. Luther was profoundly uneasy.
He regarded images as a secondary issue. In theory, he accepted most of
Karlstadt's arguments, but he was not prepared to see his own reform
of the doctrine of salvation threatened by public disorder. For Luther,
both the veneration and the destruction of images were works, human
actions which could count for nothing because they were done by sinful
humans. Like image-worship, iconoclasm could thus be a dangerous
distraction from the essential need for faith.[20]

Nevertheless, iconoclasm could be stirred up by popular feeling in
spite of the misgivings of some of the reformers. Attacks on images were
often one of the ways in which ordinary people signalled their demand
for religious change. In spite of Zwingli's reservations, images were
being destroyed in Zürich as early as 1524, when Melanchthon
expressed concern about iconoclasm there.[21] In Geneva, too, when the
city council stalled on the acceptance of the Reformers' arguments,
Protestants in the city made their feelings known by destroying statues
and paintings. There were also attacks on the relics of the saints and on
the things used by the Catholics for their sacraments. Holy water was
defiled, Communion wafers were trampled in the mud, holy oil was
taken for boot polish. It was all in accordance with the Reformers' argu-

ment that reverence for human customs and human creations was idolatry, but it was also rooted in the same crude materialism as the desecration of the statues and parodies of rituals.

Zwingli had no fundamental opposition to the use of the visual arts in church. He tried to prevent the destruction of stained glass windows, and was even prepared to defend statues in churches if no honour or worship was done to them. In practice, though, he was aware that the existence of images of holy people would lead to worship of them, so they had to be removed. Even crucifixes had to be destroyed. It was Christ's divine nature which was to be worshipped, and that could not be represented visually. All that could be depicted was his human nature, and that should not be worshipped.

The Reformation theology of iconoclasm thus linked liturgy and visual imagery: for the Reformers, false worship *was* idolatry. Their concept of idolatry thus went beyond the literal worship of idols to include all corruptions of worship by human invention. For ordinary lay people, though, the logical response to the attack on idolatry was physical iconoclasm. The abuse and desecration of crucifixes and other images of the crucified Christ went far beyond what most of the orthodox reformers would have wanted. There are, however, echoes of a similarly crude materialism in the letters of reformers like Hugh Latimer, the English bishop who described a statue of the Virgin Mary as "that great Sibyl" and suggested that a group of such images "would make a jolly muster in Smithfield. They would not be all day in burning".[22]

Meanwhile, the Reformers were creating an iconography of their own. We should not underestimate the extent to which they used visual imagery to communicate the message of the Reformation. In England, Henry VIII ordered that the royal coat of arms be painted on the walls of parish churches in place of the traditional paintings of the saints, scenes from the life of Christ and reminders of the moral code such as the Seven Deadly Sins and the Seven Corporal Works of Mercy. The Royal Supremacy was thus reinforced by an ever-present reminder in the church itself.

In Regensburg, Protestant emblems were used on the bindings of the city's books, embedding the visual message of the Reformation into civic consciousness in defiance of Imperial authority. The stamped bindings were first used in 1546, the year when the Emperor temporarily defeated the alliance of Protestant German states. The images chosen are intriguing. As well as Luther himself and the proto-Protestant martyr, John Hus, they included a secular ruler. Johann Friedrich, Elector of

Saxony, had been captured and imprisoned by the Emperor for his defence of Protestantism. His presence on the bindings in association with Luther, Melanchthon and Hus made it clear that, for the government of Regensburg, the Reformation was a civic as well as a spiritual matter.

During the same period of crisis, the city authorities in Regensburg also used depictions of the Virtues in the bindings of civic books in order to make clear the links between Protestant piety, political resistance and good government. The engravers who popularized depictions of the Virtues alongside heroes of the Old Testament also used figures from the classical tradition to emphasize the continuity between Reformation humanism and republican Rome. Particularly popular was the story of Lucretia, who was raped by the son of the king of Rome. This outrage and her subsequent suicide inspired the Romans to expel their kings and establish a republican government. Such a depiction of the justified killing of a tyrant had an obvious political charge in the context of Regensburg's subjection by the Emperor.[23]

The Regensburg emblems were refined and classical, but some of the visual imagery of the Reformation was coarse to the extent that subsequent historians have found it too offensive to consider. When Bob Scribner tried to publish an article discussing some of the German visual propaganda in 1981, the illustrations were deemed too disgusting for a general audience. Demons are depicted excreting monks, priests and a Pope; peasants fart at a Papal bull and defecate in a Papal tiara; the Pope is shown riding on a pig, with a steaming turd in his hand. Some of the grossest of these images were published in a series of woodcuts edited by Luther himself and bearing his name on each page. The visual imagery is of the type defined by Mikhael Bakhtin as "grotesque realism". It humiliates the elevated by reducing it to the level of crude bodily functions. The images had a political charge. The caption to the image of the pope on the sow, for example, alluded to the Pope's long-delayed promise to summon a General Council of the Church in Germany. Germany was the sow, spurred by the Pope and receiving only dung as its reward. But the immediate message of such crude visual propaganda was clear: the Pope was Antichrist, born of the Devil, and his servants were dung. Germany could only be saved if it was purified of the filth they represented.[24]

Celebrations in 1617 of the centenary of Luther's declaration included a number of commemorative medals and the publication of woodcuts as well as books. All this visual depiction was designed to reinforce the image of the Lutheran church as the liberator of the pure truth of the Gospel from the yoke of the Antichrist in Rome.[25] In folk myth, however, Lutheran iconography came dangerously near to the iconography of the saints which Luther himself had deplored. There were cults of miracle-working images and relics of the great man, and numerous legends of unsuccessful attempts to burn his picture, his house and his books.[26]

# 7

# *Liturgy and the Articulation of Belief*

The services of the reformed churches were dramatically different from those of the Catholic church. In place of an elaborate Latin liturgy (a liturgy is a prescribed sequence of prayers, hymns and statements of faith), accompanied by ritual movements, incense and candles and performed by priests in elaborate vestments, the reformed churches had services based on Bible readings and a lengthy sermon, with the clergy normally in ordinary clothes. However, the superficial contrast masks a complex sequence of developments and subtle shifts in ritual and meaning. In particular, changing ideas on the sacraments and their significance led to changes in the services by which those sacraments were administered. There was also considerable divergence in the nature of the rituals which replaced those sacraments of the Catholic church which had been deleted in the reformed tradition.

## The Reform of the Liturgy

Underpinning these changes was a radical change in thinking about the meaning and importance of prayer and ritual. For the medieval church, the regular repetition of prayers and the correct performance of ritual could earn God's favour and achieve specific effects. Prayer could be vicarious: monks and chantry priests were employed to pray for others and their prayers were more effective because they were ordained and (in theory) particularly holy. Many wills included bequests of money in return for prayers. The saints could be asked to intercede on behalf of the living and the dead, and requests for their intercession could shade into prayers directed to the saints rather than to God.

For the Reformers, all this was dangerously misguided. The central thesis of virtually every strand in the Protestant reformation is that you cannot bribe or coerce God. Prayers, rituals and sacraments are powerless because they are performed by sinful and inadequate humans. Prayer on behalf of others is completely ineffective. God's grace cannot be earned. All that individuals can do is to cast themselves on God's mercy and beg for forgiveness. That forgiveness will be given not because the right words have been said and the right gestures used, not because priests and saints have added their weight to the petition, but because God is good and merciful and has himself made the necessary sacrifice. Prayer, for Calvin, was the practical consequence of human realization of the wretchedness of our condition when confronted with God's mercy.[1]

Zwingli gave a great deal of thought to the problem of prayers to the saints, and summed up his conclusions in his first major statement of faith, the commentary on his Sixty-seven Propositions.[2] He admitted that he had himself offered prayers to the saints until his reading of the Bible convinced him that such prayers were idolatrous. The saints could not mediate between humans and God because even the saints were fallible, subject to human weakness and unable to fulfil God's commands without his grace. All the saints could do was to repeat human prayers, and it was better to pray yourself than to ask others to do it for you. Reliance on the intercession of the saints detracted from Christ's status as the only mediator and diminished reliance on his saving death.

Zwingli's comment on prayer to saints led him on to think about the importance of prayer in general. He described it in words drawn from St Augustine as "the reaching up of souls from earthly to heavenly things" and the contact of the spirit with God. His rethinking of the importance of prayer and ritual had obvious implications for the structuring of church services in the reformed tradition. Zwingli's emphasis on prayer as the reaching out of the soul to God, for example, led him to introduce quite long intervals of silent prayer into his liturgy.[3] The result was a radical change in public worship, where collective silent prayer was almost unknown. Zwingli had few imitators in this aspect of his liturgical practice until the English Society of Friends, the Quakers, moved from exuberant displays of religious fervour to a meeting for prayer based on silence.

There were other, more practical problems to Protestant plans for the redesigning of worship. The medieval liturgy was both familiar and aesthetically pleasing in its dignity and elaboration. Both Luther and

Zwingli were reluctant to make too many liturgical changes too quickly. For Luther, liturgy was like church discipline, not a prime concern. He had no wish to upset people by changes in worship which would only detract from the importance of his message about salvation. Nor did he see any need for uniformity of practice in church services. He was happy to accept local variations, and suggested only that pastors should be guided by the Gospel in what they did.

Some changes would obviously have to be made. The form of the medieval liturgy may have been both familiar and popular but the ideas which it conveyed were unacceptable, even in translation. However, attempts to replace it inevitably led to arguments about the precise significance of the new forms. The incomprehensibility of the Latin liturgy was undoubtedly part of its charm, as it gave mystery and significance to the sacraments it celebrated. But a liturgy in an obscure language also has practical advantages. It cloaks a wide range of doctrinal disagreements under a form of words which can be bent to suit the mind of the hearer. A vernacular form of prayers is theologically transparent: there is no way of hiding its doctrinal implications.

The demand that the liturgy should be "in the vernacular" also begs the question "whose vernacular?" In the sixteenth century, dialects of many European languages were so distinct as to constitute virtually separate languages. Translation of the Bible and the services of the church standardized languages like German and Dutch at the expense of local variants. The speakers of minority languages could be excluded more profoundly from a liturgy in an alien vernacular, particularly when that vernacular was the language of the country which ruled them. The imposition of an English prayer book on the West Country in the late 1540s led to riots and near-civil war.

A vernacular liturgy did in theory allow for more congregational participation. The parts of the medieval liturgy in which lay people had to participate – the promises of the godparents in baptism and the marriage vows – were already said in the local vernacular. It is nevertheless difficult to see how congregations could have been introduced to collective prayers in the vernacular at a time when so few people could read and even fewer could afford their own books. The solution which Cranmer adopted for his English Book of Common Prayer was to have the collective prayers said by "the whole congregation after the minister": that is, the minister read a clause of the prayer and the congregation repeated it. The practice was modelled on the method used for repeating the promises in baptism and marriage and still survives in the traditional Anglican marriage service, in which the crucial promises are read by the officiating clergy and repeated by the couple to be married. Martin Bucer was keen on this kind of interactive liturgy and suggested it to Cranmer as a way of recapturing and building on the element of participation in the medieval liturgy.[4]

Luther's revisions of the services of the medieval church placed more emphasis on the sermon and other forms of teaching. Evidence from sixteenth-century Germany suggests that sermons in the Lutheran tradition were normally based on the set Bible readings for the services. Pastors could also use material from collections of published sermons and homilies, shorter sermons with a moral purpose. In some areas pastors were required to preach regularly on Luther's catechism. Sermons could be lengthy by modern standards – up to an hour by the end of the sixteenth century – and it became increasingly necessary to provide seating in churches in order to keep the congregation in order.[5]

Even more emphasis was placed on preaching in the Calvinist tradition. Sermons became a popular form of public entertainment, and inspiring preachers could command huge audiences. It was not unusual for towns and larger parishes to have public sermons on Sunday afternoons and weekdays, and money was given to endow these. These sermons could be even longer – two or three hours – and were highly complex and structured analyses of Biblical texts.

Part of Calvin's reorganization of the church in Geneva in 1541–2 involved the provision of a new liturgy, the *Form of Prayers*. This provided services for the two remaining sacraments, baptism and the Eucharist, and rituals which replaced the sacraments which had been removed. The service of baptism, for example, was much simplified and the teaching behind it was clarified. Calvin had spent the years from 1538 to 1541 in Strasbourg, where he used and was deeply impressed by Martin Bucer's liturgy. He translated an adapted form of it as *La Forme des Prières Ecclesiastiques*, which he published in Strasbourg in 1540. When he returned to Geneva in 1541 it was Bucer's Communion service which provided him with the basis for the Communion in the Genevan *Form of Prayers*.

Bucer's liturgical innovations also provided Calvin with services which gave a form of words to the other "rite of passage" rituals. Confirmation was no longer a sacrament but was treated as an opportunity for young people to reaffirm their baptismal promises in person and in public. They were also required to be able to repeat the catechism, a simple statement of faith in question-and-answer form. The marriage service gave dignity and status to the promises which were a precondition for secure family life. The revaluing of human sexuality and the emphasis on the family were thus written into the services of the church.

Other sacraments had to be replaced for psychological reasons. The reconciliation provided by individual confession and absolution was replaced in many Protestant churches by a general confession as part of the Communion service. Calvin took the idea for a general confession from Bucer's Strasburg liturgy. The sacrament of extreme unction was revised in accordance with its Biblical origins to provide an order of prayers for the visiting of all sick people. The revision removed the final ritual which eased the dying person's passage out of the world, and it has to be said that Calvin's service for the burial of the dead is one of the least satisfactory (psychologically speaking) in the *Form of Prayers*.

Other churches in the Calvinist tradition drew on Calvin's *Form of Prayers* to a greater or lesser degree. Even Cranmer's English Prayer Books have some elements in common with the *Form of Prayers*, though in Cranmer's case it is probably because both he and Calvin were so much influenced by Bucer. Like Bucer, Cranmer made extensive provision for services other than the celebration of Communion. In Bucer's Strasbourg, there was a short early service (five o'clock in summer, six in winter) every day in each of the city's churches. (It was the assistant pastors who had to get up early for these.) The services were simple, consisting of prayers and a half-hour exhortation to piety. There was a sermon in the cathedral every morning and a daily service in the afternoon. On Sundays, each parish held an early service, intended for servants who could return to their duties while their employers attended a later service. The second service was the *Amtpredig*, the main weekly service of the parish. It began with an organ recital and hymn singing. These were followed by a general prayer of confession and other prayers including the Lord's Prayer — the prayer beginning "Our Father which art in Heaven" which was taught by Jesus to his followers and which is still the central prayer of the Christian tradition. The sermon was based on the explanation and discussion of a text from the Bible and lasted for about an hour. It was followed by prayers for the congregation and for members in need of special intercession – the sick, for example – then more hymn singing, a final blessing and an organ recital. Communion was celebrated weekly in the cathedral, fortnightly or monthly in the other churches, but for the average Strasburgher this Sunday morning service was the standard form of worship.[6]

The Sunday service of Strasbourg was broadly similar to the standard Sunday worship of the English church, though much simpler in form. Cranmer's liturgy attempted to introduce reformed ideas to a largely conservative clergy and laity. It was politically impossible to do anything with the Latin Mass while Henry VIII was alive. Cranmer therefore began his great work of liturgical revision in 1538–9 with the cycle of seven services called offices, structured sequences of prayer and praise which were followed in different ways by monastic communities, cathedral churches and other secular clergy. Cranmer recast these into two daily services of Mattins (morning prayer) and Vespers (evening prayer). They were still in Latin, possibly because they were intended primarily for use by the clergy. However, they showed the influence of the Reformation in their pruning of the list of saints to be celebrated and their insistence on a structured sequence of Bible readings.

Cranmer seems to have had plans to translate Mattins and Vespers into the vernacular but was prevented for a while by the conservative backlash in English religious politics in the early 1540s. The two services did however provide the basis for the services of Morning and Evening Prayer in his 1549 Book of Common Prayer. The translation of the Bible readings into English was another of his ambitions, and he encouraged the reading of the Bible passages in the Mass in English from 1538.[7]

We know very little about the worship of the earlier radical reformers. Many of their congregations began as groups meeting for Bible study. Their services generally followed the same framework of Bible reading and exposition accompanied by extempore prayer and (in some cases) prophetic declamations.

❊          ❊          ❊

Within the overall framework described above, we can now consider in detail the changes in each of the major services of the church, and their significance for belief and practice.

## The Eucharist

The status of the service of the Mass or Holy Communion was radically changed by the Reformation. In one way, it became more central to public worship. Lay people were expected to receive Communion regularly, and the sacrament was not considered to be valid unless it was shared. No longer would a priest celebrate the Eucharist as a mystery half-hidden behind carved screens and veiled in incense and Latin. In other ways, however, the status of the Eucharist as the central act of worship was diminished. More emphasis in the liturgy was placed on sermons and readings from the Bible, and less on the rituals leading up to the central act of consecration. This was as true in churches in the Lutheran tradition, which still believed that the consecrated bread and wine were actually Christ's body and blood, as it was in the Swiss reformed tradition in which the act of consecration created only a spiritual presence or memorial.

The leading Reformers seem to have assumed that ordinary members of their congregations would welcome the opportunity to take Communion regularly. They were wrong. Martin Bucer deplored the reluctance of congregations to receive Communion regularly:

> It is therefore shocking that they fail to see how serious an affront they offer to their Lord and Saviour when they spurn the very food of eternal life, which is commended to them in the gospel, which they clamorously demand in their prayers, and to which they are invited by our Lord's own words.

He was not prepared to accept that people might feel themselves unworthy to take part. The medieval church had insisted on complete ritual purity but the Protestant churches believed that Christ had himself done all that was necessary to purify his people.

> We cannot take seriously the excuses they offer about the reverence due to the sacrament and their own unworthiness: for no-one is regarded as unworthy of the Lord at his table except the man who retains his desire to sin, and of course this is something which we must always be casting aside. And it is a fine reverence for the sacrament which despises and repudiates the saving communion of the Son of God which is offered in it: the man who repudiates that denies Christ himself, and abandons himself to Satan.[8]

Zwingli was unusual among the early Reformers in proposing that communion be celebrated four times a year. However, the same compromise solution was subsequently adopted by other Protestant churches. The Bernese custom was for celebration on the first Sunday after Christmas and on Easter Sunday, Whit Sunday and the first Sunday in September. The town council of Geneva overruled Calvin's wish to celebrate Communion frequently and insisted on only four celebrations a year, on the Bernese model.

Even where the clergy were permitted to offer to celebrate Communion more frequently, they found that their congregations were reluctant to take part, and without their participation there could be no Communion. Therefore, the whole Communion service was said less frequently. Instead, there was an increased emphasis on other forms of worship. Churches which modelled themselves on Calvin's Geneva used the first part of the Communion service – the prayers, readings, metrical psalms and sermon – without the actual liturgy of the consecration. In England, Cranmer's Book of Common Prayer provided the services of Morning and Evening Prayer, which became the normal form of Anglican worship until the second half of the twentieth century.

As we have seen, Luther was conservative in matters of worship. He left the liturgy of the Mass in Latin for nearly ten years. It was Melanchthon who translated the Mass into German for private celebration in the summer of 1521, and Karlstadt who first used a vernacular liturgy in public on Christmas Day of that year. Luther's German Mass was a deliberate compromise, designed to retain as many familiar elements as possible. His introduction to the *Formula Missae* and the *Deutsche Messe* repeatedly emphasizes that he has no objection to most of the traditional rituals, if they are performed in the right spirit.

Luther's first German Mass was therefore largely a translation and simplification of the Latin liturgy. After a suitable introductory prayer translated from the Latin collection of "introits" (chants sung while the clergy and assistants were processing into the church), the *Kyrie eleison* ("Lord, have mercy; Christ, have mercy; Christ, have mercy", still sung in Greek), the *Gloria* ("Glory to God on high") and the traditional prayers or *collects* came readings from the Bible, interspersed with suitable chants, and the more detailed statement of faith, the Nicene Creed, which could be sung or said.

Then followed the core of the liturgy, the prayers which consecrated the bread and wine. At that point Luther moved away from the old core of the Mass in order to remove the suggestion that Christ's sacrifice was being renewed each time the bread and wine were consecrated. He achieved this largely by simplifying the prayers and removing many of the rituals associated with them. The Lutheran consecration started with a brief dialogue between priest and congregation, drawn from the Latin rite:

P: The Lord be with you
R: And with your spirit
P: Lift up your hearts
R: We lift them up to the Lord . . .

He then proceeded to a retelling of the Biblical story of Christ's last meal with his disciples: "Who the day before he suffered took bread and broke it . . . In the same way after supper he took the cup . . . " Like the introductory dialogue, these words were translated from the Latin. The difference in the Lutheran rite was that it was to be said clearly, so that all around could hear it. The Lutheran practice was that if the east end of the church was large enough, the congregation should gather there to hear the consecration.

Once the bread and wine had been consecrated, the choir sang the translation of the Latin *Sanctus*, "Holy, holy, holy, Lord God of Sabaoth", while the celebrant held the bread and wine up for the congregation to see. Luther emphasized that the elevation was done only to help people who needed some of the familiarity of the traditional ritual. However, most of the ritual gestures over the bread and wine were removed, including the ritual of breaking the bread and dipping a piece of it in the wine.

The consecration was followed by prayers including the Lord's Prayer. The traditional prayer of the Catholic Mass, "Deliver us, we beseech thee, O Lord, from all evils . . . " was explicitly removed, but the prayers were followed by the Absolution, a declaration of God's forgiveness of sin, announced by the officiating priest. The choir then sang the translation of the *Agnus Dei*, "Lamb of God who takes away the sins of the world, have mercy on us" while the officiating priest took Communion himself and then administered it to the rest of the congregation. This was the other great difference in Luther's German Mass. The consecration was always to be followed by the distribution of the bread and wine to the congregation: private Communion was meaningless. The Latin prayers to be said during the Communion were changed in translation to reflect the new practices. "Deliver *me* by this your most holy Body and Blood from all *my* iniquities" became "Deliver *us* . . . " and "The Body of our Lord Jesus Christ keep *my* soul to everlasting life" became "keep *your* soul".[9]

Much of the familiar liturgy of the Mass was thus preserved in Luther's revision. It still went too far for many congregations which were prepared to accept Luther's ideas but wanted something nearer the familiar liturgy. The reception of the Reformation by individual states and the authority which Lutheran thinking gave to heads of state meant that liturgical practices had to respond to some extent to popular demand and were consequently diverse. Luther's colleague Johannes Bugenhagen, who travelled over much of northern Germany and into Denmark setting up Lutheran churches, provided them with service books which were much closer to the pattern of the traditional Mass.

What really distinguished Luther's liturgy was the emphasis on readings from the Bible and sermons to explain them. Luther had spent part of his time in the Wartburg writing a series of short homilies on the New Testament readings which formed part of the liturgy of the Mass. These he called the *Postills*. It was not a new idea: there are plenty of medieval collections of short explanatory sermons on the readings from the Mass. Luther's incorporated his new thinking on the Bible and his stress on the importance of faith as the only precondition for salvation.

Some of the early Reformed services for the Eucharist were plain to the point of austerity in their attempt to remove everything which could not be found in the Bible. Zwingli's first attempt, in 1523, replaced the sequence of chants and responses from the central part of the Mass, the process of consecration, with a series of prayers leading up to the Biblical narrative of the Last Supper. The 1525 version was even simpler, pared down to the essentials of the Biblical account. What distinguished Zwingli's service, though, was that, after the prayer describing Christ's institution of the Last Supper, the communion was distributed in silence to the congregation who remained in their seats. Such a lengthy silence was difficult for a large congregation to sustain, and in later versions of the service it was filled with Bible readings.

In Strasbourg Martin Bucer embarked on a more thorough revision of the ritual of the Eucharist in an attempt to restore what he thought were the rituals of the early church. He added to Zwingli's model a general prayer of confession, a prayer of absolution and comfort for the minister, psalms and hymns. There was a lengthy explanation of the significance of the sacrament in the form of a prayer for understanding and proper reception, and prayers of intercession for the world, the church and the congregation. These were punctuated by repetitions of the Lord's Prayer, the "Our Father", by the whole congregation. The minister then read St Paul's account of the Last Supper and distributed the bread and wine while the choir sang a psalm. Calvin took Bucer's Communion service almost word for word for his French congregation in Strasburg and simplified it slightly for use in Geneva when he returned there in 1541. Like Bucer, he directed that psalms should be sung or suitable passages from the Bible read during the distribution of the bread and wine.[10]

The variations in Communion liturgies between Zürich, Strasburg, Geneva and the other centres of the Reformation may seem trivial, but they were the product of serious theological consideration. Even the bread of the Eucharist could be a touchstone for a doctrinal standpoint. Ordinary bread was brought into the medieval church to be blessed and distributed, but the bread which was consecrated for the Eucharist was not really bread but a hard, unleavened biscuit-like wafer. The use of wafers was defended on the theological grounds that Christ would have used unleavened bread in the first Eucharist since it was at the time of the Jewish feast of the Passover. During Passover, Jews still eat *matzoh* biscuits to remind them of the unleavened bread which the Israelites baked in their hurried preparations for the flight from Egypt. The communion wafers had the additional, practical advantage that they could more easily be distributed and eaten without the risk that crumbs of the sacred substance could fall to the ground. It was also possible to stamp them with iconographically-significant designs – the cross, the sacred monogram IHS (from the first letters of JESUS in Greek), the lamb and flag – as a reminder of their sacred nature.

Zwingli's 1525 service clearly envisaged the use of wafers. Martin Bucer accepted the use of unleavened bread and drew attention to the actual wording of the Gospel account of the Last Supper:

> all are agreed that he used bread which was unleavened and capable of being broken. For, "He broke bread and gave it to his disciples", pieces, that is, of the broken bread.

Nevertheless, while Bucer recommended uniformity of practice as "a token of harmony in the Lord and of reverence for Christ's mysteries", he was aware of the danger that the use of one distinctive type of bread could lend itself to superstitious beliefs. He was prepared therefore to accept that the use of ordinary bread made with yeast was perfectly proper in itself.[11]

In churches which accepted the argument of Zwingli and Calvin that Christ was present in the bread spiritually, in the hearts and minds of those who shared it, ordinary bread was generally considered to be more appropriate, as it was nearer to the spirit of the actual Biblical account of Christ's last meal with his followers. It seems like a minor point but it was profoundly symbolic for the Reformers. Calvin was prepared to insist on ordinary bread – to the extent that in 1538 he refused to celebrate Communion with unleavened bread and was temporarily expelled from Geneva as a result.

The changes in practice in the Church of England serve as an example of the theological weight which could lie behind such small differences in practice, and the acrimony they could cause. The 1549 Book of Common Prayer (which was ambiguous on whether the bread and wine really were Christ's body and blood) ordered that the bread for the Communion should be "unleavened and round, as it was afore, but without all manner of print, and something more larger and thicker than it was, so that it may be aptly divided in two pieces at the least . . . ". The 1552 service (which stated clearly that they were not) also stated that "the bread [shall] be such as is usual to be eaten; but the best and purest Wheat Bread that may conveniently be gotten". The same rubric was repeated in the Elizabethan Prayer Book of 1559 (which used formulae from both the 1549 and 1552 versions to produce an ambiguity which survived until recently). However, Elizabeth herself preferred wafers to be used in her own chapel and one of her 1559 Orders stated that wafers were an acceptable alternative to bread. The debate rumbled on through the sixteenth and seventeenth centuries. Bread seems to have become the norm in the eighteenth century but most churches returned to wafers in the nineteenth, under the influence of the Anglo-Catholic Oxford Movement. (Most churches also dropped the words of the 1552 Prayer Book "Take and eat/drink this in remembrance that Christ died for thee, and feed in him in thy heart by faith with thanksgiving" and went back to the 1549 version.) The issue can still cause acrimony.

The actual process of the consecration and administration of the bread and wine was also freighted with profound significance. The high point of the Latin Mass had been the moment at which the priest, having consecrated the bread, raised it above his head for the congregation to see. Luther retained the ritual elevation, not because he wanted the congregation to worship the bread, but precisely because he wanted them to see that it was just that, bread, and he wanted them to be aware of the mystery associated with its consecration:

> We do not want to abolish the elevation but retain it because it goes well with the German Sanctus and signifies that Christ has commanded us to remember him. For as the sacrament is elevated in a material manner, and yet Christ's body and blood are not seen in it, so he is remembered and elevated by the word of the sermon and is confessed and adored in the reception of the sacrament. Yet it is all apprehended by faith, for we cannot see how Christ gives his body and blood for us and even now daily shows and offers it before God to obtain grace for us.[12]

But the elevation of the consecrated bread was a clear statement that it had changed and was in some sense the body of Christ. It was therefore unacceptable to the other reformers. Even Cranmer's 1549 Communion service made it clear that the prayer of institution is to be said "without any elevation or shewing the sacraments to the people".

Much of the uproar which greeted Karlstadt's German celebration of the Mass at Christmas 1521 was caused by his decision to allow the lay recipients to take the bread and the cup into their own hands. The

Catholic practice was for the officiating priest to place the consecrated wafer into the communicant's mouth. The wafer was supposed to be swallowed without being chewed first, and the communicants might be given a sip of unconsecrated wine to help the dry wafer down.

The practice of placing the wafer into the communicant's mouth survived in some Protestant churches in the Lutheran tradition, because of the fear that people might not in fact eat the wafer but might take it away for superstitious purposes. Martin Bucer spent some time criticizing this practice, and was sceptical about the traditional excuse for it:

> I do not see how to reach the conclusion that the sacrament must only be given into the mouth. For the minister can easily see whether or not it is eaten by him to whom he has given it.
>
> In fact I have no doubt that the practice of not giving these sacraments into the hands of the faithful has been introduced to further a two-fold superstition. One part is the false honour which they wish to be given in this way to the sacrament, and the other is the ungodly arrogance by which priests claim for themselves, by virtue of the oil of consecration, a sanctity greater than that of the people of Christ . . . I wish therefore that the duty might be laid on all pastors and teachers of the people to teach their people faithfully that it is superstitious and ungodly to suppose that the hands of Christ's faithful are less pure than their mouths; or that the hands of the minister are more holy than those of the laity . . . [13]

Bucer was nevertheless prepared to allow lay people to have the bread put into their mouths if they asked for it, but he hoped that by proper education they would come to realize that they had the right to take the sacraments (the "sacred symbols" as Bucer calls them) into their own hands.

Then there was the problem of the disposal of surplus consecrated bread and wine. Because of the same fear that the consecrated elements might be taken and put to superstitious uses, pastors in the Lutheran tradition were expected to consecrate only as much as was necessary for the actual number of communicants. They were expected to take away any surplus and consume it themselves. Bucer disapproved of the practice:

> This gives rise to the superstition in some quarters that if any of the bread and wine is left over from the communion it is wrong to allow it to go into common use, as though even apart from its use at communion something spiritual or holy inhered of itself in this bread and wine . . . the Lord Christ is not offered in bread and wine but in godly minds, by means of his words and these symbols: and therefore bread and wine, even if it has

been placed on the Lord's table, is no more holy apart from its use at the communion which the Lord instituted than any other bread and wine.[14]

The Communion services of the radical reformers were explicitly made as simple as possible in an attempt to reconstruct the actual procedures of the Last Supper. The Communion might be preceded by a meeting for extempore prayer, Bible reading and discussion or the confession of sins, but these were not an essential part of the celebration. The communicants might sit around a table or in the places they had sat in for worship. The Biblical account of the Last Supper was read. The bread (an ordinary loaf) was passed around and everyone took a piece. Then a cup (an ordinary, everyday cup) of wine was passed from hand to hand. Apart from the reading, it was a silent ceremony. The silence which did not work in the worship of a whole community (as at Zürich) seems to have been more appropriate for a small group of dedicated believers.

The rôle of the pastor in the radical tradition was limited to the reading of the Biblical narrative, and some congregations dispensed with a minister altogether. In a letter to Thomas Müntzer, the Swiss radical Conrad Grebel suggested that "the server from out of the congregation should pronounce [the words] from one of the Evangelists or from Paul. They are the words of the instituted meal of fellowship, not words of consecration." He suggested that Müntzer should not administer the Supper himself, since "that was the beginning of the Mass, that only a few would partake, for the Supper is an expression of friendship, not a Mass and sacrament". No-one was to receive the Supper alone, not even on his death-bed. If Müntzer still wanted to lead the service, "we should wish that it be done without priestly garment and vestment of the Mass, without singing, without addition". Finally, he reminded Müntzer that the Last Supper took place in the evening and that the practice of the early church was to celebrate the meal in the evening also.[15] The overwhelming emphasis of the Lord's Supper in the radical tradition was on Christian fellowship, and on the Eucharist as a memorial: "we do just this, because our Lord told us to; and, as we do it, we think of him".[16]

Repetition of the actual events of the Last Supper was taken even further in some Radical congregations. On Easter Monday 1525 the German Anabaptist Balthasar Hubmaier celebrated the Last Supper at Waldshut, near the Swiss border. Before the breaking of bread, he washed the feet of the congregation as Christ had washed the feet of his apostles before the Last Supper.[17] Dietrich Philips described this ritual as one of the identifying marks of the true church. It was seen as a symbol of Christ's washing away sin and a sign of community fellow-ship.

> We should humble ourselves towards one another and ... we should hold
> our fellow believers in the highest respect, for the reason that they are the
> saints of God and members of the body of Jesus Christ, and that the Holy
> Spirit dwells in them.[18]

For at least some of the radical reformers, the important part of the Communion service was not the communion between God and humanity but between believer and believer. According to Balthasar Hubmaier:

> In baptism one pledges himself to God, in the supper to his neighbour, to
> offer body and blood in his stead, as Christ for us.[19]

The willingness of the radicals to endure martyrdom was thus in a sense an extension of their sharing of the Eucharist.

## Baptism[20]

The medieval rite of baptism had placed a heavy emphasis on the almost magical power of the ritual itself to drive out and defeat the Devil. The rite had originally been devised for adult converts who could make their own promises, but the infant's promises were made on its behalf by sponsors, the godparents. Becuase of the element of lay participation, much of the service was in the vernacular.

The rite began with a series of exorcisms: the priest blew on the infant and commanded the Devil to come out, made the sign of the cross and intoned a series of prayers. The salt to be placed in the baby's mouth, the baptismal water and the font were all separately exorcized and blessed. The priest anointed the baby's nose and ears with spittle and immersed it in the font three times, making the sign of the cross with its body. Finally, the baby was anointed with holy oil, dressed again in a white robe or a white cap, and given a candle (to be held by the godpar-ents).

The extent of lay participation in the service, the power which it was believed to have over the forces of evil and the fact that so much of the service was already in the vernacular, all made alteration to the baptism service a delicate matter. In particular, since valid baptism was so important for participation in the life of the church, it was important that change did not leave those baptized under the old rite with the impression that their baptism was inadequate. As Luther himself said in 1523, in the epilogue to his German *Little Book of Baptism*,

> I have not yet wanted to change anything in particular in the little book of baptism . . . To spare weak consciences, I let it stay almost as it is, so that they do not complain that I want to bring in a new baptism and find fault with those who have been baptized up to now, as though they were not properly baptized.

He was more concerned to add to the understanding of the ritual and to emphasize that it needed more than salt, water, spittle and oil to beat off the Devil. Christians needed to listen to God's word and to pray earnestly for the baby's spiritual well-being. Their interior faith would be more effective than outward actions.

By 1526, however, when Luther revised the *Little Book of Baptism* under pressure from the more radical reformers like Zwingli, Müntzer and Karlstadt, he was more prepared to make changes in the ritual. He removed the series of exorcisms, the blowing on the infant and anointing it with spittle and oil, and the lighted candle. All these changes were in line with the Reformation principle that non-Biblical accretions should be removed from church services as far as possible. However, there were still some quasi-magical rituals left. There was still the opening exorcism and the command to the Devil to "come out . . . and give place to the Holy Spirit". The baby was still signed with the Cross and immersed in the water.[21] Luther's insistence on preserving these traditions and his writings on the subject both suggest that he still saw the ritual actions as having some kind of independent power. In the Greater Catechism of 1529, for example, he claimed that

> no greater jewel can adorn our body or soul than baptism; for through it, perfect holiness and salvation become accessible to us, which are otherwise beyond the reach of man's life and energy.

For the Lutherans, baptism was more than an outward sign of a spiritual cleansing which had already been effected through faith. Baptism was still the essential precondition for salvation. Even children born out of wedlock were to be baptized as quickly as possible, without waiting to regularize the relationship between the parents.[22] Lutheran churches also retained for some time the custom of baptism by midwives if a newborn child was weakly and unlikely to live.

The baptism service which Martin Bucer wrote in the Strasburg liturgy was more thoroughly purged of its traditional rituals. Bucer described the exorcisms, the anointing with salt, spittle and oil and the gift of the candle as "magic tricks [which] ill become intelligent and rational Christians, who ought to pay heed to the word of the Lord and follow it alone". The changes were designed to bring the service nearer to the biblical model, but they also reflected a radical change in thinking on the significance of what was being done. For Bucer, the ritual of washing with water was a symbol of spiritual cleansing, Christ's washing away of sins. There was no need to rush to baptize sickly babies, for salvation could not be bought by human actions. Bucer even considered abolishing infant baptism, though he eventually decided against it.[23]

For Bucer, the crucial argument in favour of infant baptism was that it represented the introduction of the child into the Christian community. He therefore insisted that baptism had to take place in front of the whole congregation of the church, and preferably as part of the Sunday Communion service. The two sacraments could thus be linked, as they were in the early church. The baptismal liturgy followed the sermon, which could thus be used to explain the significance of the sacrament. The whole service was directed not at the infant but at the godparents and the other adults present.

Bucer was contemptuous of the fiction by which the godparents spoke for the infant, renouncing the Devil and declaring their faith. In his revision of the service the godparents were asked directly about their faith and were then asked to promise to bring the child up so that it would be able to renounce the devil and profess belief in God. The congregation was asked to pray that God would give the infant faith, and to help to bring it up in "Christian order, discipline and fear of God". Much of Bucer's thinking on baptism, and the form of service which it produced, was taken over by other reformed congregations. There was an increased emphasis on the importance of the promises made by parents and godparents, and godparents were questioned to make sure that they themselves understood the basics of the faith.[24]

Calvin's order of baptism was part of the 1542 *Form of Prayers*. He instructed that the service should take place on Sunday afternoon during the catechism class or on a weekday after the morning sermon. His order of service began with a lengthy discussion of the significance of the ritual. Here, Calvin explained that baptism is a sign of God's mercy and forgiveness and his wish to help us to fight against the Devil. Through baptism, God incorporates us into the church. The water is a sign of his wish to cleanse our souls. In his introduction, Calvin also outlined the Scriptural justification for infant baptism. After all that, the ritual itself was short and extremely simple. The officiating minister read the description of the blessing of the little children from St Matthew's gospel, prayed for the child and gave the charge to the godparents to have the child brought up in the faith, and then poured water on the child's head in the name of the Trinity.[25]

There was considerable debate as to whether the child should be fully immersed in the water or merely sprinkled with it. Some Catholic service books seemed to assume that water would be sprinkled or poured on the infant's head. In Cologne, however, the priest was expected to dip the baby in the font unless either the baby or the priest was too weak to cope with immersion. In general, the churches of the Reformation moved towards the custom of pouring water over the child's head, though they argued over whether or not the child should be clothed.

The rite of baptism in the churches of the radical reformation was less structured and more dependent on the initiative of the person being baptized and the congregation. The service could take place in an open meeting at the church or at home. In the early days of the movement there were mass services of public baptism in rivers. However, these seldom if ever involved the baptism by total immersion which is a feature of modern Baptist rituals. Water was poured over the head of the person being baptized. The water could come from a basin, a well or even from the town pump.

Typically, the service began with the candidate confessing his or her sins, making a profession of faith and asking for baptism. The officiating pastor asked if the congregation had any objection to admitting the candidate to baptism. If there were none, the candidate knelt down and the pastor poured water over them from his hand or a ladle, saying simply "I baptize you in the name of God the Father, God the Son and God the Holy Spirit".

As baptism became increasingly a rite for young adults from Anabaptist families rather than for converts, some form of instruction before baptism was introduced. The ritual then began with Bible reading and exposition. Candidates for baptism were examined to test their grasp of the basics of the faith. The baptism was followed by a simple celebration of the Lord's Supper to demonstrate that those who had been baptized were now part of the fellowship of those who believed they were saved by their faith.[26]

The Anabaptists had explicitly rejected infant baptism as a symbol that the baby had been born into a Christian family and was to be brought up in a Christian community. Nevertheless, members of

Anabaptist congregations still felt the need for a service which recognized and gave thanks for the birth of a new child. The German Anabaptist Balthasar Hubmaier devised a dedication service for his own congregation:

> Instead of baptism, I have the church come together, bring the infant in, explain in German the gospel, "They brought little children" [Matthew 19:13]. When a name is given it, the whole church prays for the child on bended knees, and commends it to Christ, that he will be gracious and intercede for it.[27]

# Confirmation[28]

In the early church, washing with holy water, anointing with holy oil and ceremonial blessing by a church leader (the "laying on of hands") were all part of the ritual by which new members were admitted to full membership. As baptism became increasingly confined to infants, older children needed to be given the opportunity to speak for themselves. The rituals of anointing with holy oil and the laying on with hands were separated from baptism and became a distinct sacrament, confirmation. Candidates for confirmation were expected to have been trained in the basics of the faith and to be questioned on it before they could be confirmed. There was a feeling that confirmation was necessary before a young person could receive the Eucharist and be admitted to full participation in the life of the church.

In spite of the fact that it was one of the seven sacraments, confirmation had fallen into neglect in the later medieval church. The rite could only be administered by the bishop. When many bishops were absent from their dioceses on other duties for lengthy periods, parish priests had perforce to admit young people to the Eucharist before they had been confirmed. There is considerable debate about the extent to which medieval believers were informed about the basics of their faith, but the evidence suggests that teaching and rigorous examination before confirmation had fallen into disuse. Meanwhile, the children of the powerful were still being confirmed immediately after baptism. Elizabeth I, for example, was confirmed by Thomas Cranmer himself after he baptized her.

It is ironical that, although the Reformers deleted confirmation from the list of the sacraments, many of them effectively reinstated it as part of the process of Christian education. The process began within the Catholic church. Erasmus proposed to examine children on Christian doctrine in front of the congregation.[29] Luther began by diminishing the significance of confirmation. In *The Babylonian Captivity of the Church*, he insisted that it was baptism which gave both spiritual rebirth and the gift of the Holy Spirit. He was aware of the passages in the Acts of the Apostles in which Christ's followers laid their hands on the heads of the baptized, but insisted that that was a temporary measure. By 1529, however, he had become aware of the extent of general ignorance of the essentials of Christian doctrine in his territory of Saxony. He prepared his *Short Catechism* in that year to teach the basics of the faith, and was prepared to accept that pastors should teach and examine children as a sort of extended confirmation ritual before admitting them to Communion. "I allow that confirmation be administered," he wrote, "provided that it is known that God has said nothing about it."[30]

Luther's original intention was that pastors should preach on and explain his catechism week by week. Inevitably, adults refused to attend these sessions and the church administrators were thus forced to concentrate on the children. They attempted (though without much success) to compel householders to send their children to be catechized. Martin Bucer wrote a formal ritual for examining children on their knowledge in front of the whole congregation. The congregation prayed for the increase of the Holy Spirit in the children so that they might persevere in the faith. One of the clergy then laid hands on them, praying "Receive the Holy Ghost, your protection against all that is wicked, strength and help towards all that is good, from the gracious hand of god the Father, Son and Holy Ghost".[31] The examinations of candidates for confirmation became more rigorous by the later sixteenth century. Children were then asked to promise to follow what they had learned. In some cases the church superintendent laid hands on them, and they then received Communion with the rest of the congregation.

Bucer's ritual was so similar to the medieval rite of confimation that some reformers insisted it had gone too far and was in danger of reinstating confirmation as a sacrament.[32] A similar ritual was followed in Calvin's Geneva but without the laying on of hands, which seems to have been the element that most worried the Reformers. (The laying on of hands survives as a central feature of the Anglican ritual.) Calvin insisted in the strongest terms that his ritual was not confirmation (which he deplored) but an extended form of catechism, in which children and young people made a profession of faith and were examined on it by the church leader. What concerned him about the medieval rite was that it was regarded as a sacrament and thus it detracted from the the importance of the sacrament of baptism. The laying on of hands and the anointing of the candidates with oil he condemned because these rituals were intended to look as though they conferred grace. If the laying on of hands could be regarded as simply part of the acknowledgement of the young person's profession of faith, he was prepared to accept it.[33]

The revival of confirmation, with or without the disputed ritual, thus gave children the opportunity to repeat their baptismal promises in person. It was therefore a crucial part of Christian initiation for Protestants who did not wish to go as far as the radical reformers and insist on adult baptism. As a rite of passage, it performed the same function as the medieval sacrament. The renewed insistence that children should be taught the basics of Christian doctrine and should be examined on what they had learned also contributed to the spread of a more structured approach to the understanding of the fundamental elements of the faith. Not only the children were instructed: the congregation which heard them examined also learned from the regular repetition.

There were, however, unresolved theological issues in the confirmation ritual. Whether deliberately or not, many rites blurred the crucial question of the point at which the gifts of the spirit were conferred. Too strong an emphasis on the importance of confirmation for full church membership risked devaluing the sacrament of baptism, which was believed to provide all that was necessary for salvation.

## Repentance and reconciliation

By 1520, Luther was abandoning his earlier view that penance was one of the sacraments of the Church. While writing the *Babylonian Captivity*, he convinced himself that ritual penance could only be effective for those whose faith had led them to proper repentance (technically, *contrition*). More radically, perhaps, his ideas on the priesthood of all believers led him to claim that any Christian could hear the confession of other Christians and grant them absolution. Logically, this would have allowed women to hear confession. However, the idea of the lay confessor who could also grant absolution was too much of a challenge to the organization of the church and to lay authority, and Luther abandoned it.

The doctrine of justification by faith meant that confession without genuine and heartfelt penitence was useless. The logic of the Protestant position was therefore that no human could absolve another of their sins. Nevertheless, many of the Reformers still regarded confession as a useful spiritual discipline. It encouraged reflection on sin which would lead to true penitence. Confession to an experienced spiritual guide could also console the penitent with a reminder of God's infinite mercy. Luther himself found it a source of comfort and strength.

Confession could help with congregational discipline. In the *Formulary for Mass and Communion* of 1523, Luther stipulated that only those who had shown awareness of their sinfulness could be admitted to the sacrament. This gave the pastor an unrivalled instrument for gaining information on the private lives and even the thoughts of his congregation. The potential which confession offered for the imposition of standards of moral behaviour made it useful to the secular authorities as well. The procedure of confession could also be extended to allow the clergy to test their parishioners' knowledge and understanding of the faith. Here again, they could use the sanction of refusing the Eucharist to those who were ignorant of what they should believe.

The Swiss churches influenced by Zwingli also used the practice of individual confession as a form of pastoral counselling. Martin Bucer saw individual confession as part of the framework of congregational discipline. When he tried to enforce it in Strasbourg, though, the city fathers resisted him. He was, however, able to devise a service of collective repentance for the Saturday afternoon service. In the course of the service, the pastor exhorted the congregation to repent of their sins. He stressed that anyone who took part in the Eucharist without repenting their sins would only earn God's anger. The encouragement to repent was reinforced by the general prayer of confession which began the service of the Eucharist. Bucer's liturgy had three versions of the general confession, of which the following is the shortest:

> Almighty, eternal God and Father, we confess and acknowledge unto thee that we were conceived in unrighteousness and are full of sin and transgression in all our life. We do not fully believe thy Word nor follow thy holy commandments. Remember thy goodness, we beseech thee, and for thy Name's sake be gracious unto us, and forgive us our iniquity, which is great.

The longest version is based on the Ten Commandments and enumerates the ways in which all ten have been broken.[34]

Calvin took the idea for a general confession from Bucer's Strasburg liturgy. The same prayers provided the basis for the familiar words of the General Confession which Cranmer incorporated in the service of

Morning Prayer in the 1552 version of the English Book of Common Prayer:

> Almighty and most merciful Father, We have erred and strayed from thy ways like lost sheep. We have followed too much the devices and desires of our own hearts. We have offended against Thy holy laws. We have left undone those things which we ought to have done, And we have done those things which we ought not to have done, And there is no health in us.

A slightly different form of words began Cranmer's 1552 Communion service.

Both Bucer and Cranmer followed these general confessions with a prayer of absolution. Bucer's Strasbourg liturgy gave the officiating clergyman the responsibility of declaring God's forgiveness:

> in his name I proclaim unto you the forgiveness of all your sins, and declare you to be loosed of them on earth, that you be loosed of them also in heaven, in eternity.[35]

The prayer in Cranmer's Communion service could be taken as an additional petition for forgiveness from the officiating clergyman, but the prayer in the morning service was more explicit in its claims for the powers of the clergy:

> Almighty God . . . hath given power and commandment to his Ministers to declare and pronounce to his people, being penitent, the Absolution and Remission of their sins . . .

The 1552 and 1559 Prayer Books gave no indication of *how* the officiating clergyman should say these prayers. Some chose therefore to say them kneeling, which associated them physically with the congregation being absolved. The more ritualistic Prayer Book of 1662 directed that they should say it standing while the congregation remained on their knees. This placed the clergy in a much more authoritative posture.[36]

There is no general confession in the 1549 Book of Common Prayer, and no prayers of absolution. The 1549 services of Morning and Evening Prayer are much shorter, and clearly derive from Cranmer's 1538 Latin services of Mattins and Vespers, which were mainly designed for use by the clergy. The Communion service includes an exhortation to the congregation to repent their sins, confessing them to God "with inward sorrow and tears", to be reconciled with their neighbours and to make due restitution to those they have wronged; but the service then moves straight to the point at which the congregation make their offerings to the church, followed by the ritual of consecration.

The 1549 Book of Common Prayer is generally regarded as a compromise between the desire of the English Protestants for a reformed liturgy and the need to make the services acceptable to the majority of the population. The Communion service in the 1552 version is certainly much clearer about the essentially commemorative nature of the sacrament. At first sight, though, the prayers of confession and absolution move the liturgy in a more Catholic direction. What was Cranmer doing? He and Bucer were in close contact in the 1540s and Cranmer relied heavily on Bucer's ideas for the 1549 communion service.[37] In the spring of 1549 Bucer finally came to England to take up a chair at the University of Cambridge. He arrived too late to have any further impact on the 1549 Book of Common Prayer, but Cranmer seems to have drawn more widely on his ideas for the 1552 version to produce services which were in general liturgically richer. There is no direct reference to the desirability of prayers of confession and absolution in the critique of the 1549 Prayer Book which Bucer drew up some time between 1549 and his death in 1551 at Cranmer's request.[38] The idea of a general confession is, however, implicit in what Bucer says about the need for the congregation to be aware that they should repent and make amends for their sins before approaching the Lord's Table.

It is possible that Cranmer had already told Bucer of his plans to include a general confession, at least in the Communion service. Bucer suggested in a general section on behaviour in church that "it would be suitable if the people were to recite, together with the minister, both the confession of sins and that prayer before the reception of the sacraments . . . or to follow him as he recites them".[39] There was already a prayer of absolution in the 1549 order for the Visiting of the Sick.

Calvin's Genevan liturgy included a general confession but no prayer of absolution. The pronouncement of a general absolution was after all fundamentally opposed to everything that Calvin stood for. How could a minister pronounce absolution, when only God knew which of the congregation had been predestined to salvation? Nevertheless, towards the end of his life, Calvin admitted that he regretted not having included a general absolution to be spoken by the minister after the general confession. Though the rituals of penance and absolution were no longer theologically acceptable, there was still a profound human need for reconciliation and closure.

For the radical reformers, penitence and reconciliation was part of the ritual of baptism. Dietrich Philips made the sequence of spiritual development clear: "the penitent, believing and reborn children of God must be baptized".[40] Caspar Schwenckfeld, too, considered that the sacrament of adult baptism was a better form of the dubious sacrament of penance.[41] The penitence and reconciliation which candidates underwent before baptism was a one-off event. However, the Anabaptist congregations also had a mechanism for dealing with social discord in their exercise of excommunication, the imposition and lifting of the ban. According to Philips:

> What the congregation binds on earth shall be bound in heaven, and, on the other hand, what they loose on earth shall be loosed in heaven. This must not be understood as meaning that men have power to forgive sins, or to retain them . . . for to no prophet or apostle on earth has it been given to forgive sin, to hear confession and to absolve the people . . . But the congregation has received the Holy Spirit and the gospel from Jesus Christ (Isa. 43:25; Matt. 9:6; Ps. 51:4) in which is proclaimed and promised forgiveness of sins, reconciliation with God and eternal life to all who truly repent and believe in Jesus Christ.[42]

## The Solemnization of Matrimony

Marriage was one of the seven sacraments of the medieval church, a symbol of the relationship between Christ and the church. Its celebration involved prayers and readings designed to emphasize the dangers of sexuality and female influence and the indissoluble nature of the bond being contracted. The priest blessed the wedding ring and sometimes even the bed. In spite of this sacramental approach, the medieval church clearly treated marriage as a second-class state, and those who aspired to a more holy life had to remain celibate.

All the Protestant churches rejected the idea that a celibate life was inherently more holy. Nevertheless, virtually all the magisterial reformers retained a sense of underlying unease about sexual activity. There was often a tension between their anxiety to value the married state and their wish to control sexual excess. Cranmer, of all people, should have valued marriage highly: he had married a niece of the Nuremberg reformer Andreas Osiander in 1532 and he remained defiantly in the married state in spite of all the difficulties it caused him in the later years of Henry VIII's reign. Even so, the marriage service in his Prayer Book, like a number of other Protestant marriage services, described marriage as being for "the procreation of children, to be brought up in the fear and nurture of the Lord" and "a remedy against sin, and to avoid fornication", and only then "for the mutual society, help and comfort that the one ought to have of the other". It was Martin Bucer who suggested that Cranmer should reverse the order of these causes and place mutual help at the head of the list.

> And so it is that in the first institution of marriage, to which the Lord Christ taught us to look back, God did not say that its purpose was children, or a remedy, but this: "It is not good for man to be alone, let us therefore make a help for him, to be with him." He says "help" in general terms, by which we may understand that a wife has been given to the man by the Lord, a help not only to avoid fornication and not only to procreate children, but for all the purposes of human life. "For now," says the Lord, "they are not two but one flesh," that is, one person, "and for this reason a man shall leave his father and mother and shall cleave to his wife," meaning, for the work and intercourse of every aspect of life which is lived in gratitude to God. It is very useful if these things can be explained and instilled into engaged and married couples, so that they may fully cultivate and faithfully perform the whole law of marriage.[43]

This was one of the suggestions which Cranmer did not take up, and the wording remained as in the 1549 Prayer Book until the twentieth-century revisions.

Nevertheless, in spite of their reservations, it was the Protestant reformers who revalued the married state. It is ironical, therefore, that they also removed marriage from the list of sacraments. Luther initially considered marriage as a civil contract with an optional religious blessing. His rite for the blessing was closely modelled on the medieval Catholic rite, but with some significant differences. Luther's rite placed less emphasis on the dangers of sexuality in general and female sexuality in particular, but more emphasis on the need for the husband to be the head of the household and for the woman to be subordinate and confined to the private sphere. Marriage was thus seen less as a strategy for dealing with the challenge of human sexuality (though that emphasis was always there) and more as the foundation of the Christian household. The Christian couple were to be models of godly behaviour.

The marriage rites of the Lutheran states became more detailed and prescriptive by the later sixteenth century, and rulers attempted to enforce marriage in church as part of their strategies for increasing social discipline. A number of states required their ministers to keep written registers of the marriages they performed. In addition, ministers were expected to check the status of the prospective couple, to make sure that one of them was resident in the parish and, in some cases, that the bride was not pregnant. The couple were required to make full statements of acceptance of the marriage vows, which stressed the duty of the male to protect and care for his wife, and the duty of the woman to be subservient and obedient to her husband. A sermon or written homily reinforced the message of the liturgy.

## Death and burial

The rite of extreme unction was the last of the seven sacraments of the Catholic church. The full ritual involved blessing with holy water, after which the dying person made as full a confession of sins as their medical condition allowed. The priest absolved their sins, anointed them with holy oil and gave them a final Eucharist. The anointing was considered to be so powerful that anyone who received extreme unction and subsequently recovered was required to live as if dead to the world, abstaining from eating meat and from sexual activity. For this reason, most people were reluctant to ask for anointing until death was really imminent. However, the other parts of the ritual, the confession and Eucharist, were considered enough to ensure the soul's safe passage into salvation. Without them, though, the soul might well be damned. Sudden and unforeseen death was thus the greatest of threats, and the medieval Christian was regularly exhorted to prepare for death and to live always with the imminence of death in mind.

Luther, too, regarded death as something which could be prepared for. The preparations he suggested in his "Sermon on Preparing to Die" (1519) were surprisingly similar to the traditional Catholic practices, but it is already possible to see changes in the spirit behind them. At this point he still believed in the sacrament of penance and in purgatory, and he was still prepared to recommend Extreme Unction. However, he emphasized that "the sacraments are nothing other than signs that serve to stimulate faith" though they do "constitute a staff on which one can lean for support". Like the authors of medieval books of advice on preparing for death, he believed that the greatest danger to the dying person was the temptation to doubt and despair. For Luther, the one remedy for this was an unswerving faith in the salvation which had been bought by Christ's sacrifice. Like the medieval authors, he recommended that this faith should be cultivated throughout life: you should not approach death unprepared.[44]

Luther's priority was promoting faith and preaching the Word. His suggested deathbed rituals were designed to comfort the dying and reinforce their faith at the last. Consequently, he left much of the detail of deathbed ritual practice to the discretion of the individual pastor, who he trusted to know what the individual member of the congregation needed. His successors were more prescriptive. The orders of worship of a number of Lutheran states included detailed instructions for visiting and offering Communion to the sick. A similar ritual, prescribing the exact words to be said by both the minister and the sick person, is in the English Book of Common Prayer.

These instructions were broader in scope than the Catholic liturgy, which was geared specifically to the dying. The widening of the scope of the ritual was in line with the Protestant critique of the sacrament of Extreme Unction. Catholic sacramentology had derived the ritual of Extreme Unction from the instructions in the general letter of St James: "Is one of you ill? He should send to the elders of the congregation to pray over him and to anoint him with oil in the name of the Lord". Based on St James's instructions, Protestants argued that the prayer and anointing of Extreme Unction was not a sacrament reserved for the dying but something which should be offered to all those who were ill. Indeed, Martin Bucer suggested that it should be completely abolished. He regarded it as "an absurd imitation of what the apostles did" and considered that it had been so corrupted by its misuse in the Catholic church that it was inevitably a source of superstitious belief.[45]

The Lutheran rituals were thus geared to comforting the sick rather than the dying, though the prayer of absolution suggests that the rite was normally reserved for those who were seriously ill and unlikely to recover. It is clear from the complaints which parishioners levelled against absent or lazy clergy that what most people still wanted was a final Communion before they died. The rituals laid down in a number of Lutheran states make it clear that Communion could not be offered to those who refused to repent of their sins or be reconciled with their neighbours, and to those who were ignorant of the essentials of their faith. For this reason, the rituals for visiting the sick and offering them Communion were frequently separated. The English Book of Common Prayer stressed that the sick were not to be offered Communion alone: there had to be "three, or two at the least" except in the most exceptional circumstances. A Communion which was not shared was not a valid Communion.

After death came burial. The medieval liturgy stressed the continued presence of the dead in the spiritual community of the living. The burial service was normally followed by at least one mass for the soul of the dead. The underlying principle of requiem and anniversary masses, like that of the Catholic burial service, was that absolution could be effective even after death, and that the prayers of the living could benefit the dead.

Lutheran burial rites attempted to remove the element of prayer for the dead while retaining the comforting ceremonial of a formal funeral. In some parts of Lutheran Germany, candles could still be burned around the bier and family and friends could pray around it. There were still funeral processions (with detailed regulations of the size of procession appropriate for the different ranks of society) and the church bells could be rung while the body was carried to the cemetery. Women who died in childbirth were attended to the grave by female friends, who lowered to body into the grave. There were attempts to control the amount of display at funerals. Wooden coffins were becoming increasingly popular in the sixteenth century, and some states issued regulations for the decoration of coffins – the amount by which they could be decorated varying according to the age and sex of the deceased. As well as the regulations on the size of funeral processions, there were attempts to limit the extravagance of post-funeral entertainment. Above all, commemoration of the dead after the funeral was forbidden. There was to be no extended period of mourning, no anniversary masses, no prayers for the dead in church, no readings from the parish roll of those whose anniversaries of death were imminent. The dead were with God and the living were to leave them there.

Bucer attempted to overcome the inevitable austerity of funeral rituals when the dead were beyond all human influence by encouraging the living to remember the dead with thanksgiving, to follow their example where appropriate and to remind themselves of their faith in the resurrection. They were also to meditate on their own sins and to prepare for their own passage "from this lost world to the Lord Christ".[46]

Funerals in the Swiss Calvinist tradition were more austere. John Knox's Genevan Book of Common Order suggested that the bodies of the dead should be "decently attended" from the house to the place which had been designated for public burial. However, the burial area was in no sense to be seen as consecrated ground. Nor was there to be any ritual activity there: the body was simply to be interred. There was no need even for the presence of the minister, though he might turn up if it was convenient. According to the Book of Common Order, he "goeth to the church if he be not far off, and maketh some comfortable exhortation to the people touching death and resurrection". Apart from that, there was no ceremony, and certainly no scope for rites of separation and remembrance.

# Singing the ritual: music and liturgy in the Protestant tradition

There were other more practical issues which had to be addressed in the form of the church services of the Protestant tradition. In particular, there was concern about the amount and nature of the music which was considered allowable and appropriate as part of worship.

Luther's great contribution to the services of the German church was his musical abilities. He wrote music and played several musical instruments himself, and was interested in collecting traditional German tunes. His first hymn book, which included the hymn *Aus tieffer not schrey ich zu dir* ("From trouble deep I cry to thee"), was published in 1524. It was a resounding success and he went on to publish several more. Possibly his best known is *Ein' Feste Burg* ("A safe stronghold our God is still"), published in 1527 to a tune which he probably wrote himself; it was a sort of Battle Hymn of the Reformation.

Luther also encouraged the use of music elsewhere in the liturgy and took advice from musical experts to ensure that the music recommended was less "monotonous" than Gregorian plainchant.[47] Surprisingly, in spite of his insistence on the importance of reading and understanding the Bible, he encouraged the clergy to sing the Bible readings in the Communion service. He wrote music for his translations of the Creed and assumed that the celebrant at Communion would sing the crucial words of institution, the words by which the bread and wine became the body and blood of Christ. He also suggested hymns to be sung during the distribution of the bread and wine and wrote for that purpose the "German Sanctus" a paraphrase of the passage from Isaiah 6 which describes the angels surrounding God and singing "Holy, Holy, Holy, Lord God of hosts". The song of the angels had been part of the Latin liturgy but Luther's translation placed it in its Biblical context. For Luther, music was not a barrier to understanding but an enhancement of it. He may also have been aware that members of the congregation were more likely to remember the Creed if they had music to help them.

The more austere Calvinist churches were reluctant to allow any music other than psalms, songs from the Old Testament which were often translated into verse by the Reformers. Calvin's Geneva service book, the *Form of Prayers*, consists largely of metrical versions of several of the Psalms. These were translated not by Calvin himself but by the poet Clément Marot. Calvin's successor, Théodore de Bèze, completed the translation of the psalter by 1561. Some of their translations are still in use.

The English church also made considerable use of metrical translations of the psalms. Some of these translations also survive in modern hymn books. The best known are probably the various versions of "The Lord's my shepherd", translations of the 23rd psalm. The traditional chorales which Luther collected were sung in harmony, but the versified psalms of the Calvinist tradition were customarily sung in unison. This was not because the Reformers were opposed to the beauty of harmony and polyphony. On the contrary: Calvin's preface to the 1543 metrical psalter shows that he was aware of the power of music to move and to delight:

> Among other things which can refresh man and give him delight, music is either the first or one of the first. It is a gift of God intended for this use ... We know by experience that music has a hidden and almost incredible power to sway hearts in one sense or another.

It was precisely because music had such power that care must be taken in choosing suitable music for worship. The Reformers had criticized the complex polyphonic settings of the medieval liturgy because they made the words unintelligible and subordinated the sense of the text to mere musical trickery. As Calvin said:

> One must always take care that the music should not be frivolous or flighty; it should have weight and majesty ... So there is a great difference between the music one makes at home, round the table, for enjoyment, and the psalms which one sings in church, in the presence of God and his angels.[48]

Singing in harmony, even for sacred songs, was quite permissible at home. The Genevan psalter was republished in 1565 with four-part harmonizations of the tunes – "not for singing in church, but in order to rejoice in the Lord, especially at home". In church, however, the "weight and majesty" of the psalms meant that they should be sung in unison and unaccompanied. The resulting music was powerful in its simplicity and directness and deeply moving: there are accounts of refugees new to Geneva who broke down in tears on hearing the psalms sung in this way for the first time.

There was also the question of instrumental music in church. Luther liked it; Calvin felt it detracted from the "weight and majesty" he was trying to achieve with his unaccompanied unison singing. In many

Protestant traditions, the music of the organ (and later the harmonium) was felt to be suitable in an ecclesiastical context but the music of groups of instrumentalists was not. In late sixteenth-century Strasbourg, the main Sunday service began and ended with an organ recital, and was punctuated by the singing of hymns accompanied by the organ.

## Shaping ritual: architecture and the visual appearance of worship

The reinterpretation of the sacraments and the restructuring of the liturgy inevitably led to changes in the appearance of Protestant churches. In the medieval church, the altar was the focal point of worship. Situated in the most richly decorated part of the church, framed and even partly concealed by elaborately carved screens, placed under a carved and painted canopy of honour and decorated with embroidered cloths, this was where God was made visible and tangible in the form of the consecrated bread. The words of consecration were a priestly mystery. They were muttered rather than declaimed, and they were of course in Latin. The priest celebrated with his back to the congregation, at an altar set firmly against the east wall of the church.

Wealthier churches had a clear division between the chancel, the east end of the church where the clergy celebrated the Mass, and the nave, where the congregation remained except for the rare occasions on which they actually took Communion. The chancel might have wooden stalls for a choir: for that reason, the chancel is sometimes called the choir (or *quire*). Larger churches had aisles to the side of the nave, or transepts, projecting wings on either side of the chancel. Aisles and transepts might have private chapels in them, with their own screens, and almost all had additional altars at which the Mass was regularly celebrated. The congregation could move freely around the church from service to service, summoned by the little bells which were rung to announce the moment of consecration.

All this ritual and mystery was removed by the Reformation. Screens and side altars were removed. The priest spoke the Gospel narrative openly and in the vernacular, facing the congregation. The altar had therefore to be moved to make a space behind it. In some churches the main stone altar was destroyed. In others, it was left at the east end of the chancel but a new table-like altar was installed in front of it. In churches of the Lutheran tradition, the altar stayed in the chancel, and in many cases the people came to sit in the choir for the Communion service. The chancel thus remained as a sort of holy of holies, the most sacred space in the church. In his review of the liturgy of the Church of England, Martin Bucer was highly critical of the continuing practice of the clergy performing services in the chancel, removed from the congregation and thus not fully heard or understood. In an interesting reference to architectural history he added:

> We know from the appearance of the most ancient churches and from the records of the Fathers that in ancient times the churches were nearly round and that the place of the clergy was in the centre. From that position the holy things of God were set before the people so that whatever was said could be heard and understood by everyone present.[49]

Bucer stopped short of recommending a comprehensive rebuild of all churches, but it was possible to achieve the effect he wanted even within the constraints of the traditional medieval church building. In churches in the Swiss Reformed tradition, the Communion table (no longer even described as an altar) was often moved to stand at one side of the nave. Its position as the focus of church services was taken by the pulpit. Medieval churches did have pulpits, but their focal point was the altar. Protestant pulpits became increasingly elaborate, culminating in the triple-decker pulpits of the seventeenth and eighteenth centuries with their separate lecterns for the parish clerk, Bible reading and the sermon.

In the medieval church, the congregation normally stood, knelt or sat on the floor. Some churches had benches around the walls for those who could not stand, and the wealthy had pews, backed wooden benches which could be elaborately decorated. As sermons became a more important part of worship, devout people brought stools and cushions into church to sit more comfortably. More and more Protestant churches were provided with pews for the whole congregation. The provision of pews meant that people could sit through the increasingly lengthy sermons, but it also meant that they were physically restrained. Instead of moving about the church from altar to altar, engaged in their own devotions, they sat obediently through readings, lengthy prayers and the sermon. They might sit in hierarchial order or separated by age and gender. In churches in the Swiss Reformed tradition, these pews were often oriented not towards the altar but towards the pulpit. The focus of attention and liturgical activity was thus directed away from the sacrament and towards the preaching of the Word.

The sixteenth-century prayer books of the Church of England make it clear that altars were expected to be movable. Kept in the chancel when not in use, they were supposed to be carried into the nave for the

Communion service. These instructions were not followed in all churches, possibly because the size of the congregation did not warrant it. By the end of the sixteenth century, some congregations (and some members of the clergy – though not always in the same parishes) wanted more respect paid to the altar, and went back to the traditional practice of placing the altar against the east wall. In some cases it was railed off and communicants knelt at the rail. These rails became more common in the 1630s, when Charles I's Archbishop Laud encouraged them, but they were not universal until the later seventeenth century.

The reinterpretation of the sacrament of baptism also had an impact on the physical appearance of the church and its decorations. Medieval fonts were often substantial stone structures, designed to reflect the power of the holy water they contained and the importance of the ritual which was celebrated with it, and were often carved with instructive imagery. Since the water in the font had been blessed and charged with spiritual power, it could be stolen and used for magical rites. Many fonts therefore had lockable covers of varying degrees of elaboration. The font was traditionally placed at the west end of the church, near the lay people's door, so that baptism was physically as well as symbolically an entry into the Christian life.

The changing emphasis of baptism in the Protestant tradition meant that all these traditions were swept away. The water itself was no longer considered as holy: it had no powers of itself, outside the baptism service. Elaborate fonts were defaced or removed. In some churches they were replaced by simple metal bowls in a deliberate break with the ritualism of the past. Churches in the Lutheran tradition retained the font but placed it towards the east end of the church, near the Communion table and the pulpit, so that the process of baptism could be clearly seen by the whole congregation. Calvinist churches used basins placed near the pulpit or Communion table, again so that the congregation could see and participate in the ritual.

In the Anabaptist tradition, of course, facilities would eventually be provided for adults to be baptized by total immersion. However, baptism by immersion was very unusual in the early Anabaptist tradition. It seems to have developed first in England and the Netherlands and spread to the rest of Europe in the later eighteenth century. Early Anabaptists were baptized by water being poured over them. There was no special font or container for the water, and frequently no special building for the ceremony. Services were frequently held in the open air – on a river bank, at a well or even at the town pump.

Other changes in the visual appearance of Protestant church services were the result of changing ideas on the value and significance of vestments and ritual gestures. In spite of Luther's insistence that the bread and wine of the Eucharist really were the body and blood of Christ, he disapproved of outward gestures of adoration. In *The Adoration of the Sacrament of the Holy Body of Christ* (1523) he argued that the heart of the sacrament was actually the word of God – the word by which Christ declared that the bread and wine of the sacrament were his body and blood. The congregation should therefore be led to concentrate on the Word rather than the bread and wine. They would then give true honour to the sacrament, rather than the "bowing, bending, kneeling and adoration" of Catholic worship. He reminded his readers of Christ's own statement that "God is spirit, and those who worship him must worship in spirit and in truth" (John 4: 24). They *might* then kneel, but need not necessarily do so. Worship was a spiritual activity and those who worshipped the word of God properly would forget about physical postures.[50]

In the early stages of the Protestant Reformation, refusal to kneel at the Communion was a touchstone for reformers. The 1552 English Book of Common Prayer insisted that

> the communicants kneeling should receive the holy Communion: which thing being well meant, for a signification and grateful acknowledging of the benefits of Christ given unto the worthy receiver, and to avoid the profanation and disorder which about the holy Communion might otherwise ensue: lest yet the same kneeling might be thought or taken otherwise, we do declare that it is not meant thereby, that any adoration is done, or ought to be done . . .

Kneeling for prayer (as opposed to kneeling to receive Communion) was not immediately abandoned even in the radical tradition. During Hubmaier's service for the dedication of infants, "the whole church prays for the child on bended knees".[51]

The clergy of the Catholic church wore elaborate vestments which changed according to the ritual they were celebrating and the seasons of the ritual year – purple for Lent and Advent, green for Easter and so on. Clergy in the Lutheran tradition were expected to wear distinctive clothing in church though without the elaborate symbolism of Catholic vestments. Luther was prepared to be flexible about candles, incense and vestments and about the tonsure, the Catholic practice of shaving part of the priest's head. Such rituals, he said, were of no importance. Christ did not forbid them, so humans are free to do them. To argue otherwise would be to suggest that *not* doing these things was a meritorious work which could contribute to salvation. As the Pope is wrong to insist on these things so the radicals are wrong to forbid them. Christ (Luther said) has given us the freedom to choose.[52]

As a result, Lutheran civil authorities were able in practice to decide what was to be done and what was to be forbidden in their territories. Brandenburg, for example, kept much of the visual regalia of the Mass as well as the ritual of elevating the consecrated host, long after these had been abolished elsewhere.[53] Luther might have regarded physical movements as unimportant, but the Lutheran churches in Germany retained many of the rituals of the Catholic church – kneeling for prayers, laying offerings on the altar, the ritual gestures of the celebrating priest.

Martin Bucer recommended that vestments should be abolished, not because they were in themselves wrong but because they were a source of superstitious belief and contention. While not actually wicked, they were inconsistent with the Christian aspiration to reflect the simplicity of Christ and his apostles and were a reminder of the Antichrist of Rome.[54] The clergy of the Calvinist and Radical Reformed traditions generally wore ordinary dress even for the Communion service. With the increased emphasis on university education for the clergy, it became the custom in many Calvinist churches for the clergy to wear academic gowns, especially for preaching, as a symbol of their intellectual (rather than spiritual) authority.

# 8

# *Ritual and Society: The Reshaping of Popular Religious Practice*

Thus far, we have been looking at how the intellectual leaders of the Reformation reinterpreted and reshaped the beliefs, sacraments and worship of the church. However, these sacraments and rituals were more than theological concepts. They shaped the fabric of ordinary people's lives. Baptism, confirmation, marriage and extreme unction were rites of passage, indicating major changes in social status. Baptism welcomed a new baby into the community. Confirmation, for most young people, came at the transition to adulthood. Marriage gave independence and a fuller rôle in the life of the community. Extreme unction eased the soul out of this world and into the next.

The other sacraments and their associated rituals also had social functions. The confession and reparation involved in the sacrament of penance could bring healing for an individual and reconciliation with the community. In the Eucharist, the lay community was ritually united in itself. Even if lay people participated only occasionally, the Eucharist brought them together to worship their God in the consecrated bread and wine and to share a symbolic loaf of bread which had been blessed but not consecrated. The sacrament of ordination created a separate group of priests, ritually pure by virtue of their abstention from sexual activity and able to administer and control access to the other sacraments.

The traditional sacramental structure of the medieval church was thus a crucial part of the practicalities of everyday life. The changes which the reformers made to the sacraments had immense social consequences. For example: in declaring that marriage was no longer a sacrament, the reformers had cast doubt on the validity of the marriage ceremony. But if a marriage was not valid, the children of the union would be illegitimate. Without the marriage ceremony, how could a couple make proper provision for the care of their children and the inheritance of property? Changing attitudes towards baptism had implications for the membership of the church and the right to burial in consecrated ground. Changes in funeral rites changed the status of the dead, who were still in some senses members of the ritual community in the Catholic church but were completely excluded by the reformers.

The sacraments could define a community and bind it together: but they could also be used to establish and negotiate status in the community, and even to subvert authority. Recent studies in the social anthropology of religious ritual have extended our understanding of the ways in which one can "read" the actual performance of a ritual activity as if it were a complex and multi-layered document – what the American writer Clifford Geertz called "thick text". The same ritual will have different meanings for different participants and will be used for different purposes at different times. Those who are in power may try to use ritual to impose and strengthen their own authority, but they do not always succeed. Those who take part in rituals laid down by others can nevertheless manipulate what they do, changing the emphasis, even deliberately misinterpreting their instructions in order to appropriate the rituals to their own purposes.[1]

The sacraments were also hedged about with other rituals, some of them not altogether approved of by the church hierarchy. The tangible physical elements of the sacraments – the wafer from the Eucharist, the holy water of baptism – could be taken out of the church and used for a range of quasi-magical practices. Baptism, marriage and burial were all focal points for the celebration of social relations. The sacred rituals of the church were accompanied by other more secular rituals which involved feasting and drinking and offered opportunities for the display of conspicuous consumption.

The process by which these communal rituals were brought under some sort of civic control had begun well before the Reformation. Secular governments were increasingly concerned about the expense of some of the social celebrations associated with the rite of passage rituals, and about the opportunities they offered for unruly and socially subversive behaviour. In Zwickau, for example, restrictions were placed on the celebrations at baptisms and churchings from 1490. The *Fastnacht* or Mardi Gras, the day of celebration and self-indulgence in early spring before the period of self-denial known as Lent, was finally abolished in 1525. *Fastnacht* was a celebration of communal unity which could even overturn established values for a brief period of license. It was replaced after the Reformation by more restrained private celebrations which were based on existing social class groupings. This social stratification, too, probably preceded the Reformation. From the late fifteenth century, increased prosperity for manufacturers and merchants was accompanied by increased poverty for the labourers. These economic changes had their own independent dynamics but they could create a climate of opinion which the Reformers could use for their own purposes.[2]

The Lutheran reformation attempted only a partial reform of this ritual underpinning of communal life. Luther's own belief, repeatedly expressed, was that it was no more virtuous to refrain from ritual activities than to engage in them. The Lutheran liturgy therefore left room for the social as well as the spiritual significance of ritual. A more complete purging was envisaged first by the radical reformers and then by the Calvinists, but their efforts did not always affect the ritual practices of the wider community.

## Baptism

The medieval rite of baptism had been as much as anything a rite of exorcism, by which the devil was cast out of the infant. The prayers and rituals by which this was done – blowing on the child, anointing it with spittle and oil as well as water – were rapidly written out of the order of service by the Reformers. The Lutherans retained an abbreviated form of the prayers of exorcism in their baptismal rite. The Calvinists tried to remove it completely but met with considerable public opposition. When the Elector Christian of Saxony tried to introduce a more Calvinist liturgy in 1586, the ordinary people opposed him vehemently, backed by some of their pastors. In Dresden, a butcher wielding a cleaver forced the pastor to include the words of exorcism in baptizing the butcher's daughter. Elsewhere, people took their babies over the border to a neighbouring principality where they could still be exorcized, or simply failed to baptize them at all.

For the ordinary people of Saxony, it seems, baptism without exorcism was no baptism at all. The ritual was seen as just one of the ways in which the child could be protected against evil influences. It might well be accompanied by more obviously magical methods – as in seventeenth-century Weimar, where women customarily bound herbs in the christening clothes to give the baby added protection against evil influences. Christening was in some senses a liminal rite – that is, the baby was moving from one state of being to another during the process of casting out the Devil. It was therefore in particular danger and in need of special protection.[3]

For many lay people, though, the most important part of baptism was in the implications of the appointment of godparents. Through their choice of godparents, parents could widen and strengthen family links. Ordinary parishioners could declare their allegiances to leading local families, and the wealthy and powerful could demonstrate the extent of their influence. In parts of Germany the chance to secure the patronage of the local landowner was seen as more important than the defence which baptism offered against the powers of the Devil. Parents were accused of delaying baptism when the nobleman was away, so that the children risked dying unbaptized. Poorer families might have only one godparent for each child, but wealthier families sometimes asked large numbers of godparents in order to ally themselves with as many other families as possible. This too could mean baptism was delayed as messengers were sent to distant godparents to ask their consent.

The choice of names was also a crucial part of the function of baptism in the popular mind. Babies could be named in honour of their sponsors, or named after senior members of their families. However, there was also a tendency in the later medieval church to see baptism as a ritual pertaining purely to infancy and early childhood and to baptize the baby under a diminutive or pet name: Willikin instead of William, Jack instead of John. The Reformers were generally opposed to this practice. Whatever the sacramental significance of baptism, they regarded it as a serious ritual with lifelong implications.[4]

The social symbolism of baptism and sponsorship was cemented by lavish entertainment for neighbours and godparents. Neighbours and visitors brought gifts for the baby and helped with the entertainment. If the baby was baptized within a few days of birth, the mother was still likely to be lying in, and it was in any case unlikely that she would yet have undergone the ritual purification of churching. She would not therefore be expected to attend the child's christening. Most of the women at the party would go to church with the godparents, though there were complaints that fathers often failed to attend. After the Reformation as before, baptism was seen as being in some senses a women's ritual. The priest might consecrate the water and baptize the child, but it was the women who tied herbs into the child's clothes as an additional protection against the devil.[5]

The pre-Reformation emphasis on the need for baptism gave the midwife an important rôle as the person charged with baptizing children who were likely to die before they could be taken to the priest. Folk tradition also gave the midwife an important part in baptisms in church. It was often the midwife who took the baby to church and for poorer children she might be the only godparent. Women of low social status thus had a mystique from their association with the birth process and the sacrament of baptism. Their standing was, however, being eroded in the sixteenth century. The rôle of the midwife in the birthing process was under pressure from male doctors, and her right to baptize sickly infants was attacked by Protestant churches for whom the ritual of baptism was not necessary for salvation and a private baptism was no baptism at all.

These social rituals associated with baptism could become enormously expensive. Feeding all-comers for three or four days could place immense strain on resources. The festivities were also an excuse for all kinds of unruly behaviour: this was, after all, a celebration of fertility. Friends and neighbours gave presents both to the baby and to the mother. Some of these gifts had symbolic significance. In Germany, for example, the mother's friends and neighbours often gave her gifts of food, especially eggs and laying hens. The gifts had a practical purpose: the food would help her recover her strength and contribute to the entertainment expenses. However, the eggs and the hens were also a powerful symbol of fertility and reproduction.

Civic authorities were already expressing disapproval of the ensuing disruptive behaviour by the late fifteenth century. Their efforts were increased after the Reformation, when it became possible to use religious arguments to enforce secular restrictions. Poorer people were ordered to limit the entertainment they offered at christenings. The city authorities in Geneva even attempted to control the names that were given to children at baptism, outlawing names associated with Catholic "superstition" even when those names had family and social connections.The extent of resistance to these attempts to curtail traditional religious practices testifies to their stubborn popularity and the importance they had for ordinary people.

The Reformation thus had little impact either on popular perceptions of baptism or on the folk rituals which hedged it about. Baptism remained as a crucial protection against the forces of evil and an important part of the structure of social networks. Lutheran visitation records throughout the sixteenth century suggest that water which had been blessed for baptism was still in demand for all kinds of semi-magical purposes. It was thought to be able to heal livestock and even people. Pastors and sextons were repeatedly instructed to pour the water away immediately after each baptism, but the regularity with which these instructions were given suggests that they were widely ignored. In spite of the increasing professionalization of the clergy, it seems that there was a gulf not only between lay and clerical perceptions but between the outlook of the local clergy and the hierarchy. The gulf may have been dictated partly by the fact that the local clergy had to look to the community for support, but it may well reflect deeper differences in sympathy as well.

## Ritual purification: childbirth and the churching of women

The sacrament of baptism, by which the new infant was welcomed into the church, thus survived the Reformation. There were changes and areas of dispute, but the essentials of the ritual remained the same. There was more uncertainty about some of the other beliefs and rituals which surrounded and followed childbirth.

Jewish law included complex taboos to be observed during menstruation and after childbirth. One well-known episode in the Biblical life of the young Jesus describes how his mother went to the Temple to be purified after childbirth and to present the baby. The Biblical story was (and is) commemorated by the Christian church in the feast of Candlemass, with a service which involved processions carrying candles.

The early church rejected the ideas about the ritual impurity of women which were the basis for these ceremonies. However, forms of prayers giving thanks for the birth of a child and blessing women who had given birth survived, and gradually the ideas about ritual purity and danger crept back in. Childbirth was (and still is) in some senses a liminal process. One body becomes two, and the moment of transition is fraught with physical and spiritual danger.

By the end of the medieval period, there was an established liturgy for a ceremony forty days after the confinement. There were a number of local variants, but the service involved the woman going to church with the midwife and other women friends. They all carried candles, a reminder of Mary's purification and the feast of Candlemass. They were greeted and led into the church by the priest, who said prayers and led them around the altar. The woman being churched made an offering and was blessed with holy water. The ceremony was followed by the usual food and entertainment. Like baptism, it was emphatically a women's rite, one which simultaneously emphasized women's ritual impurity and gave them status in society.

Officially, the ceremony was optional. It was not a sacrament, and it could be refused to unmarried or otherwise disobedient women. (It was even possible for a woman who had miscarried or had a stillbirth to be churched, but in some areas the candle she carried was not lit.) The official Catholic church insisted that women who had died in childbirth or before they could be purified could still be buried in consecrated ground, with the full burial service. Folk tradition insisted that a woman who died in childbirth or before she had been churched could not receive a Christian burial. However, the harshness of the tradition was considerably modified in practice. In northern France and the Channel Islands, for example, women who had died in childbirth could be churched by proxy, a friend of the dead woman standing in for her in the ceremony.[6]

Martin Luther regarded churching as a human custom but one for which there was evidence in the Bible and which could therefore be retained in the reformed church. He was also aware from his own experience of its practical advantages. Until a woman had been churched, she was not expected to return to her household work. Nor was she supposed to have sexual intercourse. The six weeks rest which this gave her was vital for her well-being and that of the child, and the prohibition on intercourse made it less likely that she would conceive again before her body had recovered from the previous birth.

The instructions to parish visitors in Lutheran Saxony in 1528 make clear that the church was prepared to lend its authority to a custom which was seen as practical and socially useful:

> For the period of six weeks is ordained in the law of Moses . . . Even though that law is now suspended, this particular piece, which is taught us not just by the law but by nature too, is not suspended . . . For that reason, women shall be spared until they return to their full strength, which cannot well happen in less than six weeks . . . So in this case, one should consider the needs of the body and do what is proper, and not use Christian liberty to injure the body or for lewdness.[7]

The Lutheran ritual cut out the candles and holy water involved in the Catholic ceremony, and the priest no longer led the women into the church. Instead, they entered and sat together through the service and were called up to the altar by the priest. The prayers and readings concentrated on thanksgiving for the wonder of birth and emphasized that marriage and reproduction were gifts from God. The clergyman was instructed to remind the congregation that the new mother was not ritually impure or under the power of the Devil – no more than she had been before, at least.

Religious belief also intervened in the question of the feeding of the baby. The medieval belief was that breast milk was a form of modified blood, and that the baby would derive its intellectual and moral qualities from the milk with which it was fed. Wealthy and aristocratic women who sent their children to wet-nurses were therefore risking their future development. The lives of medieval saints are full of stories of women of high status who nevertheless fed their babies themselves, and the Virgin Mary was often depicted suckling the infant Jesus.

These beliefs survived and were even strengthened by the Reformation. They suited the Protestant emphasis on women's domestic functions and the virtues of a temperate and retiring life. The Protestants also continued the medieval belief that sexual intercourse during lactation was dangerous as it would both diminish the milk supply and make it unwholesome. Wet-nurses were thus required to abstain from sexual activity, and a nursing mother was also required to abstain for longer than the minimum six weeks.

Churching in the Lutheran tradition remained as a women's rite, though shorn of much of its near-sacramental elements. Lutheran governments also attempted to restrict and control the entertainments associated with churching, arguing that they placed too much strain on family finances. There is of course a suspicion that what they were trying to control was women's freedom of action and association, and the danger that elaborate festivities represented a harking back to Catholic practices. Churches in the Calvinist tradition removed the rite completely, seeing it as unnecessary and misleading. They retained the practical aspects of churching by insisting that newly-delivered mothers were to remain in seclusion for six weeks. However, the rituals by which women had been able to undermine the service of purification and make it a celebration of women's rôle in bringing children into the world were lost.

## Repentance, confession and the Eucharist

There are two ways of looking at the communal significance of the medieval Eucharist. On the one hand, some historians have seen it as an increasingly privatized form of worship. The priest muttered the crucial words of the consecration in Latin, with his back turned to the onlookers. The members of the congregation were largely absorbed in their own devotions or in everyday concerns, so that their attention had to be called to the moment of consecration by the ringing of a bell. Private endowments for private masses and chantries meant that the power to bring God down to earth and the whole mechanism of salvation was up for sale and could be privately owned.

On the other hand, it has been stressed (notably by Jack Scarisbrick and Eamon Duffy) that attendance at Mass was an essentially communal activity. The extent to which members of the congregation took the initiative in establishing their own devotional practices and even in organizing services meant that there was a high level of community involvement in the activities of the church. Many private Masses were funded by parish guilds whose membership was open to most members of the congregation. Ordinary worshippers might not partake of the consecrated bread but they still shared in the ritual activity. They passed around and kissed a *pax*, a plaque of wood or metal which usually depicted the Crucifixion, and they shared a loaf which had been separately blessed. The Mass, for all its remote and esoteric aspects, was also a profound symbolic expression of the identity of the community.

The preparations for the annual Communion also had important implications for community life. Devout people were encouraged to confess their sins regularly, and the confessional could function as a form of counselling. For most people, though, an annual confession preceded the Easter Communion. This was a private ceremony, a time for individuals to take stock of their own spiritual condition. However, it also had a communal function in that it provided a framework for reparation and reconciliation.

Change in the community functions of the Eucharist was if anything even more gradual than change in the liturgy. Luther's insistence that Christ was really present in the consecrated bread and wine meant that shared Communion could still express the identity of a community in the most profound way. The consecrated bread and wine retained their almost magical significance for ordinary people. The minister was expected to consecrate only as much as was needed, and to eat and drink anything that was left. Lutherans also continued to use specially-formed wafers instead of bread. Churches in the Swiss and Calvinist tradition used ordinary bread, which was less inherently likely to have magical qualities attributed to it. Surviving churchwardens' accounts for the purchase of bread and wine suggest that the portions given were quite generous – certainly more than the tiny sip of wine which is customary in most modern churches.

Ironically, it was the Reformers' insistence on the importance of sharing Communion which made it less significant in the life of the church. For the Protestants, the Eucharist was only valid if it was shared. Instead of repeated celebrations of the Mass every day, at which worshippers would share in the adoration of the consecrated Host and in ceremonies like the kissing of the *pax*, the Protestant church offered an occasional Communion service when there was a big enough congregation to warrant it. The service was in the vernacular, but in some ways it offered less in the way of participation than the Mass had done. Individual prayer and collective worship of a God made physically present was replaced by a service based on prayer, Bible reading and sermon in which members of the congregation were increasingly passive participants and recipients of instruction. On the other hand, evidence from early seventeenth-century England suggests that by that time the vernacular services of the Prayer Book had considerable popular support. Congregations seem to have valued the shared activity and the limited measure of participation in the actual words of the liturgy which the English translation made possible.[8]

The Protestant insistence that the Eucharist had to be a shared ritual also created problems for those who did not wish to take part. Although the Protestant churches did not place the same emphasis on ritual purity, they insisted that participants in the Communion service had to be "in charity" with each other. All disputes had to be laid aside, all quarrels resolved and all enemies forgiven. Such a counsel of perfection was too much for some people, who felt that their rights would be threatened if they did not defend them. It is an ironical testimony to their piety that so many people were unwilling to receive Communion when they were not in charity with their neighbours. They obviously took seriously the Lutheran doctrine that those who receive Communion unworthily do so to their own damnation. A study of parishioners in late sixteenth-century Württemberg suggests that many of them were prepared to refuse to attend Communion if they were not on good terms with their neighbours, in spite of all the attempts of the church visitors to compel them to do so. These cases suggest that the shared Eucharist was still seen as a powerful social bond.[9]

## Marriage and the ritual control of sexuality

In later medieval society, the religious ceremony was only a small part of the social rituals which were involved in a marriage. Aristocratic weddings took place in the home; ordinary people were married in church, in a brief ceremony with few attendants. Virtually all the Protestant churches tried to enhance the religious element in marriage, with varying (and limited) degrees of success. Far more important for most couples were the social ceremonies which accompanied betrothal and marriage.

In Germany, the Reformation appears to have had little impact on these social customs. They were focused primarily on feasts and entertainment for the families and friends of the young couple. Some of the rituals – drinking freshly-made beer from a brand-new drinking bowl, the wreath with its silk or gold cord which the bride gave her prospective husband – have an obvious and secular symbolism. It was always publicly assumed that the bride was a virgin on her wedding night. In fact, registers of baptisms suggest that many couples consummated their relationship once the betrothal arrangements were complete. The church – Catholic as well as Protestant – deplored the practice but could do little or nothing about it.

The church was involved at an early stage, as the location for the preliminary negotiations on financial arrangements, but only to make the agreements reached more binding. The family then adjourned to a suitable house for a lengthy round of ceremonial eating and drinking. The church part of the actual wedding was similarly brief. In some states the couple came to church on a Sunday morning and were joined before the whole congregation. This gave the pastor a good audience for his wedding sermon and an opportunity to attempt to inculcate the whole congregation in the significance of Christian matrimony. In some areas, however, Sunday was the one day on which a wedding could not take place. The prohibition may have been rooted in residual Catholic unease about the sexual activity which would follow the wedding, but it may equally reflect a Protestant dislike for the excessive eating and drinking which could follow the church service.

The church service and ensuing feast were followed in wealthier peasant families by a ceremonial procession which took the bride and her trousseau to her husband's house. The procession was followed by even more extravagant feasting, in the course of which the bride was introduced to the company and seated in the place of honour by the stove. After the wedding night the couple might return again to church for a blessing before the final feast. Those clergy who describe and comment on these rituals particularly deplore the vulgarity and obscene behaviour involved in the ritual bedding of the couple. Secular authorities were more likely to be concerned about the expense of the elaborate feasting, which could be ruinous for a family with several daughters. They used the language of religious reform to attempt to enforce moderation on the festivities, but the issues at stake had little to do with the Reformation.[10]

Broadly speaking, the magisterial reformers valued marriage and the controlled expression of human sexuality. The radicals had more conflicting ideas. Even within a small town like Zwickau there were two opposing standpoints. Thomas Müntzer, the earliest of the Zwickau radicals, taught that a married couple should have sexual relations only if they were sure that the wife would become pregnant. Anything else was prostitution. As a result, several of his female followers refused to have sexual intercourse with their husbands. One of them, Mrs Teucher, explained Müntzer's teachings in some detail. The core of the argment was that she considered herself to be married to Christ and that she could not serve two masters. "The city must be worthy that God is supposed to enter". She declared herself ready to be martyred three thousand times for Christ's sake.

On the other hand, Niclas Storch and the other radicals known as the "Zwickau prophets" advocated complete sexual freedom for members of the true church. Storch was accused of being unchaste himself and of opposing marriage. Instead, he was said to recommend that each man should take as many sexual partners as he wished. His advocacy of sexual liberation did not appeal to the radically-inclined women of Zwickau, who probably saw how easily they could be used and discarded. In general, they preferred Müntzer's teachings.[11]

The Schleitheim Confession of 1527 was drawn up in part to control the antinomian tendency in the Radical Reformation. It does not actually mention marriage, though it does suggest that believers should end all relationships with unbelievers – including separating themselves from unbelieving spouses. The implication is that most of the radical reformers were working towards an idea of marriage as a covenant rather than a sacrament. Marriage was only valid if both partners were true believers. The apostasy of one would therefore invalidate the contract.[12]

## Death, burial and the ritual community

The medieval Catholic approached death as part of a community. There was an extensive popular literature on the *ars moriendi*, the way to make a good death. Depictions of medieval deathbeds show them surrounded by people who have come to comfort, encourage and pray with the dying person. A final confession and communion guaranteed forgiveness and salvation, but there would still be penances to be undergone in Purgatory. And what about those who died in their sin, unshriven and unhouselled, without the saving rituals of the final Communion and extreme unction? The living could still help them. In the medieval world picture, the dead were still very much part of the community. Buried in consecrated ground at the heart of the settlement, they were prayed for by the living community. The charitable endowments they had made before death served as a reminder of their continued existence. Church bells, stained glass windows, a light before the statue of a particular saint, a chantry priest offering the Mass daily for the souls of the departed, all served to keep the memory of the dead in the minds of the worshipping community.

The basis of the incorporation of the dead in the community of the living was under threat in the great cities of continental Europe by the end of the fifteenth century. Overcrowded graveyards were a threat to the health of the living, and many cities took to burying their dead in more spacious graveyards outside the walls. The rupture in the community of living and dead made it easier for the Protestant reformers to effect a more conclusive break.[13]

Luther's challenge to the doctrine of indulgences was ultimately a challenge to the idea that the living can have anything to do with the fate of the dead. Although he seems to have retained a belief in purgatory until 1530, his suggested ritual for the burial of the dead effectively removed any suggestion that the prayers of the dead could benefit the living. Nevertheless, post-Reformation deathbed and funeral traditions in Lutheran Germany still had a great deal in common with those of the medieval Catholic tradition.

The Lutheran idea of a "good death" was exemplified in funeral sermons and books of spiritual advice. Luther insisted that faith alone could bring salvation, and Lutheran descriptions of a "good death" emphasize the faith of the dying person. However, the ways in which that faith was demonstrated – reading and meditating on the Bible, confessing and receiving Communion, and above all the calm assurance which was supposed to keep the dying person serene in spite of pain – are very similar to the prescriptions of medieval books on the *ars moriendi*, the "art of dying well". Lutheran accounts of the behaviour of the dying are more likely to stress their pious exhortations to their families and friends, but these are a commonplace in the accounts of the deaths of medieval saints. The difference with the Lutheran good death is that it is offered as a model for all, not as a demonstration of exceptional sanctity.[14]

The good Lutheran's deathbed was also likely to involve the ministrations of a clergyman. In spite of Luther's insistence on the priestly capabilities of all believers, only those who had been ordained to the ministry could consecrate and administer the Eucharist, and it was the Eucharist which dying people wanted as an assurance of their eventual salvation. The price they paid for the Eucharist was to submit to clerical questioning about their morals and their understanding of the faith. These requirements in fact put the Lutheran clergy in a more powerful position than that enjoyed by their Catholic counterparts. They were treated as an intellectual élite with the responsibility to instruct and admonish their congregations. They could control access to the remaining sacraments, using their local knowledge to ensure that the penitent made a full confession and proper reparation. Those who ignored their powers and stayed away from church when they were in good health would have to submit in order to receive the Eucharist in the hour of their death.

The link between the living and the dead might have been broken by Luther's theological challenge, and in the great cities of continental Europe the dead were increasingly being buried away from the centre of the community. In rural areas, however, the dead were still interred in the church and its enclosure – for a while, at least. The clergy and the wealthiest of the laity were still likely to be buried in the church itself. Those with a lesser status in the community were likely to be buried outside but near the south wall of the church. The north side of the church continued to be the less favoured. In the Lutheran tradition, burial in the consecrated ground of the churchyard remained a privilege for those who were members of the worshipping community. Those who died excommunicated or guilty of serious sin were buried with no ceremony and might well be interred outside the churchyard.

Even burial in the churchyard did not guarantee that the body would remain there. Expanding populations of the living meant expanding populations of the dead, and once a graveyard was full, each new interment would displace the bones of earlier burials. Many medieval graveyards had charnel houses, where disinterred skulls and other large bones were kept in some degree of safety. The existence of a charnel house was a constant reminder both of the omnipresence of death and of the presence of the dead in the community of the living. Even these de-fleshed remnants were treated with respect in the medieval tradition. In the town of Brecon in south Wales, for example, a priest was paid to celebrate the Mass of St Michael in the town charnel house for the souls of all the dead.[15]

Charnel houses survived in England and Wales at least until the eighteenth century. Elsewhere in Europe, however, Protestant reformers considered that ossuaries were too much associated with Catholic superstitious practices, in spite of their obvious practical purpose. Where possible, they were removed, and where that was not possible they had to be concealed.

The omnipresence of the dead in medieval society was backed by the possibility that they might return as ghosts and could again take part in or influence the affairs of the living. In particular, ghosts were believed to have access to information which they could impart if they chose. There were rituals for the burial of (for example) women who died in childbirth, suicides and those executed for serious crimes, to ensure that they did not return to harm the living. The Protestant breaking of the link between the living and the dead meant that such rituals were no longer acceptable. Belief in ghosts continued – and continues to the present day. However, the official interpretation was that ghosts were not the spirits of the dead but evil powers, emissaries of the Devil. In Shakespeare's *Hamlet*, much of the central figure's internal debate centres around the question whether the apparition he has seen is really his dead father's ghost imploring him for revenge or an evil spirit sent to tempt him to the crime of murder.

## The ritual of everyday life

The reformation has been interpreted as a break with the concept of the "ritual year". The medieval church observed a complex cycle of feasts and fasts, keyed to the anniversary celebrations of events in Christ's life and the births and deaths of the saints. The reformers regarded these days with suspicion, as they detracted from the central message of salvation. Zwingli suggested reducing them to four: Christmas Day and the following day, which was the feast of the first martyr, St Stephen; the feast of the Annunciation (25 March, the beginning of the medieval year and the celebration of the anniversary of the Incarnation, when God became human and began the process of salvation); the birth of St John the Baptist on 24 June, in order to commemorate all the prophets; and the combined feast of St Peter and St Paul on 29 June, to remember the apostles and evangelists. His statement of principle was soon modified in fact. Zwingli acknowledged that the routine of the working year needed breaks, and other feasts crept back into the Zürich calendar.

To some extent, the ritual year of medieval Catholicism was replaced by a ritual year whose celebrations were geared to the Protestant tradition. The Lutherans celebrated the anniversaries of Biblical events: Christmas, Easter, Ascension and Pentecost. (Some Calvinists notoriously removed Christmas from the list, mainly because of its associations with excessive indulgence and the pagan feast of midwinter.) Some festivals remained in the popular calendar but their significance was changed. All Hallows Eve was the evening before the feast of of All Saints, when the church celebrated the lives and witness of the heroes of the church. In the post-Reformation calendar it became Hallowe'en, a time when evil spirits walked abroad and witches had special powers. This inversion was a propaganda coup comparable with the depiction of ruined monasteries as graveyards haunted by the ghosts of evil monks and nuns bewailing their incarceration.

With the removal of so many saints' days from the calendar, the Protestant churches increasingly concentrated on Sunday as a day for religious devotion. Sabbatarianism – the insistence on Sunday as a special day of religious observance on which everyday work should be avoided – was not an invention of the Reformation. Texts such as the "Jesus Letter" encouraged its observance, and many churches had warning paintings of Jesus surrounded by craft implements showing how everyday work on a Sunday had wounded him.[16] What distinguished the Protestant Sunday was the nature of the religious observance and the restrictions on other activities.

Worship in a medieval Catholic church could be chaotic and individualized, with the congregation free to move around the church, talking or absorbed in their own personal religious rituals while the priests celebrated Mass quietly and in the Latin which few lay people could understand. It was possible to spend much of the day in a large church listening to a sequence of services and watching the performance of the Mass several times. But it was also possible to crowd in at the church door to watch the elevation of the host and to leave immediately afterwards.

Protestant worship was more structured and as a result more controlled. There was no one high point to the service. The readings, prayers and sermons were all geared to increasing the congregation's knowledge and understanding, and all were important. The congregation had to be able to hear and understand all the prayers and echo them in their thoughts if they did not repeat them out loud. The prayers would achieve nothing on their own: they had to be shared. Perhaps most important of all was the sermon; and sermons were long by modern standards, taking an hour or more to deliver a structured argument or discuss and explain a section of the Bible. It was crucial, therefore, that all the congregation attended for the whole of a lengthy service, and that they concentrated and paid attention to what was being said.

> Let there be an end of that ungodly strolling and chattering in churches, the whole infantile uproar. Behaviour in church of this kind at any time, even when the sermons are preached and the ceremonies performed, is extremely disrespectful.[17]

Wealthier parishes might have a separate afternoon sermon or prayer meeting; independent congregations might meet a second time for prayer or Bible study. The whole day needed to be devoted to worship and study and must therefore be freed from all other distractions – not just work but social activity as well. Bucer again:

> On these days, apart from the necessity of carrying forward the salvation of men, it is not right to do any work other than to go to the sacred assemblies and there to hear the word of God, to pray and praise God with the rest of the saints, to offer the sacred oblations and to receive the sacraments. The other hours of these days when there is no meeting in the churches should be spent at home in establishing the children, the family and the neighbours in devotion, injured brothers making peace with each other, visiting the sick, and conversing about the teaching and discipline of Christ.
>
> For not only physical labour and activities useful for human purposes, but also all other business of the flesh and profitable occupations, much more untimely and extravagant festivity and other harmful delights, profane games and merriment, ought to be left and put on one side on these days; in the same way indeed as they have been forbidden by the laws of godly princes in accordance with the law of God.[18]

Luther was uneasy about the emphasis on Sunday observance. Part of his unease derived from his fear that Sabbatarianism was part of a Jewish propaganda campaign to spread their beliefs.[19] He was also influenced by his distaste for any restrictions on Christian behaviour which might suggest that people could earn spiritual merit by obeying them. It was not until the second or third generation of reformers that Sabbath observance became one of the identifying characteristics of doctrinaire Protestantism.

The Protestant ritual year also acquired new festivals, some of them with a political as well as a religious charge. Saints' days were replaced by days of prayer and fasting, often for a political purpose. These days might celebrate the anniversaries of important events in the Reformation. In England and Wales, for example, the death of the Catholic queen Mary Tudor and the accession of the Protestant Elizabeth I on 17 November 1558 was celebrated for over half a century. From 1605 it was somewhat overshadowed by the celebrations of the defeat of the Catholic plot to blow up James I and his parliament on 5 November. Both these celebrations were near the traditional autumn festival which had featured in the Catholic ritual year as the feast of All Saints.

The Reformation also had a ritual calendar with a longer perspective, celebrating the centenaries of major events in the story of religious change. In Lutheran Germany, the centennial of Luther's 1517 declaration was the occasion for major ecclesiastical and academic festivals. These included fireworks and specially-written school plays as well as academic sermons and solemn processions. It was the 1617 centennial which finally embedded Luther's legacy into a hagiographical tradition:

> The Reformation centennial consolidated the legacies of Luther into a coherent tradition and reshaped his life into the secular focus of a church in need of symbols of identity. History itself thus became a principle of legitimation; commemorations of the years 1517, 1530 and 1555 in subsequent centuries served as historical rituals confirming the identity of Lutheran Germany.[20]

# 9

# Popular Belief and Folk Culture

For a long time, historians assumed that medieval Catholicism had been able to absorb a lot in the way of "popular" or "folk" religion but that post-Reformation Protestantism was less tolerant. It has even been suggested that Protestant rejection of traditional beliefs resulted in the resurgence of more overtly magical practices, since the church was no longer fulfilling the need of the peasants for processions to bless their crops, holy water to heal their animals and prayers to the saints for assistance with life's difficulties.[1]

The idea of a dichotomy between "popular" religion and "official" or "elite" religion does not always work. There are plenty of examples of what we would describe as gross credulity and superstition in the spiritual lives of the wealthy and powerful. Nevertheless, much of the resistance to Protestant ideas in the sixteenth and seventeenth centuries seems to have come from those who were comparatively poor and powerless.

In some cases, the arguments of the reformers were simply not understood. When Karlstadt visited Rothenburg at the beginning of the Peasants' War in 1525, he preached against both the Catholic and the Lutheran interpretations of the sacrament of the Eucharist. The congregation heard him with apparent approval, and his preaching led to an outbreak of iconoclasm. By May, however, the townspeople had turned against him and were demanding "true Christian preachers who teach and preach the holy gospel and God's word with forthrightness and clarity without any finespun glosses or human additions". On the surface it looked as though Karlstadt's attempts to make himself into a man of the people had failed. However, the real problem was that, for all the enthusiasm with which they greeted his preaching, the townspeople had not really understood his arguments about the unique nature of Christ's sacrifice and the symbolic nature of the Eucharist. They wanted to receive both the bread and the wine of the Eucharist at least once a year, but they described it as "under the form of bread and wine, [Christ's] blessed body and his rose-coloured blood".[2]

There is also later evidence of resistance to state-enforced conformity. When the Landgrave Moritz of Hesse-Kassel converted to Calvinism in the early seventeenth century, he attempted to introduce Calvinist church discipline in his Lutheran territory. Those who opposed the Landgrave's Calvinist reforms included leaders of local society like the Bürgermeister Georg Freundt, but there were also a number of ordinary villagers who refused to receive communion. Some gave as their excuse the fact that they were ill, or that they were in dispute with their neighbours (in all Christian traditions, people who share Communion are expected to be on good terms with each other). Others were prepared to give reasons of belief. Some claimed that they still believed in the Lutheran doctrine of the Real Presence, which was denied by the Calvinist order of service. Others said openly that they were confused by the disagreements among theologians. Georg Wursteschmidt claimed to have received communion in three ways in three consecutive weeks: not surprisingly, he now described himself as utterly confused.[3]

Where the beliefs of ordinary people are concerned, the dichotomy between Protestantism and Catholicism breaks down. Many communities took what they wanted from the Reformation – married clergy, communion in both kinds. They rejected what they did not want – predestination, Bibliolatry, the state enforcement of moral codes. Finally, they retained what they valued from the old religion – pilgrimages, sacramentals, prayers to the saints. Counter-Reformation Catholicism had as many problems with these eclectic believers as the Protestant churches did.

Nor was there an integrated "Protestant" response to "traditional, "popular" or "folk" religion. Rooted as it was in the countryside and in intensely superstitious industrial communities, orthodox Lutheranism proved able to absorb a fair amount of traditional belief. Much of the Catholic folk culture which the Protestants wanted to sweep away was simply replaced by a Protestant folk culture.

## Popular religion and the cults of the saints

Not all the Reformers rejected the idea that the saints had a place in the life of the church. Martin Bucer, for example, in his *Brief Summary of*

*Christian Doctrine*, suggested that they could provide an example and an inspiration:

> We teach that the blessed saints who lie in the presence of our Lord Christ and of whose lives we have biblical or other trustworthy accounts, ought to be commemorated in such a way, that the congregation is shown what graces and gifts their God and Father and ours conferred upon them through our common Saviour and that we should give thanks to God for them, and rejoice with them as members of the one body over those graces and gifts, so that we may be strongly provoked to place greater confidence in the grace of God for ourselves, and follow the example of their faith.[4]

However, the Reformers rejected the veneration of the saints and the appeal to their intercessory powers. Saints in the medieval tradition were people set apart by their exceptional holiness, but the Reformers considered that all humans were equally sinful. They could nevertheless all be equally sanctified by Christ's sacrifice. Their reading of the Bible taught them that St Paul referred to all Christians as saints – in the addresses of his letters, "To all that be in Rome, called to be saints", "to all the saints in Christ Jesus who are at Philippi", "to the saints and faithful brothers in Christ who are at Colossae", in his references to "ministering to the saints" (2 Cor 8:4, 9:1) and in numerous other references. For the Reformers, as all believers were in some sense priests, so they were all saints. The celebration of saints' cults was thus a dangerous delusion. It detracted from Christ's status as the only mediator between God and humanity, and could distract Christians from the need for faith in his sacrifice as the only path to salvation.

It is therefore ironic that so many of the Reformers themselves became the focus of cults very like the medieval cults of the saints. Luther was almost venerated as a saint, in a way which must have caused him considerable embarassment. Even during his own life, woodcuts and popular broadsheets represented him as a holy prophet. He was even depicted with a halo, linking him even more closely with the saints of the Catholic tradition.

A number of German folk tales present Luther as something between a saint and a mythical hero. His stand against abuses in the church was said to have been foretold by prophecy. Stories about his life drew parallels not only with the Old Testament prophets and leaders but with the saints of the medieval church and even with Christ himself. He was credited the ability to perform miracles, healing the sick and causing springs of water to flow, but also miraculously punishing those who opposed him. Places were named after him, and stories explaining the origins of the place names were elaborated and made more extravagant. Pictures of him showed him receiving his inspiration from the Holy Spirit depicted as a dove, and in some pictures he is portrayed as haloed, again like a medieval saint. Even pictures of him were believed to have miraculous powers.[5]

Like traditional Catholic visual imagery, these pictures were far more than cheap propaganda for the ignorant masses. Some of the finest artists of the time produced portraits and woodcuts of Luther and the other Protestant leaders. The biographies which were written in the years after Luther's death are the Protestant equivalent of the legends of the Catholic saints, and the stage plays based on his life substituted for the mystery plays of the medieval guilds.

The more thoughtful representations of the Luther-cult associated him with the early saints and the martyrs of the Reformation. Andreas Hondorff's *Calendar of Saints* (first published in 1573) offered stories of episodes from Luther's life alongside events from the lives of the early martyrs. However, there were other stories current in the later sixteenth and seventeenth centuries which were more reminiscent of the later saints' legends. As well as the famous story of his throwing his inkwell at the devil, there were traditions that pictures of him could not be burned. Hsia suggests that some of these may have originated in the Catholic custom of burning effigies of Luther and his wife Katherina.[6]

The story of Luther and the field of oats has a particularly interesting pedigree. Luther is said to have been escaping from the imperial forces when he met a peasant who was sowing oats in his field. After Luther had gone, the oats grew with miraculous speed, so that the peasant was able to begin harvesting them. When the imperial forces came past and asked the peasant whether he had seen Luther, the peasant was able to reply with complete honesty that he last saw him while sowing the oats which he was now harvesting. The imperial forces then gave up their search. The same story appears in a fifteenth-century version of the mystery play of the Three Kings as an episode during the flight of Jesus and his family to Egypt. There are several other versions in the legends of St Cornelius, St Macrine and St Radegund of Poitiers. It is also found in a folk story from the Poitou region of France about some children escaping from the Devil.[7]

Luther was a large-scale character. It was easy for folk tradition to cast him in the heroic mould. Calvin's reputation seems to have been less amenable to such treatment. Nevertheless, he was revered by a number of his followers in ways which are surprisingly reminiscent of medieval devotion to the saints. The people of Geneva are said to have buried him in an unmarked grave so that there would be no cult devoted to him, and no search for relics.

The English compendium of Protestant biographies commonly known as "Foxe's Book of Martyrs" also stands in this tradition of veneration of heroes of the Reformation. The full title, *Acts and Monuments of the English Martyrs*, does not do justice to the scope of the book. It was originally intended as a collection of the lives and deaths of the English Protestant martyrs of the Henrician Reformation. The final version included the European Protestant martyrs and linked them with the martyrs of the early church. Foxe presented history as a cosmic struggle between Christ and Antichrist in which the Protestant churches were the latter-day representatives of the True Church. The book is in line with the Protestant conception of the true church as a suffering and persecuted church. However, it also provided the Protestant Reformation with a cult of martyrs to replace those of the Catholic church.[8]

## The Pursuit of the Millennium

One central motif of both Catholic and Protestant propaganda was *eschatology*, the study of the end of the world (from the Greek *eschaton*, the Last Things). In the Christian tradition the picture of the end of the world was dominated by the strange visions attributed to Christ's closest disciple St John. These form the final book of the Bible, the Book of Revelation or the Apocalypse.[9] Much of the imagery of these visions centres around the figure of the Antichrist, who will be allowed to rule the earth for a short time before Christ himself returns. There will be a time of wars and natural disasters, in which the people of the true God will be purified by their suffering. These will be followed by the Last Judgement and by Christ's rule on earth for a thousand years.

The prophecy of the thousand years of Christ's reign has given the words "millenarian" (from the Latin *mille*, a thousand) and "chiliast" (from the Greek word for a thousand) for those who looked forward to Christ's reign and felt it was imminent. These prophecies were naturally appealing to the people of the Protestant churches, as they struggled to defend their beliefs against the power of the Holy Roman Empire and the revived Catholic church.

Millenarianism is generally associated with the Radical Reformation. Much of the extremism of the radicals was the result of their conviction that the final battle between Christ and Antichrist was imminent. They simply did not have time to wait for the reformation of the whole of their society. Further, the prophecies in both Old and New Testaments led them to believe that the reformation of the whole of society was not going to happen. The people of God would be reduced to a persecuted remnant before Christ returned to rule the world.

The Hutterites, German spiritualist radicals, had a particularly clear view of the processes which they anticipated would lead to the Millennium. The first three of these, the Hutterites believed, they had seen in their own time. First was the threefold baptism by water, suffering and the Spirit which they all believed they had themselves received. The second was the introduction of the Kingdom of God for those who were poor in spirit – that is, those who claimed nothing for their own but were ready to work for and share with all other true Christians. The third was the establishment of congregations based on the principles of complete interdependence and mutual aid. These would have no need of secular government. They were to be followed imminently by the end of the world, Christ's resurrection, the Last Judgement and the eternal punishment of the wicked.[10]

The apocalyptic tradition was also surprisingly powerful in the Lutheran tradition. Hsia even goes so far as to suggest that eschatological fervour was a unique feature of Lutheranism in the late sixteenth and early seventeenth centuries, though its importance waned thereafter.[11] Lutheranism was certainly not unique in its stress on the last things, but Luther himself was deeply interested in eschatology and repeatedly identified the Pope as the Antichrist. The prophecies of suffering and oppression and the rule of Antichrist were particularly appropriate to the Lutherans by the end of the sixteenth century, when they were under intense political pressure both from the Calvinists and from the revived Catholic church.

Eschatology thus provided comfort for those who were experiencing persecution, "the church under the cross". However, the millenarian outlook was not necessarily allied to political or social protest. In late sixteenth- and early seventeenth-century England, orthodox mainstream Protestants confidently anticipated the end of the world, the final struggle with Antichrist and the rule of Christ the King. They considered monarchs like Elizabeth I and James I and VI to be the godly rulers whose duty was to fight the Antichrist. They were no more radical in their political and religious beliefs than a modern Anglican who sings

> Thy kingdom come, O God!
> Thy rule, O Christ, begin!

at Choral Eucharist then buys the Mail on Sunday in the supermarket on the way home.

Eschatological thought was not even confined to the Protestant churches. There was a long tradition of apocalyptic vision in the medieval Catholic church. The Catholic outlook became more eschatological in the sixteenth and seventeenth centuries: like the Protestants, but for different reasons, they too saw the end of the world as imminent.

## Witchcraft and witch persecution

Closely associated with eschatology was the fear of witchcraft. The period of the Reformation was also the period of the great European witch craze. Persecution of witches does not seem to have been associated with any particular confessional stance. Lutherans, Calvinists and Catholics all pursued, tortured and executed witches with equal fervour. Even the supposedly tolerant people of Strasbourg executed several women for witchcraft in the later sixteenth century.

Evidence from Germany suggests that the high points of the waves of persecutions, 1586–91 and 1626–31, coincided with severe farming crises. Famine and resulting epidemics created social tension. In a period when people were accustomed to looking for supernatural explanations for their problems, witches were one possible scapegoat.

The English evidence suggests that witch persecution fits into more deeply-rooted patterns of social tension. Community and church-based arrangements for poor relief were breaking down under pressure from social and economic change. Traditional Catholic charitable provision had offered a rather haphazard safety net for the poorest people in society, but it had also given a spiritual value to poverty. The prayers of the poor were regarded as being particularly effective, just because they were poor. The increasing commercialism of later medieval society meant that this attitude was changing, even before the Reformation. A distinction was drawn between the deserving and the undeserving poor. Poor relief was becoming the responsibility of the state and was increasingly structured to help the "deserving poor". It was thus easier for people to refuse to offer charity to their poorer neighbours. Nevertheless, they still felt guilty, and this guilt led them to accuse their neighbours of witchcraft.[12]

The witch craze was thus not a direct consequence of the Reformation. However, like so many other changes of the sixteenth century, it seems to have been influenced by social tensions created by the break-up of the universal medieval church. What fostered belief in witches was not so much the specific beliefs of different religious groups as the fact that they were different – and that because they were different, they were seen as radically wrong. The witch was one of the most extreme expressions of the "other", so alien that she (or he – but they were most frequently women, particularly in England) could provide a target for communal hatreds. The persecution of witches was never as intense in Britain as it was elsewhere in Europe. This may be significant: religious divisions were not as marked in Britain, and the islands were to some extent insulated from the extremes of religious tension in central Europe.

While they were prepared to attack witches (who were seen as a threat), Protestants were as likely as Catholics to turn to the services of prophets, soothsayers and diviners of all sorts. Folk ritual and Lutheranism co-existed in many parts of Germany at least until the late sixteenth century – to the despair, in some cases, of the official church visitors. According to the visitation officials in Nassau-Wiesbaden in 1594,

> the use of spells is so widespread among the people here that no man or woman begins, undertakes, does or refrains from doing, desires or hopes for anything without using some special charm, spell, incantation or other such heathenish medium.

But these spells were inextricably linked with the formulae of traditional medieval Catholicism:

> They practise them with familiar and strange words, with names, rhymes and especially with the names of God, the Holy Trinity, some special angels, the Virgin Mary, the twelve apostles and the three kings, also with numerous saints, with the wounds of Christ and his seven last words . . . with gospel verses and certain prayers.[13]

Strasbourg had its *warsagers*, who claimed to be able to find lost or stolen objects and to see events at a great distance or in the future. The clergy preached against them as agents of the Devil but that did not stop their parishioners from consulting them, or from buying books of prophecies and stories about the Devil, witches and magic. The secular authorities also attempted to prevent people from consulting soothsayers and banned the publication of their books, with limited effect.[14]

Nor were these beliefs confined to ignorant lay people. According to Luther, Melanchthon had an "incurable belief in astrology". He insisted on Luther delaying a journey from Schmalkalden to Gotha (when Luther was seriously ill with kidney stones) "for it was new moon".[15] Luther's account of the episode indicates his own scepticism. But Luther was himself thoroughly old-fashioned in many of his beliefs. The story of his throwing an inkpot at the Devil may be a myth, but he was convinced that the Devil was a real, corporeal presence, the embodiment of absolute evil.

## Anti-Semitism

Luther was also convinced that the Jews were the arch-enemies of Christianity. Although he claimed at one point early in his career, "The Jews are blood-relations of our Lord; if it were proper to boast of flesh and blood, the Jews belong more to Christ than we", in 1514 he was already prepared to say:

> I have come to the conclusion that the Jews will always curse and blas-pheme God and his King Christ, as all the prophets have predicted.[16]

And in 1543, in *The Jews and their Lies*, he warned his readers:

> Therefore be on your guard against the Jews, knowing that wherever they have their synagogues, nothing is found but a den of devils in which sheer self-glory, conceit, lies, blasphemy, and defaming of God and men are practiced most maliciously and veheming his eyes on them . . . Moreover, they are nothing but thieves and robbers who daily eat no morsel and wear no thread of clothing which they have not stolen and pilfered from us by means of their accursed usury. Thus they live from day to day, together with wife and child, by theft and robbery, as arch-thieves and robbers, in the most impenitent security.[17]

Luther's ideas have plenty of parallels with medieval anti-Semitism. Like the witch persecutions, anti-Semitism was intensified during the period of the Reformation. However, both were found right across the spectrum of religious belief rather than being the province of one partic-ular confessional group. It was probably the tension caused by inter-confessional conflict, rather than the beliefs of individual groups, which lay behind the intensification of attacks on witches and other groups on the margins of society. In an attempt to prove their own doctrinal purity, most of the mainstream groups (Catholic as well as Protestant) turned against all kinds of dissenters.

Some of the most violent expressions of anti-Semitism came from radical reformers such as Balthasar Hubmaier. He was involved in the anti-Jewish violence in Regensburg which culminated in the expulsion of the Jews and the destruction of their synagogue. On the other hand, for some of the radicals, the genuine ignorance of both Jews and Muslims was preferable to the deliberate denial of the truth of magisterial and Catholic Christians. The Hutterite mystic John Schlaffer explicitly listed Jews, Turks and pagans as people who could still receive the light of God's illumination. Michael Sattler declared at his trial that he would rather fight against the "spiritual Turks", the false Christians who persecute God's people, than against the real Turks who make no pretence of following Christ.[18]

Many of the radical groups also drew on the inspiration of Jewish history and prophecy for their vision of the suffering and persecuted church awaiting the second coming of the Messiah. The most extreme in his willingness to cooperate with the Jews was the apocalyptic prophet Augustine Bader. His visions of the Jewish Old Testament leader Moses led him to study Hebrew and to seek out Jewish religious leaders to help him understand the Old Testament and the other prophecies of the Jewish people. He wanted to remove from the worship of the church all the sacraments which could offend Moslems and Jews. His prophecies of the end of the world included the crushing of the false Christian churches – but even he assumed the final conversion of both Jews and Moslems to Christianity.[19]

# *Conclusion*

---

The Protestant Reformation bulks so large in our picture of the influences which shaped modern Europe that it is easy for us to imagine that the contemporaries of Luther and Calvin would have seen it in the same way. With hindsight we can trace the influences which brought Luther to his personal theological breakthrough. From our perspective, the consequences of his actions seem to have an inevitability which blurs the importance of individual human decisions. With hindsight, too, the ideas of the Protestant reformers – ideas on salvation, on worship, on the duties of the Christian as a member of civic society – take on a coherence and consistency which they did not necessarily have for their contemporaries.

That is not to say that we should view the Protestant Reformation as a series of discrete and unconnected episodes. But we need to remember that the defining incidents – Luther's outburst in 1517, Zwingli's sausage supper, Henry VIII's declaration of independence – all started trains of events which the participants could not have anticipated and which they might not even have wanted. These trains of events were lengthy and might be inconclusive. Some of the German states adopted the Lutheran Reformation fairly rapidly. Others dithered for many years: the Regensburg city council was appointing Lutheran sympathizers to posts in the city from the 1520s but did not officially align itself with the Lutheran communion until 1542. There was a point in the early 1530s when it seemed that France might have a moderate Reformation on the English model, and for a brief period in the mid-1550s it even seemed possible that England might return to the Catholic fold.

Although the split in the church had the power to divide societies and even families, we should not assume that the whole population of Europe can be put neatly into a series of boxes – Catholic or Protestant, Lutheran, Calvinist or Radical. Even more so, for whole communities, like the German city of Strasbourg, it can be difficult to decide how to classify their confessional stance. Strasbourg was officially Lutheran: but its great religious leader Martin Bucer clearly disagreed with Luther on such crucial issues as the meaning of the Communion service. The city council was technically committed to enforcing the Lutheran confession on all the inhabitants, but in effect Calvinists, Catholics and even some radicals were tolerated, and many members of the council themselves refused to take a clear doctrinal line.

Nor should we over-emphasize the impact of the Reformation on the thoughts and beliefs of ordinary people. Professional theologians could refine their definitions of the exact nature of Christ's presence in the Eucharist or the difference between imparted and imputed righteousness. But the basics of the faith, as outlined in the Apostolic and Nicene Creeds, remained; and the Creeds continued to be recited by all but the most extreme Protestant churches as their statement of fundamental belief. What Wolfgang Schütterlin said to his fellow-members of the Strasbourg senate in 1577 could have been said by virtually any Christian:

> I am neither Zwinglian, Calvinist nor Lutheran, for I follow Christ who saved me. I believe in the teachings of the Christian faith, simple and unbeclouded. I believe that God created me, that Christ saved me, and that the Holy Ghost leads us to the truth. I was baptized in the name of the Trinity. Of the sacraments I believe what every Christian can and should believe from God's Word.

His fellow member of the Senate, Josias Rihel, spoke in similarly broad terms:

> I was born into a Christian family and brought up to be the opponent of error. I learned my worthlessness from the Ten Commandments, my salvation and sanctification from the articles of faith, take my comfort and resolution from hearing God's word and receiving the sacraments. Let people pin what party label on me they will, I recognize no name but Christian.

As Lorna Jane Abray says, "they might just as well have stood up and recited the Apostles' Creed".[1] The emphasis on God's Word might lead us to suspect that they were towards the Protestant end of the spectrum of belief, but that is all.

Both these men explicitly refused to take up positions in theological debate. Their fellow magistrates saw no need to push them to go further. Some of them had already expressed their unwillingness to get involved in doctrinal subtleties. As Carl Mieg said about the Tetrapolitan Confession in 1534, "I hope that as a layman I won't be trapped into something I don't understand and then forced to confess and believe in it". A generation later, Barthel Keller had the same feelings about the Formula of Concord: "This is over my head and I am reluctant to bind my conscience to it".[2] But there is more in Schütterlin and Rihel's statements than simple reluctance to become embroiled in doctrinal subtleties which they could not understand. There is a perceptible distaste for the multiplication of differences and a wish that the church should be one.

There were of course public order issues involved. The Strasbourg senate urged the clergy to focus their sermons on ethics rather than dogma. They wanted to be able to use religion to impose morality, and they feared that too much concentration on doctrine would lead to disagreements and civil discord. Eventually the clergy too came to accept that theology should be left to the experts rather than being offered to ordinary people.[3]

The Protestant Reformation has been credited with a powerful influence on many aspects of modern life.[4] Capitalism, the Scientific Revolution, modern democracy, rationalism, toleration and the development of affectionate family life, all have been seen as having their roots in the Reformation. This is to credit the Reformation with more importance than it should have. In many cases, these arguments have their origins in a wish to legitimize some aspect of modern society. If capitalism (or democracy, or rationalism, or whatever) has its origins in the Protestant Reformation, then capitalism (or whatever) has a moral and religious aspect to it.

It was the American anthropologist Max Weber who first popularized the idea that the Protestant spirit (with its emphasis on the virtues of sobriety and hard work and the merits of delayed gratification) created the preconditions for nineteenth-century capitalism. His thesis was neatly inverted by Marxist historians like R. H. Tawney, who argued that capitalism (with its emphasis on individual responsibility and its challenge to the old feudal hierarchy) created the preconditions for the Reformation. Both these theories have been challenged by more recent historians who have pointed out that capitalism has its roots in Italy, which was and remained Catholic.

There is a connection between the Reformation and economic development but it is a more remote and accidental one. It is based not so much on the actual ideas of the Reformers as the social disruption they caused. All over Europe, people were forced to leave their homes because of religious persecution of one kind or another. Frequently, the refugees were the most capable and enterprising members of their communities. Some of the more pragmatic rulers were prepared to make concessions on matters of religious belief in order to attract traders and manufacturers. The Elector Palatine, Friedrich IV, founded the new city of Mannheim in 1607 specifically to promote industry and commerce in the Palatinate by attracting Calvinist refugees from the Netherlands. Its toleration was subsequently extended to the radical Hutterites and even to the Socinians, who rejected the doctrine of the Trinity. Existing trading and industrial centres like Augsburg and Frankfurt also prospered by encouraging religious refugees. When the Lutheran population of Frankfurt eventually turned against the Calvinist newcomers, the latter moved *en masse* to the Palatinate, where they set up new communities like Frankenthal.

When Louis XIV of France abandoned the limited toleration which had been offered to the French Protestants (the *Huguenots*) by the Edict of Nantes, a wave of refugees left the country, taking their professional and craft skills with them. A number came to England where their impact on (for example) the weaving industry was considerable.[5] In England the Protestant nonconformists were prevented from attending university or entering the major professions until the nineteenth century. Instead, they set up independent academies which had a more up-to-date curriculum, and they turned their energies to manufacturing and trade.

The connection between Protestantism and individualism is even more remote. Luther's doctrine of the priesthood of all believers, and Calvin's insistence that even the most illiterate clown should be able to give a reason for his faith, both suggest the importance of the individual as a spiritual agent. But the breakdown of the concept of the church as a spiritual community predates the sixteenth century. One of the commonest modern criticisms of late medieval worship is its atomized character. Priests muttered the liturgy in an obscure language, half-hidden behind screens. The wealthy sat in private side chapels reading their primers. Individual worshippers were encouraged to concentrate on their private devotions, attending to the service only when the sacring bell rang to signal the elevation of the consecrated bread. The picture is of course an exaggeration: but the worship of the Protestant churches, with its emphasis on the vernacular, was at least as communal as that of the Catholics. The rise of individualism has arguably more to do with economic change, the increasing commercialization of farming and changing ideas on social welfare.

It has been suggested that the Reformation influenced family life by promoting the development of the affective family. On the one hand, Protestants idealized the married state rather than celibacy. Early reformers like Luther and Bullinger spoke warmly of the joys of family life. On the other hand, virtually all the reformers stressed patriarchal authority and the need for children to be controlled in order to break their will and turn them away from evil. The stern, distant father is as much part of the image of the Reformation as the Lutheran new man, changing nappies and getting up when the children cry in the night. The kind of marriage which the Protestants idealized was a marriage of the head rather than the heart, a marriage contracted under parental guidance rather than a love match. The Welsh landowner John Gwyn, who we have met already (above p. 37), listed "5 qualifications indispensably required in persons who make wise choice in marriage":

1. piety in respect of salvation & present blessing
2. person in respect of comfort
3. parts in useful end of marriage [i.e. abilities which will lead to a prosperous partnership]
4. parentage in respect of success and advice
5. portion [the dowry]: be ever your mistake in making the last of these to be the first as you will answer it hear and after.[6]

It is equally difficult to establish a connection between Protestantism and intellectual developments like scientific rationalism. With its appeal to the authority of a sacred text, Protestantism was arguably less rational than late medieval Catholicism with its appeal to rigid scholastic logic. The Protestantism of the sixteenth and seventeenth centuries was certainly able to co-exist with a fair measure of folk tradition and superstition. Our Welsh landowner John Gwyn was a personal friend of the Puritan leaders Walter Cradock and Henry Walters. His commonplace book contains prayers from the Puritan tradition, cures based on both herbs and astrology, spells and charms. He made rigorously scientific observations of different grafting techniques which he had tried out on his fruit trees – but the observations include the planetary aspects and the phases of the moon.[7] Folk ritual and the Reformation co-existed in many parts of Europe at least until the late sixteenth century.

Nor did the Protestant Reformation produce any noticeable advance in toleration. Attacks on those on the margins of society intensified rather than diminished. Witch persecutions and attacks on Jews increased in the century up to 1648. Thereafter, tensions between confessional groups decreased, toleration became more common and anti-Semitism

also decreased. An increasing number of German states adopted policies of toleration for commercial reasons, and some were even prepared
to encourage Jews to settle in their trading communities.

In the sixteenth century, though, other dissenters were also the object
of fierce attacks. At its outset, the Protestant Reformation had nothing
to do with tolerance or the ecumenical spirit. The followers of radical
reformers like Schwenkfeld and Socinius were persecuted wherever
they were found. Many fled from Germany to eastern Europe and eventually to the New World.

The American anthropologist Bob Scribner has argued that the rise
of rationalism and the retreat from a sacramental view of the world may
have little or nothing to do with the Reformation. Popular religion and
folk belief in a sacred and sacramental universe persisted well into the
seventeenth and even the eighteenth centuries. The very gradual change
in popular attitudes may be more closely linked with the rise of other
ways of ordering and controlling the material world – improvements in
medicine, the development of new agricultural techniques, the concept
of insurance – so that the sacred is less necessary.[8]

The Reformation has also been held to account for changes in cultural
life. Like its social and intellectual impact, many of these links are not
straightforward. The profound distaste which many of the reformers
felt for the visual imagery of late medieval Catholicism undoubtedly led
to the destruction of much fine art. However, it also led to the destruction of plenty of third-rate sentimentalism. The early reformers had a
rich visual culture of their own, to which leading artists like Dürer and
Cranach contributed.

The impact of the Reformers on Europe's musical heritage was probably accidental. It was pure happenstance that the man who was
prepared to go public about St Augustine's doctrine of salvation
through faith was also a keen and competent amateur musician. The
chorales which Luther collected and adapted for use in his church
services have become part of the cultural property of Europe. Many of
J. S. Bach's greatest works are based on them. But the Protestant
Reformation was also responsible for some musical disasters: psalms
translated into doggerel verse and set to dreary tunes. There was no
necessary connection between worship in the vernacular and great
music.

It is easier to trace the impact of the Reformation on the development
of language. The Protestant reformers were people of the word, spoken
as well as written. Where the late medieval church had asserted doctrine
through complex visual imagery, the Protestant reformers argued their

case in sermons and pamphlets. Their influence on the development of the languages of modern Europe can be seen most clearly in the vernacular translations of the Bible. Luther's translations of the Bible both validated and standardized a language which is recognizably modern German. The translation of the Bible also led to the standardization and validation of many minority languages. Successive translations of sections of the Bible into Welsh culminated in the production of the Welsh Bible in 1588, and the Welsh Bible set the forms of written Welsh for centuries. This is a continuing phenomenon: many Third World languages in the nineteenth and twentieth centuries have been preserved by the fact that they were used for translations of the Bible.

Other key Protestant texts have also influenced the development of vernacular languages. Calvin's *Institution of the Christian Religion* has long been held up as a particularly fine piece of French writing. Calvin wrote his *Institution* first in Latin but soon translated it into French. Most of his Biblical comentaries were also written first in Latin but were rapidly published in French translations. He also wrote a series of shorter pamphlets explaining particular points of the faith, and these were written directly in French. His aim was always, as he said in the introduction to *Against the Anabaptists*:

> to fit my writing to the lack of training of simple folk . . . to use a simple and straightforward language not far removed from everyday speech . . . to the best of my ability I strive to put in order what I am saying, so that it can be more clearly and easily understood.[9]

Francis Higman's analysis of Calvin's French prose style identifies one of the secrets of his success: "To put it crudely, Calvin discovered the short sentence".[10] The complex sentence structure of classical Latin with its range of subordinate clauses was ill suited to translation into French. Calvin broke these complex sentences up into shorter units which moved his argument along a step at a time. Sentences were linked by clear signposts – "consequently", "but on the other hand", "however" – and the ideas were always in the right order.

These debates over the long-term consequences of the Reformation are in danger of giving more importance to incidentals than to substance. The Reformation was a movement for religious change and as such it should be judged. In the final analysis, though, the impact of the Reformation was not so much the impact of individual doctrines as the breaking of the mould of the community of belief. The medieval world in western Europe had one church, one overarching framework for the expression of belief and spirituality. The authority of this "one holy Catholic and Apostolic Church" (as the Nicene Creed puts it) could be used by secular rulers to legitimize and bolster their own power, and as a result they were in return prepared to defend the unity and authority of the church. On the other hand, the existence of such a powerful spiritual organization provided an alternative source of authority in society, a higher court of appeal which could be used against the secular powers.

All that changed with the Reformation. However much the early reformers claimed to want to preserve the unity of the church, the reality was that they fractured it beyond repair. Henceforward, there would be choice. It might be a choice which could only be exercised by those prepared to risk appalling suffering and death, or to leave their homes and all that they had to follow their own beliefs, but nevertheless it was a choice.

The resulting pluralism inevitably influenced thinking on the relationship between political and spiritual life. Indeed, the idea that there was such a relationship, implying as it does a separation between church and state, is in some senses a creation of the Reformation. For over a century, there was normally only one accepted religious standpoint in each state, and the choice between (say) the Lutheran and Calvinist traditions could change with the preferences of the individual head of state. The concept of religious unity and the power of the church could still be used by the secular powers to reinforce their own authority. However, the potential for religious dissent, the existence of an alternative which was the accepted orthodoxy in other countries, meant that religious doctrines could also be used to support political dissent. In the "one nation, one creed" framework, religious dissent would almost inevitably produce political dissent. In order to change the accepted religious orthodoxy of the individual state, it was necessary to change the standpoint of the secular authority, and that meant entering into the political process. This was what happened in England in the early 1640s, when some of the more Protestant members of the established church, desperately worried about Charles I's moves towards what they saw as Catholicism, took their resistance to him into Parliament and eventually to the desperate remedy of a civil war.

There were two alternatives to the politicization of religion. One was to opt completely out of civic society, as some of the radical reformed communities did, and for over a century that meant opting for a life of persecution and suffering. The other was to leave the homeland and found a new society elsewhere, an alternative adopted by some of the more extreme (or desperate) of the English Protestants in the 1630s as well as by more radical groups like the Mennonite Brethren from Bohemia. In most cases, however, the new societies established by these religious dissidents were not noted for their tolerance. What the Puritans of New England wanted was not religious freedom, but the freedom to practise and impose their own brand of extremely rigorous conformity. The third alternative, the secular state which does not seek to impose religious conformity on its subjects, was rare before the end of the seventeenth century.

Did this fracturing of the unity of the church, the creation of a climate of choice, however limited the alternatives actually were, contribute to the end of the era in which Christian belief shaped the lives of the majority of people? It is no longer possible to view the Middle Ages as an age of faith. We know too much about the extent of superstition, residual paganism, and crude sceptical materialism in medieval society. However, there was a sense in which the belief systems of the medieval church could be said to speak for the whole society, and the language of religion was used to express people's deepest concerns and priorities.

The Reformation resulted in many societies in an intensification of religious feeling and experience, as communities from Germany to New England found their identity defined in religious terms. However, that identity was defined as much as anything else by its opposition to the religious identities of neighbouring communities. The Welsh have a story about a castaway who builds two chapels on his desert island. Amazed at his devoutness, his rescuers ask him, "Why two?" In reply, he points to one and says, "That's the one I don't go to".

For most Christians before the advent of the ecumenical movement in the twentieth century, acceptance of one doctrinal standpoint has meant rejection of another, often in the crudest and most violent terms. Many historians of the Reformation have remarked on the fact that the Reformers were generally better at attacking and destroying what they disapproved of than they were at replacing it with something better. This was ultimately destructive of the whole belief system over which they were arguing. If both sides in a doctrinal dispute could produce compelling refutations of the other side's arguments, they could not both be right: but they might both be wrong.

# Notes

## Introduction

1 Heiko Oberman, *Forerunners of the Reformation* (London: Lutterworth, 1967) translates a number of key texts including Thomas Bradwardine's "The Cause of God against the Pelagians".

2 See, for example, the writings of Ernst Walter Zeeden, Wolfgang Reinhard and Heinz Schilling. Most of these are in German but Schilling summarizes his arguments in "Between the Territorial State and Urban Liberty: Lutheranism and Calvinism in the County of Lippe" in R. Po-Chia Hsia, ed., *The German People and the Reformation* (Ithaca, NY: Cornell University Press, 1988), pp. 263–83. For a discussion of these ideas in English see R. Po-chia Hsia, *Social Discipline in the Reformation* (London and New York: Routledge, 1989), pp. 2–4.

3 *Why the Reformation?* (Geneva: Institut d'Histoire de la Réformation, 1996), p. 66.

4 In the introduction to the first edition, which was addressed to Francis I of France: for the text see John T. McNeill, ed., *Calvin: Institutes of the Christian Religion* (Library of Christian Classics, vols xx, xxi. London: SCM Press/Philadelphia: Westminster Press, 1960), i, pp. 7–31.

5 For a translation of the *Confession of faith sworn to by all the citizens of Geneva* see J. K. S. Reid, ed., *Calvin: Theological Treatises* (Philadelphia: Westminster Press, 1954). Reid's translation is reprinted in M. A. Noll, *Confessions and Catechisms of the Reformation* (Leicester: Apollos, 1991), pp. 126–32.

6 For details of this process in the English church see J. A. Scarisbrick, *The Reformation and the English People* (Oxford: Oxford University Press, 1984).

7 Hsia, *Social Discipline*, p. 183.

8 See, for example, Eamon Duffy, *The Stripping of the Altars* (New Haven and London: Yale University Press, 1992), pp. 147–53 for some English examples.

9 Susan Karant-Nunn, *Zwickau in Transition*, pp. 106, 155–6.

10 Alister McGrath, *A Life of John Calvin* (Oxford: Blackwell, 1990), pp. 131–2.

11 For details of these visitations see Gerald Strauss, *Luther's House of*

*Learning* (Baltimore and London: Johns Hopkins University Press, 1978), pp. 249–99.

## 1 Sin and Salvation

1 "Doctrina non reformata, frustra fit reformatio morum" – "Unless doctrine is reformed, the reformation of conduct will be in vain." This is from the Table Talk, the notes which Luther's friends made of his conversations. The original is in the German edition of his work, *D. Martin Luthers Werke: Tischreden* (Weimar: H. Böhlaus Nachf, 1912–21), vol. 4.4338.

2 In, for example, *Reformation Thought: An Introduction*, 3rd edn (Oxford: Blackwell, 1999), pp. 33–5; *Luther's Theology of the Cross* (Oxford: Blackwell, 1990), pp. 8–12.

3 Hubert Jedin, "Contarini und Camaldoli", *Archivo per la storia della pièta* 2 (1959), p. 64: quoted in McGrath, *Luther's Theology of the Cross*, p. 10.

4 Hubert Jedin, who discovered the Contarini letters in the archives at Camaldoli, has compared Contarini's spiritual revelation with Luther's: "Ein Turmerlebnis des jungen Contarinis", *Kirche des Glaubens – Kirche der Geschichte: Ausgewählte Aufsätze und Vorträge* I (Freiburg, 1966), pp. 167–80. For a summary in English see McGrath, *Luther's Theology of the Cross*, pp. 9–10.

5 S. Jayne, *John Colet and Marsilio Ficino* (Oxford: Oxford University Press, 1963), esp. pp. 58–68, 74–5; see also J. K. McConica, *English Humanists and Reformation Politics* (Oxford: Oxford University Press, 1965).

6 *LW* 34, pp. 336–7.

7 *A Short Exposition of the Decalogue, the Apostles' Creed and the Lord's Prayer* (1520). B. L. Woolf, *Reformation Writings of Martin Luther*, vol. 1 (London: Lutterworth Press, 1952), pp. 83–4.

8 The extent to which there can be said to be a distinct "Augustinian school" in theology is still debatable: for a summary of the issues see, for example, McGrath, *Luther's Theology of the Cross*, pp. 63–71.

9 *Commentary on True and False Religion* (1525): *The Latin Works and the Correspondence of Huldreich Zwingli, together with selections from his German works*, ed. S. M. Jackson (New York and London: G.P. Putnam's Sons, 1912–29), vol. 3, p. 97.

10 *Latin Works*, vol. 3, p. 92.

11 G. R. Potter, *Zwingli* (Cambridge: Cambridge University Press, 1976), p. 44.

12 *Latin Works*, vol. 1: 1510–1522, pp. 70–112.

13 *Latin Works*, vol. 3, p. 94.

14 H. J. Hillerbrand, *The Reformation: a narrative history related by contemporary observers and participants* (New York: Harper & Row, 1964), p. 115.

15 Andreas Musculus, *Gründliche Anzeygung . . .* (1552), trans. Gerald Strauss, *Luther's House of Learning* (Baltimore and London: Johns Hopkins University Press, 1978), p. 206.

16   *Inst.*, III, xii, 4 (McNeill, i, p. 759).

17   *Inst.*, II, vii, 14–17 (McNeill, i, pp. 362–6).

18   *Inst.*, III, iii, 9 (McNeill, i, p. 610).

19   Caspar Aquila, *Des kleinen Catechismi Erklerung . . .* (1538), trans. Gerald
     Strauss in *Luther's House of Learning*, p. 209.

20   The General Confession from the Communion Service in the English 1552
     Book of Common Prayer.

21   W. P. Stephens, *The Holy Spirit in the Theology of Martin Bucer*
     (Cambridge: Cambridge University Press, 1970), pp. 63, 25.

22   See Stephens, *Holy Spirit in Martin Bucer*, pp. 23–41, for a detailed study
     of Bucer's theology of predestination.

23   Stephens, *Holy Spirit in Martin Bucer*, p. 28.

24   *Inst.*, III, ch ii, 35 (McNeill, i, p. 583).

25   *Inst.*, III, ch xxi (McNeill, ii, pp. 920, 931–2).

26   The Thirty-Nine Articles are found in a number of old editions of the Book
     of Common Prayer. A convenient modern text is reprinted in Noll,
     *Confessions and Catechisms*. Article 17 is on p. 219.

27   In the 'Reply by John Calvin to the letter by Cardinal Sadolet to the Senate
     and People of Geneva': see J. K. S. Reid, ed., *Calvin: Theological Treatises*
     (Library of Christian Classics, vol. xxii, London: SCM Press, 1954), p. 228.

28   Reid, *Calvin: Theological Treatises*, p. 91.

29   *Inst.*, III,. xi, 1 (McNeill, i, p. 726).

30   Williams, *Radical Reformation*, p. 40.

31   For a discussion of Karlstadt's changing views on free will and predestina-
     tion see Calvin Augustine Pater, *Karlstadt as the Father of the Baptist
     Movements: The Emergence of Lay Protestantism* (Toronto, Buffalo and
     London: University of Toronto Press, 1984), pp. 25–46.

32   Williams, *Radical Reformation*, pp. 170–1.

33   *Ibid.*, p. 194.

34   "Against the Heavenly Prophets in the Matter of Images and Sacraments"
     (1525): *LW* 40, p. 128.

35   From the Schleitheim Articles. For the text of the articles see John Wenger,
     "The Schleitheim Confession of Faith", *Mennonite Quarterly Review* xix
     (1945), 243–53; Wenger's text is reprinted in M. A. Noll, *Confessions and
     Catechisms of the Reformation* (Leicester: Apollos, 1991), pp. 50–8, and is
     also available online at http://www.Anabaptists.org/history/schleith.html

36   On Antinomianism see Williams, *Radical Reformation*, pp. 351–60.

37   Gwent Record Office D. 43. 4216 p. 117: I am grateful to Alexandra
     Kendal-Tye for drawing my attention to this reference.

38   For details of the debate and references to the two men's writings see
     Timothy Wengert, "We Will Feast Together in Heaven Forever: the epis-
     tolary friendship of John Calvin and Philip Melanchthon" in Karin Maag,
     ed., *Melanchthon in Europe* (Grand Rapids, MI: Baker Books, 1999), pp.
     28–33.

39 Markus Schär, *Seelennöte der Untertanen, Selbsmord, Melancholie und Religion im alten Zürich, 1500–1800* (Zürich, 1985); for a discussion of his conclusions in English, R. Po-chia Hsia, *Social Discipline in the Reformation: Central Europe, 1550–1750* (London and New York: Routledge, 1989).

## 2 Sacrament and Ritual

1 See, for example, Eamon Duffy, *The Stripping of the Altars*, p. 313.
2 What follows is based on *The Babylonian Captivity of the Church* (1520: *LW* 36, pp. 106–17).
3 *LW* 36, pp. 112, 117.
4 *LW* 36, pp. 112, 115–16.
5 *LW* 36, p. 18.
6 *LW* 36, p. 124.
7 *LW* 36, pp. 86, 90.
8 *Inst.*, IV, xix, 34 (McNeill, ii, p. 1481).
9 See, for example, Luther's *Large Catechism* or *German Catechism*: Tappert, Theodore G., ed. and trans., *The Book of Concord* (Philadelphia: Fortress Press, 1959), esp. p. 440, 443–4. See also Paul Althaus, *The Theology of Martin Luther*, trans. R. C. Schultz (Philadelphia: Fortress Press, 1966), pp. 351–2.
10 *That the words of Christ "This is my body" etc shall stand firm against the fanatics* (1527): *LW* 37, p. 73.
11 *LW* 36, pp. 18.
12 Euan Cameron, *The European Reformation* (Oxford: Clarendon Press, 1991), p. 158.
13 *Propositions on the Mass* (1521), quoted in Alister McGrath, *Reformation Thought*, 3rd edn. (Oxford: Blackwell, 1999), p. 172.
14 *Letter to the Princes of Germany*, quoted in W. P. Stephens, *The Theology of Huldrych Zwingli* (Oxford: Clarendon Press, 1986), p. 190.
15 *Baptism, Rebaptism and Infant Baptism* (1525), quoted in Stephens, *Huldrych Zwingli*, p. 185.
16 *De Vera et Falsa Religione*, p. 202, quoted in Fisher, *Christian Initiation: the Reformation period*, p. 129.
17 *Inst.*, IV, xiv, 7–9 (McNeill, ii, pp. 1281–5).
18 Matthew 19.14. For a detailed discussion of Luther's developing views on baptism see Pelikan, *Spirit versus Structure*, pp. 17–20, 77–97.
19 Pelikan, *Spirit versus Structure* pp. 96–7.
20 *LW* 36, p. 57.
21 *LW* 40, p. 23.
22 *Inst.*, IV, xix, 17 (McNeill, ii, pp. 1465).
23 *LW* 43, pp. 245–50.
24 See, for example, David Cressy, *Birth, Marriage and Death: ritual, religion and the life-cycle in Tudor and Stuart England* (Oxford: Oxford University

Press, 1999), p. 114. See also M. Gray, "Ritual space and ritual burial in the early modern Christian tradition", forthcoming.

25  For the text of the articles see John Wenger, "The Schleitheim Confession of Faith", *Mennonite Quarterly Review*, xix (1945), 243–53; Wenger's text is reprinted in M. A. Noll, *Confessions and Catechisms of the Reformation* (Leicester: Apollos, 1991), pp. 50–8, and is also available online at http://www.Anabaptists.org/history/schleith.html

26  Gordon Rupp, *Patterns of Reformation* (London: Epworth Press, 1969), pp. 296, 320–1.

27  Williams, *Radical Reformation*, p. 173. (On a personal note: my own daughter was baptised at the age of 9. We found that a very appropriate age for the ceremony. She was able to take part in the service, making her own responses, choosing favourite hymns and so on. However, she was clearly not ready for a personal profession of faith. As I am an Anglican, she will be able to do that when she is older and receives Confirmation.)

28  For a translation see *Zwingli and Bullinger*, ed. G. W. Bromiley, Library of Christian Classics, vol. xxiv (London: SCM Press, 1953), pp. 129–75.

29  Williams, *Radical Reformation*, p. 193.

30  *Babylonian Captivity of the Church*: *LW* 36, p. 34.

31  *Ibid.*: *LW* 36, p. 32.

32  In *The Adoration of the Sacrament of the Holy Body of Christ* (1523): *LW* 36, p. 287.

33  *Babylonian Captivity*: *LW* 36, p. 51.

34  *Epistola Christiana admodum*: translated in Heiko Oberman, *Forerunners of the Reformation* (London: Lutterworth, 1967), pp. 268–78.

35  On the early development of Karlstadt's Eucharistic theology see Williams, *Radical Reformation*, pp. 42–4.

36  For a translation see *Zwingli and Bullinger*, ed. G. W. Bromiley, Library of Christian Classics, vol. xxiv (London: SCM Press, 1953), pp. 185–238.

37  *On the Lord's Supper*: see *ibid.*, p. 188.

38  Translated in Bromiley, *Zwingli and Bullinger*, pp. 245–79.

39  Bromiley, *Zwingli and Bullinger*, p. 256.

40  Ibid, pp. 258–9.

41  Ibid, pp. 259–60.

42  Noll, *Confessions and Catechisms*, pp. 221–3.

43  *Babylonian Captivity*: *LW* 36, p. 22.

44  Carter Lindberg, *The European Reformations* (Oxford: Blackwell, 1996), p. 103.

45  Mark U. Edwards, *Luther and the False Brethren* (Stanford: Stanford University Press, 1975), pp. 82–111.

46  For a discussion of the whole debate see Timothy Wengert, "Luther and Melanchthon, Melanchthon and Luther", *Luther-Jahrbuch* 65 (1998).

47  Wengert, "Epistolary Friendship", 37–8.

### 3 *"By this book": Authority and Interpretation*

1 *LW* 13, p. 272.

2 Timothy Wengert, "The day Philip Melanchthon got mad". *Lutheran Quarterly* 5 (1991), 419–33.

3 By S. Raeder, in a series of books in German: *Das Hebräische bei Luther untersucht bis zum Ende der ersten Psalmenvorlesung* (Tübingen, 1961); *Die Benutzung des masoretischen Textes bei Luther in der Zeit zwischen der ersten und Zweiten Psalmenvorlesung* (Tübingen, 1967); *Grammatica Theologia: Studien zu Luthers Operationes in Psalmos* (Tübingen, 1977). For a summary in English see McGrath, *Luther's Theology of the Cross*, pp. 47–8.

4 For a translation of the 67 Articles see *Luther and Zwingli's Propositions for Debate: the 95 Theses of 31 Oct 1517 and the 67 Articles of 19 January 1523*, ed. Carl S. Meyer (Leiden: E.J. Brill, 1963).

5 In the *Preface to the New Testament* (1525): *LW* 35, p. 362; see also *LW* 35, pp. 395–9 for his later thoughts on James and Revelation.

6 Calvin Augustine Pater, *Karlstadt as the Father of the Baptist Movements: The Emergence of Lay Protestantism* (Toronto, Buffalo and London: University of Toronto Press, 1984), pp. 15–18.

7 Translated in Bromiley, *Zwingli and Bullinger*, pp. 59–95.

8 Bromiley, *Zwingli and Bullinger*, p. 75.

9 *Ibid.*, p. 89.

10 In his exposition of the 67 Zürich propositions of 1523, *Auslegen und Gründe der Schlussreden* (Z II 11–457: Potter, *Zwingli*, p. 105.

11 Potter, *Zwingli*, p. 106.

12 *On Christian Liberty. LW* 31, p. 345.

13 Alister McGrath, *A Life of John Calvin* (Oxford: Blackwell, 1990), pp. 131–2.

14 *Inst.*, I, viii.2 (McNeill, i, p. 83).

15 Williams, *Radical Reformation*, pp. 824–5.

16 Karant-Nunn, *Zwickau in Transition*, pp. 106–7.

17 Summary of Umblauft's ideas in Williams, *Radical Reformation*, p. 825.

18 *Letter to the princes of Saxony concerning the rebellious spirit . . .* (1524: LW 40, pp. 47–59); *Letter to the Christians at Strassburg in opposition to the fanatic spirit* (1524: LW 40, pp. 65–71). For a discussion of these points see Zapalac, *In His Image and Likeness*, p. 15.

19 Lorna Jane Abray, *The People's Reformation: magistrates, clergy and commons in Strasbourg, 1500–1598* (Oxford: Basil Blackwell, 1985), p. 23.

20 *On Translating. LW* 35, pp. 182–202.

21 Williams, *Radical Reformation*, pp. 816–17.

## 4 The True Church in the Protestant Tradition: Theory and Organization

1 Torrance, Thomas F., ed., *Tracts and treatises on the doctrine and worship of the church, by John Calvin* (Edinburgh and London: Oliver and Boyd; Grand Rapids, MI : Eerdmans, 1958), vol. 1, p. 102.

2 McGrath, *Theology of the Cross*, p. 20; S. H. Hendrix, *Luther and the Papacy: Stages in a Reformation Conflict* (Philadelphia, 1981), pp. 77–8.

3 For a translation of the *Apologeticus Architeles* see *The Latin Works and the Correspondence of Huldreich Zwingli, together with selections from his German works* ed. S. M. Jackson. Vol. 1: 1510–1522. (New York and London: G. P. Putnam's Sons, 1912), pp. 197–292.

4 McGrath, *Theology of the Cross*, p. 21.

5 Eire, *War against the Idols*, pp. 234–75.

6 Abray, *The People's Reformation*, p. 120.

7 *LW* 40, p. 7.

8 In *The Blessed Sacrament of the Holy and True Body of Christ* (1519): LW 35, pp. 49–73; for a discussion see Jaroslav Pelikan, *Spirit versus Structure*, pp. 130–1.

9 For a discussion of Bucer's doctrine of the church see Peter Stephens, "The church in Bucer's commentaries on the Epistle to the Ephesians" in D. F. Wright, ed., *Martin Bucer: reforming church and community* (Cambridge: Cambridge University Press, 1994), pp. 45–60.

10 For an extended discussion of Luther's ideas on the rôle of the ministry see Pelikan, *Spirit versus Structure*, pp. 11–17, 32–76.

11 *LW* 41, pp. 148–66.

12 *LW* 41, pp. 194–219.

13 *LW* 13, p. 90.

14 For the text of Augsburg Confession see Tappert, *The Book of Concord*; reprinted in Noll, *Confessions and Catechisms*.

15 *LW* 39, pp. 301–14.

16 *LW* 40, pp. 5–44.

17 *LW* 36, p. 116.

18 *LW* 1 p. 272.

19 Avis, *The Church in the Theology of the Reformers*, pp. 27–9.

20 For discussions of the technicalities see A. S. Barnes, *Bishop Barlow and Anglican orders* (London & New York: Longman Green, 1922); Claude Jenkins, *Barlow's consecration and Archbishop Parker's Register: with some new documents* (London: SPCK, 1935); J. C. Whitebrook, *The Consecration of Matthew Parker* (London: A. R. Mowbray & Co, 1945); F. J. Shirley, *Elizabeth's First Archbishop* (London: SPCK, 1948). The main argument against the validity of Anglican orders, however, was that enshrined in the bull *Apostolicae curae* of 1896, based on the inadequacy of the form of consecration in the Edwardian and Elizabethan ordinal and the lack of intention on the part of the consecrating bishops to ordain a sacramentally valid priesthood.

21 *Exposition of the 67 Articles*: Stephens, *Zwingli*, pp. 260–1.
22 *Inst.*, IV, xii, 1 (McNeill, ii, p. 1230).
23 *Inst.*, IV, xii, 2 (McNeill, ii, p. 1231).
24 Andrew Pettegree, "The Calvinist church in Holland, 1572–1590" in Pettegree et al., *Calvinism in Europe 1540–1620* (Cambridge: Cambridge University Press, 1994), esp. pp. 173–4.
25 Williams, *Radical Reformation*, p. 118.
26 Pater, *Karlstadt as the Father of the Baptist Movements*, p. 57.
27 "On the Ban: Questions and answers by Menno Simons" in G. H. Williams, ed., *Spiritual and Anabaptist Writers* (Library of Christian Classics, vol. xxv. London: SCM Press, 1957), pp. 261–71.
28 Williams, *Radical Reformation*, pp. 123–4.
29 "Cherished Instructions on Sin, Excommunication, and the Community of Goods, by Ulrich Stadler" in G. H. Williams, ed., *Spiritual and Anabaptist Writers*, pp. 272–84.
30 *Ibid.*, p. 284.
31 "The Church of God, by Dietrich Philips" in Williams, ed., *Spiritual and Anabaptist Writers*, p. 251
32 H. J. Hillerbrand, *The Reformation: a narrative history related by contemporary observers and participants* (New York: Harper & Row, 1964), p. 115.
33 Potter, *Zwingli*, pp. 80–1.
34 Scribner, "Preachers and People in the German Towns" in his *Popular Culture and Popular Movements in Reformation Germany*, pp. 123–44.
35 *Latin Works*, ed. Jackson, vol. 1, p. 267.
36 Richard Hoyle, *The Pilgrimage of Grace and the Politics of the 1530s* (Oxford: Oxford University Press, 2001), pp. 252–3.
37 Reid, *Calvin: Theological Treatises*, p. 59.
38 Abray, *The People's Reformation*, pp. 70–1.
39 M. Gray, "The Diocese of St Asaph in 1563", *Journal of Welsh Religious History* 1 (1993), 1–40.
40 *Social Discipline in the Reformation*, p. 19; see also D. W. Sabean, *Power in the Blood: popular culture and village discourse in early modern Germany* (Cambridge: Cambridge University Press, 1984), p. 17. For some comparable English examples see Rosemary O'Day, "The Reformation of the Ministry, 1558–1642" in O'Day and Felicity Heal, eds., *Continuity and Change: Personnel and Administration of the Church in England, 1500–1642* (Leicester: Leicester University Press, 1976), pp. 55–75; Ian Green, " 'Reformed Pastors' and *Bons Curés*: the changing rôle of the parish clergy in early modern Europe" in W. J. Sheils and Diana Wood, eds., *The Ministry: Clerical and Lay* (Studies in Church History xxvi, 1989).
41 Williams, *Radical Reformation*, p. 184.
42 Pater, *Karlstadt as the Father of the Baptist Movements*, pp. 66–8.
43 *The Freedom of a Christian* (1520): *LW* 31, p. 345.

5  *Church and State: the Protestant Churches and Secular Authority*

1   *LW* 44, pp. 115–220.
2   *LW* 46, pp. 45–56.
3   *The Christian State / In which Christendom asserts itself against the atheists and such people* (1685).
4   Karant-Nunn, *Zwickau in Transition*, pp. 48–55, 153–65.
5   Abray, *The People's Reformation*, pp. 44–65.
6   Zapalac, *In his Image and Likeness*; R. Po-chia Hsia, *Social Discipline*, 10–11.
7   Abray, *The People's Reformation*, pp. 84–141.
8   Z I, 467; Potter, *Zwingli*, pp. 95–8.
9   Potter, *Zwingli*, p. 100.
10  Noll, *Confessions and Catechisms*, pp. 214–27.
11  Williams, *Radical Reformation*, pp. 362–81.
12  Karant-Nunn, *Zwickau in Transition*, pp. 111–13.
13  "Dr Martin Luther's Warning to his Dear German People": *LW* 47, esp. pp. 19–21.
14  Hsia, *Social Discipline*, pp. 57–63.
15  For a recent study of the Pilgrimage see Richard Hoyle, *The Pilgrimage of Grace*.
16  Keith Wrightson and David Levine, *Poverty and Piety in an English Village: Terling, 1525–1700* (revised edition: Oxford: Clarendon, 1995).
17  Diarmaid MacCulloch, *Thomas Cranmer*, p. 356–8 and references therein.
18  McNeill, i, pp. 9–31.
19  R. Gwynn, *Huguenot Heritage*, 2nd rev. edn. (Brighton and Portland: Sussex Academic Press, 2001).
20  For examples see Karant-Nunn, *Reformation of Ritual*, p. 102.
21  Gerald Strauss, *Luther's House of Learning* (Baltimore and London: Johns Hopkins University Press, 1978), ch. 8, pp. 151–75, "Techniques of Indoctrination: Catechism", esp. pp. 163–9.
22  Bob Scribner, "Police and the Territorial State in Sixteenth-Century Württemberg" in Kouri and Scott, *Politics and Society in Reformation Europe*. See also D. W. Sabean, *Power in the Blood*, esp. pp. 37–60.
23  Wrightson and Levine, *Terling*.
24  Karant-Nunn, *Zwickau in Transition*, pp. 216.
25  *The Sermon on the Mount*, in *LW* 21.
26  *The Ordinance of a Common Chest* (1523), in *LW* 45: passage quoted on p. 172. For a discussion of Luther's ideas see Pelikan, *Spirit versus Structure*, pp. 59–67.
27  J. K. McConica, *English Humanists and Reformation Politics* (Oxford: Oxford University Press, 1965).
28  *Common Chest: LW* 45, p. 170.
29  Karant-Nunn, *Zwickau in Transition*, p. 217.
30  Whitaker, *Martin Bucer and the Book of Comon Prayer*, pp. 36–9.

31  Abray, *People's Reformation*, pp. 58, 188, 210, 214.
32  *Inst.*, IV, iii, 9 (McNeill, ii, pp. 1061–2).

### 6  Literacy, Education and the Popular Response to the Reformation

1  As they have been for Brunswick and Kitzingen in the sizteenth and seven-teenth centuries: Erdman Weyrauch, "Die Illiteraten und ihre Literatur" in Wolfgang Brückner *et al.*, eds., *Literatur und Volk* (Wolfenbütteler Arbeite zur Barockforschung; Wiesbaden: Harrassowitz, 1985), vol. 2, 465–74; for a discussion of his findings in English see Hsia, *Social Discipline*, pp. 110–11.

2  For details see Bob Scribner, "Oral Culture and the Diffusion of Reformation Ideas" in *Popular Culture and Popular Movements in Reformation Germany* (London and Ronceverte: Hambledon Press, 1987), pp. 17–48, on which the following paragraphs are based.

3  *LW* 41, p. 149.

4  Karant-Nunn, *Zwickau in Transition*, pp. 106–7.

5  *LW* 45, pp. 365–6.

6  Gerald Strauss, *Luther's House of Learning* (Baltimore and London: Johns Hopkins University Press, 1978), pp. 155–6. On the whole subject of the use of catechisms in the Lutheran tradition see ch. 8, "Techniques of Indoctrination: Catechism" in *Luther's House of Learning*, pp. 151–75.

7  W. P. Stephens, *The Holy Spirit in Martin Bucer* (Cambridge: Cambridge University Press, 1970), p. 150.

8  *Inst.*, III, ii, 2 (McNeill, i, p. 545).

9  Reid, *Calvin: Theological Treatises*, p. 243.

10  Hsia, *Social Discipline*, p. 114.

11  *The Judgement of Martin Luther on Monastic Vows* (1521): *LW* 44, pp. 245–400; *To the Councilmen of All Cities in Germany that they Establish and Maintain Christian Schools* (1524): *LW* 45, pp. 341–78.

12  Strauss, *Luther's House of Learning, passim,* esp. pp. 135–202.

13  *LW* 45, pp. 356–7.

14  R. Po-chia Hsia, *Social Discipline*, pp. 116–19.

15  Abray, *People's Reformation*, p. 169.

16  Duffy p. 68: refers to Charles Jackson, ed., "The Life of Master John Shaw" in *Yorkshire Diaries and Autobiographies in the Seventeenth and Eighteenth Centuries* (Surtees Society LXV, 1877), pp. 138–9.

17  *Selected Works*, ed. Jackson, p. 54.

18  For a study of iconoclasm as part of carnival rituals see Bob Scribner, "Reformation, Carnival and the World Turned Upside-Down" in his *Popular Culture and Popular Movements in Reformation Germany*, pp. 71–102.

19  On iconoclasm and its theological implications see C. M. N. Eire, *War against the Idols: the reformation of worship from Erasmus to Calvin* (Cambridge: Cambridge University Press, 1986).

20  This argument is made most clearly in Luther's 1524 letter of advice to the Protestant church in Strasburg, *Letter to the Christians at Strassburg in opposition to the fanatic spirit* (1524): *LW* 40, esp. pp. 68–9.

21  Karin Maag, ed., *Melanchthon in Europe* (Grand Rapids, MI: Baker Books, 1999), p. 48.

22  In a letter to Thomas Cromwell in 1538. London: Public Record Office, SP 1/133.

23  Zapalac, *In His Image and Likeness*, pp. 108–126.

24  Scribner eventually published his discussion of these woodcuts as "Demons, Defecation and Monsters: Popular Propaganda for the German Reformation" in his *Popular Culture and Popular Movements*, pp. 277–99.

25  Hsia, *Social Discipline*, pp. 12–13.

26  Bob Scribner, "Incombustible Luther: the image of the Reformer in early modern Germany" in *Popular Culture and Popular Movements*, pp. 323–53.

## 7  Liturgy and the Articulation of Belief

1   *Inst.*, III, xx, 8–11 (McNeill, ii, pp. 859–64).

2   In the *Exposition* of his 67 Principles: Potter, *Zwingli*, pp. 112–13.

3   Potter, *Zwingli*, p. 121, based on the *Exposition*.

4   E. C. Whitaker, *Martin Bucer and the Book of Common Prayer*, Alcuin Club Collections no 55 (Great Wakering: Mayhew-McCrimmon for the Alcuin Club, 1974), pp. 144–5.

5   For a review of sixteenth-century Lutheran preaching see Karant-Nunn, *Reformation of Ritual*, 125–7.

6   Abray, *The People's Reformation*, pp. 166–7 and references therein.

7   For details of these developments see MacCulloch, *Cranmer*, pp. 221–6.

8   Whitaker, *Martin Bucer and the Book of Common Prayer*, pp. 26–9.

9   The outline of the services is summarized and the prayers of institution are translated in Jasper and Cuming, *Prayers of the Eucharist*, pp. 122–8.

10  *Ibid.*, pp. 132–42.

11  Whitaker, *Bucer and the Book of Common Prayer*, pp. 22–5.

12  *Deutsche Messe*, 1526, translated in Jasper and Cuming, *Prayers of the Eucharist*, pp. 127–8.

13  Whitaker, *Bucer and the Book of Common Prayer*, pp. 34–5.

14  *Ibid.*, pp. 40–1.

15  "Letters to Thomas Müntzer by Conrad Grebel and Friends", in Williams, ed., *Spiritual and Anabaptist Writers*, pp. 76–7.

16  D. H. Tripp, "Protestantism and the Eucharist" in Cheslyn Jones *et al.*, eds., *The Study of Liturgy* (London: SPCK / New York: Oxford University Press), p. 295.

17  Williams, *Radical Reformation*, p. 136.

18  In "The Church of God": Williams, ed., *Spiritual and Anabaptist Writers*, pp. 244–5.

19  Williams, *Radical Reformation*, p. 222.

20  The standard authority on this is J. D. C. Fisher, *Christian Initiation: the Reformation Period* (London: SPCK for the Alcuin Club, 1970); for a summary, see his chapter "Lutheran, Anglican and Reformed Rites" in Cheslyn Jones *et al.*, eds., *The Study of Liturgy*, pp. 154–66.

21  Fisher, *Christian Initiation*, pp. 3–25.

22  An extensive German literature on this subject is summarised by Karant-Nunn, in *The Reformation of Ritual*, p. 60 and notes.

23  Hughes Oliphant Old, *The Shaping of the Reformed Baptismal Rite in the Sixteenth Century* (Grand Rapids, MI: William B. Eerdmans, 1992), pp. 51–62.

24  Fisher, *Christian Initiation*, pp. 30–42.

25  *Ibid.*, pp. 112–17.

26  W. M. S. West, "The Anabaptists and the Rise of the Baptist Movement" in A. Gilmore, ed., *Christian Baptism* (London: Lutterworth Press, 1959).

27  Williams, *Radical Reformation*, p. 135.

28  The literature on confirmation in the Reformation period is largely in German. For material in English see Fisher, *Christian Initiation: the Reformation period* and A. C. Repp, *Confirmation in the Lutheran Church* (St Louis, MO: Concordia, 1964); for a summary, Susan Karant-Nunn, *The Reformation of Ritual*, pp. 66–70.

29  In the appendix to *Paraphrasis in evangelius Matthei*: see John B Payne, *Erasmus: His Theology of the Sacraments* (Richmond, VA: John Knox Press, 1970), pp. 172–4.

30  Fisher, *Christian Initiation*, pp. 171–3.

31  Karant-Nunn, *Reformation of Ritual*, p. 68; though see Fisher, *Christian Initiation*, pp. 174–8 for a slightly different liturgy.

32  For details of the debate over this see Bjarne Hareide, *Die Konfirmation in der Reformationszeit: Eine Unterschuung der Lutherischen Konfirmation in Deutschland 1520–1585*, Arbeiten zur Pastoraltheologie 8 (Göttingen: Vandenhoeck & Ruprecht 1971), pp. 250–73, summarised in Karant-Nunn, p. 69.

33  Fisher, *Christian Initiation*, pp. 254–60.

34  Thompson, *Liturgies of the Western Church*, pp. 168–9.

35  *Ibid.*, p. 170.

36  J. H. Blunt, *The Annotated Book of Common Prayer* (London: Longman, 1903), compares all versions of the Book of Common Prayer in detail. For the Prayers of General Confession and Absolution see esp. pp. 182–3.

37  MacCulloch, *Cranmer*, esp. pp. 399–403 for Bucer's influence.

38  For an edition and translation of this, see E. C. Whitaker, *Martin Bucer and the Book of Common Prayer*.

39  Whitaker, *Martin Bucer and the Book of Common Prayer*, pp. 144–5.

40  "The Church of God" in Williams, *Spiritualist and Anabaptist Writers*, p. 242.

41  Williams, *Spiritualist and Anabaptist Writers*, pp. 34–5.
42  "The Church of God" in Williams, *Spiritualist and Anabaptist Writers*, p. 248.
43  Whitaker, *Martin Bucer and the Book of Common Prayer*, pp. 120–3.
44  *LW* 42, pp. 97–115.
45  Whitaker, *Martin Bucer and the Book of Common Prayer*, pp. 124–5.
46  *Ibid.*, pp. 126–9.
47  Karant-Nunn, *Reformation of Ritual*, p. 118.
48  From Calvin's introduction to the 1543 metrical psalter: see F. M. Higman, *Who was John Calvin? or Calvin and his Times* (University of Geneva, Faculty of Theology, 1992), pp. 44–5.
49  Whitaker, *Martin Bucer and the Book of Common Prayer*, pp. 16–17.
50  *LW* 36, pp. 271–305.
51  Williams, *Radical Reformation*, p. 135.
52  "Against the Heavenly Prophets" (1525), *LW* 40, pp. 129–30.
53  Karant-Nunn, *Reformation of Ritual*, p. 251 n 141.
54  Whitaker, *Martin Bucer and the Book of Common Prayer*, pp. 18–19.

## 8  *Ritual and Society: The Reshaping of Popular Religious Practice*

1   For a fuller discussion of these ideas, see Catherine Bell, *Ritual Theory, Ritual Practice* (Oxford and New York: Oxford University Press, 1992).
2   Karant-Nunn, *Zwickau in Transition*, pp. 182–8, 210–11.
3   Karant-Nunn, *Reformation of Ritual*, p. 64.
4   I am grateful to Dr Prys Morgan for this point.
5   Karant-Nunn, *Reformation of Ritual*, p. 63.
6   This is based on a discussion on the medieval religion online discussion group: see http://www.mailbase.ac.uk/lists/medieval-religion/1998-04.htm
7   *WA* 26: 175–240; Karant-Nunn, *Reformation of Ritual*, p. 79.
8   Judith D. Maltby, *Prayer book and people in Elizabethan and early Stuart England* (Cambridge: Cambridge University Press, 1998).
9   D. W. Sabean, *Power in the Blood*, pp. 37–60.
10  For a detailed discussion and analysis of German marriage ceremonies see Lyndal Roper, " 'Going to Church and Street': Weddings in Reformation Augsburg", *Past and Present* 106, Feb. 1985, 62–101; Karant-Nunn, *Reformation of Ritual*, pp. 22–42.
11  Karant-Nunn, *Zwickau in Transition*, pp. 104–5, based on Georg Spalatin's notes of the interrogation of Müntzer's followers in 1529.
12  Williams, *Radical Reformation*, pp. 184, 505–17.
13  Craig M. Koslofsky, *The Reformation of the dead : death and ritual in early modern Germany, 1450–1700* (Basingstoke: Macmillan; New York: St. Martin's Press, 2000).
14  There is an extensive literature on Lutheran funeral sermons and deathbed literature, almost all of it in German. For a summary of the conclusions in

English, see Karant-Nunn, *Reformation of Ritual*, pp. 155–66.

15  PRO E178/3503.

16  For a detailed study of medieval Sabbatarianism see Athene Reiss, *The Sunday Christ* (Oxford: BAR, 2000) .

17  From Bucer's *Censura*: see Whitaker, *Martin Bucer and the Book of Common Prayer*, pp. 144–5.

18  Whitaker, *Martin Bucer and the Book of Common Prayer*, pp. 142–3.

19  *LW* 47, pp. 60–1.

20  Hsia, *Social Discipline*, p. 14.


**9  *Popular Belief and Folk Culture***

1  Keith Thomas, *Religion and the Decline of Magic* (London: Weidenfeld & Nicolson, 1971).

2  Williams, *Radical Reformation*, pp. 72–3.

3  R. Po-chia Hsia, *Social Discipline in the Reformation*, London and New York: Routledge, 1989, pp. 135–6; Bob Scribner, "Police and the Territorial State in Sixteenth-Century Württemberg" in Kouri and Scott, *Politics and Society in Reformation Europe*. See also Sabean, *Power in the Blood*.

4  Kevin Donovan, "The Sanctoral" in Jones *et al.*, *The Study of Liturgy*.

5  For a detailed account of this strange phenomenon see Bob Scribner, "Luther Myth: a popular historiography of the Reformer" and "Incombustible Luther: the image of the Reformer in early modern Germany" in his *Popular Culture and Popular Movements in Reformation Germany*, pp. 301–22 and 323–53.

6  *Social Discipline*, p. 107: see also Scribner, "Incombustible Luther".

7  For references to these see F. Brittain, ed., *The Lyfe of Saynt Radegunde, edited from the copy in Jesus College Library* (Cambridge: Cambridge University Press, 1926), pp. xv–xvi.

8  William Haller, *Foxe's Book of Martyrs and the Elect Nation* (London: Cape, 1963).

9  *Apocalypse* is not another word for the end of the world: it derives from the Greek word for a revelation.

10  Williams, *Radical Reformation*, p. 174.

11  *Social Discipline*, p. 112.

12  See, for example, Alan MacFarlane, *Witchcraft in Tudor and Stuart England: a regional and comparative study*, 2nd edn. (London: Routledge, 1999).

13  Strauss, *Luther's House of Learning*, pp. 303–5; Scribner, *Popular Culture and Popular Movements*, pp. 46–7.

14  Abray, *People's Reformation*, pp. 171–3.

15  Oberman, *Luther*, 330.

16  Letter to George Spalatin, Wittenberg, January or February, 1514: translated in http://www.fordham.edu/halsall/source/luther-jews.html

17  *LW* 47, pp. 172, 242.

18 Williams, *Radical Reformation*, pp. 170, 186, 834.
19 Williams, *Radical Reformation*, pp. 188–9.

## Conclusion

1 *The People's Reformation*, p. 179.
2 Abray, *People's Reformation*, p. 178.
3 *Ibid.*, p. 181.
4 For a discussion of many of these issues (and conclusions which differ in some aspects from mine) see Richard van Dülmen, "The Reformation and the Modern Age" in C. Scott Dixon, ed., *The German Reformation* (Oxford: Blackwell, 1999).
5 Gwynn, *Huguenot Heritage*.
6 Gwent Record Office, D. 43. 4216, p. 7.
7 Gwent Record Office, D. 43. 4216.
8 *Popular Culture and Popular Movements*, pp. 15–16; "The Reformation, Popular Magic, and the 'Disenchantment of the World' ", *Journal of Interdisciplinary History* 23 (1993), 475–94, reprinted in Dixon, *The German Reformation*, pp. 262–79.
9 F. M. Higman, *The Style of John Calvin in his French Polemical Pamphlets* (Oxford: Oxford University Press, 1967).
10 *Who was John Calvin? or Calvin and his Times*, p. 82.

# Glossary of Reformers

**Arminius, Jacobus (1559–1609)**
Dutch protestant theologian who criticized the prevailing idea of salvation through predestination. He argued that humans had the power to make their own choices – to choose to accept grace, for example – and that even those who had been saved could fall from grace. He also pleaded for a reconciliation of the differences among Christians. After his death, his ideas on salvation were eventually debated and rejected at the Synod of Dort (1618–19) but they continued to influence a number of otherwise Calvinist thinkers.

**Bucer, Martin (1491–1551)**
Protestant reformer at Basle. Born in Alsace and entered the Dominican order of friars as a young man. Studied at Heidelberg 1517–18, where he was influenced first by Erasmus* then by Luther*. Moved to Strasburg in 1523 and became one of the leaders of the Reformation there. His theology is complex and at times almost contradictory. He could not accept that Christ was really present in the bread and wine of the Eucharist. However, he was reluctant to accept the splits in the Protestant reformation on this issue. He tried to reconcile Luther's doctrine of the Real Presence with Zwingli's* memorialism. His insistence on God's sovereignty influenced the development of Calvin's* doctrine of predestination*. At the same time, he clearly believed that human actions ("good works") could help in the process of salvation.

Bucer left Strasbourg in 1549 after the defeat of the Protestant Schmalkaldic League. He was invited to England, where he became Regius Professor of Divinity at Cambridge University, but he died two years later. An important Reformation leader in his own right, with a clear vision of a united Protestant church, he is now considered important mainly for his influence on Calvin* and on Thomas Cranmer* and the Church of England.

**Bullinger, Heinrich (1504–75)**
Zwingli's* successor at Zürich; he codified and developed Zwingli's ideas and wrote a history of the Reformation in Zürich. He was one of the main promoters of the First Helvetic Confession on 1536, which was intended to settle differences of approach between the Swiss Protestant cantons. In 1549 he and Calvin* eventually reached a settlement of their differences over issues like predestina-

tion\* and the Eucharist\*. This was embodied in the *Consensus Tigurinus* (the "Zürich Agreement") and united the Zwinglian and Calvinist churches.

### Calvin, John (1509–64)

Second-generation Protestant reformer at Geneva. Born at Noyon, near Paris; studied law at Paris and published an edition of Seneca's *On Clemency* before coming under the influence of French reformers. He was forced to flee from Paris during the crack-down on Protestants there. He settled briefly in Basle, where he wrote the first version of the *Institutes of the Christian Religion*. His clear and comprehensive outline of the basics of the Christian faith brought him to the attention of the early reformers in Geneva and he was invited to join them. Opposition to his ideas forced him to leave Geneva briefly in 1538 and he sought refuge in Bucer's\* Strasbourg. He was asked to return to Geneva in 1541 and became the city's religious leader. He spent the next twenty years developing his rigorously analytical approach to church organization and belief. He is best known for his doctrine of salvation through *predestination*, the idea that God has already chosen who will be saved and that humans can do nothing to alter that choice. It was not a central doctrine for him but it became one of the hallmarks of the church which he established.

### Cranmer, Thomas (1489–1555)

Reforming English archbishop. A Protestant academic, he was appointed Archbishop of Canterbury in 1532 to facilitate Henry VIII's marriage to Ann Boleyn. For the remaining 15 years of Henry's reign he attempted with varying degrees of success to defend and extend the limited Protestant advance in England. During the reign of the young Edward VI he was one of those who led the country towards a more thorough reformation. He compiled and translated the standard liturgy of the English church, the Book of Common Prayer. During the Catholic revival under Mary Tudor he briefly abandoned his Protestant beliefs, but returned to them and was burned as a heretic.

### Erasmus, Desiderius (1466–1536)

Leading Christian humanist; acutely aware of the need for reform but always remained a member of the Catholic church. He was the illegitimate son of a priest and was brought up by members of the late medieval clerical reform group the Brethren of the Common Life. After studying theology in Paris he became a travelling scholar, living largely on money from the sale of his books. He wrote some savagely witty satires against the worldliness and corruption which he saw in the Church. His influential *Enchiridion Militis Christi* (the "Handbook of the Christian Soldier"), first published in 1503, attacked the unintelligible language of late medieval scholasticism and called for a return to the Bible and the writings of the early Christian fathers. His accurate and comprehensive editions of the writings of the early church fathers made their ideas accessible to a wider audience. His edition of the Greek New Testament, the *Novum Instrumentum* *omne*, published in 1516, influenced a number of the early reformers. However, he disagreed with Luther* both on the importance of human free will and on Luther's willingness to allow ordinary people to take part in theological debate. Ultimately the unity of the Catholic church was more important to him than the need for reform.

### Farel, Guillaume (1489–1565)

The French protestant pioneer who first invited Calvin* to Geneva. He studied at Paris, then moved to Basle, where he met Erasmus*. He then travelled around the Rhineland and spent some time with Bucer* and the other early reformers in Strasbourg. He was never formally ordained, but he believed that he had been been called to the pastorate by God and that that was what enabled him to celebrate the sacraments. He visited Geneva briefly in 1532 but was forced to leave by a popular uprising. He returned in 1535 and invited Calvin to join him, but their proposals for the reform of religious life were so unpopular that they were forced to leave again. He settled in Neuchâtel where he worked as a pastor and published a number of books of guidance for French Protestant communities.

### Grebel, Conrad (*c.* 1497–1526)

Leader of the radical Protestant group in Zürich. He was initially a supporter of Zwingli* but by 1524 he was in touch with the radicals Thomas Müntzer* and Luther's former colleague Karlstadt*. He shared their vision of an exclusive church made up of true believers and of the need for adult baptism as a sign of faith. In spite of his advanced views, though, he was never prepared to leave the church of Zürich.

### Hofmann, Melchior (?1495–1543)

Furrier and Anabaptist lay preacher. He travelled around the Baltic cities in the 1520s, becoming more radical in his views. In 1530 he settled in Strasbourg, where he published a series of pamphlets announcing the imminent end of the world. He was arrested in Strasbourg in 1533 on the grounds that he was a threat to civil order, and he died in prison in 1543. His followers, the "Melchiorites", eventually gave up his violent ideas and became seekers after spiritual enlightenment.

### Hubmaier, Balthasar (*c.* 1485–1528)

Early Anabaptist leader from near Augsburg. It was probably he who drafted the demands of the peasants in 1524. After the crushing of the peasants' uprising he emigrated to Moravia, where he settled at Nikolsburg and attracted a sizeable congregation. Unlike many Anabaptists, he believed in the legitimacy of secular government and the need for an established church: but he considered that only rebaptized Christians were qualified to serve as magistrates. He was eventually arrested and condemned by the Habsburg authorities and burned at the stake in Vienna.

### Karlstadt, Andreas (Rudolf) Bodenstein von (1480–1541)

Luther's colleague at Wittenberg, collaborator and later critic. As Dean of the faculty of theology at Wittenberg, he initially opposed Luther's interpretation of the theology of salvation of Augustine. Convinced after acquiring a copy of the new edition of Augustine's works in 1516, he cooperated with Luther in a radical overhaul of the theology syllabus and took a leading rôle with him in the Leipzig disputation of 1519. While Luther was in the Wartburg, Karlstadt's ideas became more radical: he celebrated a reformed Mass, campaigned against images in churches and got married. Eventually, he left Wittenberg to serve as parish priest of Orlamünde in Thuringia. He was an active leader in the Peasants' War. After a period of wandering he settled at Basel, where he became professor of biblical theology. His distinctive approach to theology drew on the traditions of the German mystics as well as Augustine's theology of salvation. Karlstadt had a powerful vision of the church as a community of the godly. His emphasis on the importance of the divine will within the individual believer makes him one of the forerunners of the Society of Friends (the "Quakers") and of the modern theology of "God as the ground of our being".

### Martin Luther (1483–1546)

Father of the Protestant Reformation. Born in Eisleben in Saxony, son of a mine-owner. Studied law and theology at University of Erfurt. Entered the Augustinian priory at Erfurt in 1505. Chair of Biblical Studies at University of Wittenberg 1512, where he developed a theology of salvation through faith similar to that of St Augustine. His challenge to the church over the sale of indulgences* eventually led him to defy the Pope's authority. His stress on the rôle of secular authorities in the reform and defence of the church made his ideas attractive to a number of German rulers. His influence on virtually every aspect of the Reformation was immense: the theology of salvation, the doctrine of the church and the sacraments, Biblical translation, liturgical reform, education, social welfare. His ideas on the Eucharist* – his insistence that Christ was physically present in the consecrated bread and wine – led to a split with the more radical reformers like Zwingli, Bucer and Calvin who believed that Christ's presence was spiritual or metaphorical.

### Melanchthon, Philip [Philipp Schwartzerdt] (1497–1560)

Luther's colleague at Wittenberg; the systematizer of the Lutheran Reformation. Born into a respectable merchant's family, he received a strongly humanist education and became professor of Greek at Wittenberg in 1518. There, he came under the influence of Martin Luther and placed his humanist scholarship on the side of the Reformation. His *Loci Communes*, a systematic analysis of the themes of the Bible, provided a Protestant textbook of theology which was firmly based on Scripture. He was also the main administrative organizer of the early Lutheran church, advising several of the German Lutheran principalities, drafting statements of belief like the Augsburg Confession and acting as mediator in disputes. His belief in the need for peace and unity led him to emphasize the concept of *adiaphora*, "matters of indifference" over which it was possible to disagree. However, his willingness to compromise, particularly during the Catholic revival after the defeat of the Schmalkaldic League by Charles V in 1546–47, made him unpopular with the hard-line Lutherans and split the Lutheran church for some time.

### Müntzer, Thomas (before 1491–1525)

Early militant radical. Born in the mountain region of central Germany, studied at Leipzig and Frankfurt, ordained a priest, worked briefly in Wittenberg then in the Saxon town of Zwickau. There he developed a theology influenced by the late German mystics, which stressed the importance of the spirit within, the imminence of the end of the world and the need for radical human action as part of the final conflict foretold in the Book of Revelation. After a few years as a travelling preacher he took control of a peasant army during the Peasants' War, which he interpreted as the beginning of the apocalypse; but his army was crushed and he was executed.

### Oecolampadius, Johannes (1482–1531)

Early Swiss Protestant reformer. From the Rhineland, a humanist scholar and ordained priest. Appointed city preacher at Basle in 1515; became an enthusiastic proponent of Luther's ideas.

### Sozzini, Lelio (1525–62) and Fausto (1539–1604)

Uncle and nephew from Padua in northern Italy. Lelio's radical scepticism led him to doubt the nature of the Trinity, the basic Christian doctrine of one God but with three separate identities, Father, Son (Christ) and Holy Spirit. Fausto settled in Poland and developed his uncle's ideas, arguing that Christ was an entirely human being.

### Zwingli, Huldrych (1483–1531)

Early Swiss Protestant reformer and humanist scholar. Born at Wildhaus in St Gall; educated at Bern, Vienna and Basel; chaplain to Swiss military forces at battle of Marignano. Settled at Zürich, where his preaching on the New Testament led him to rethink the Christian doctrine of salvation. He began in 1522 by attacking the dietary restrictions and seasonally-imposed abstinence of the medieval church and moved on to attack idolatry, clerical celibacy and the imposition of all kinds of outward observances. For Zwingli, the only binding observances were those which God asked for in the Bible. What mattered was not outward restrictions and a supposedly austere lifestyle but the faith of the individual Christian in Christ's sacrifice. Thus far he was in agreement with Luther (though he always claimed to have reached his views independently) but he went beyond Luther in his interpretaition of the Eucharist. For Zwingli, Christ could not be present in the bread and wine because he was in Heaven.

The Eucharist was a memorial of Christ's sacrifice and a pledge of his love and forgiveness. Zwingli also wanted a more thorough recasting of the worship of the church. He began the conversion of the Swiss cantons to his vision of a reformed church but was killed at Kappel while serving as the army chaplain of the Swiss Protestant forces fighting the army of the Catholic cantons.

# Glossary of Terms

---

**absolution**
In the Catholic tradition, remission of the penalties of sin, offered by the priest on behalf of the Church to those who have confessed their sins and shown contrition.

**Anabaptists**
Literally, 'rebaptizers': refers to those radical reformers who believed that baptism was only valid for those who could make a personal commitment and profession of faith. They thus insisted on rebaptizing converts who had been baptized as infants.

**Antinomians**
Those who reject all legal restrictions and moral codes. In the Reformation period the antinomians were a group of radical reformers who believed that, once they were in a state of grace, they could do no more wrong.

**apostasy**
Complete defection from the faith. An apostate is one who has been a believer but who then rejects the faith, rather than an unbeliever who has never accepted it.

**Arminianism**
A seventeenth-century form of the doctrine that humans have free will and can contribute to their own salvation. Named after the Dutch protestant theologian Jacob Arminius*.

**Augustinianism**
The theology of salvation associated with Augustine of Hippo, stressing the importance of divine grace and the powerlessness of sinful humans to achieve their own salvation.

**baptism**
Ritual washing with consecrated water, which either effects or symbolizes the

washing away of sin. Baptism is accompanied by promises made by adults for themselves and made on behalf of infants by godparents or sponsors.

**blasphemy**
Speaking offensively of God, or speaking in a way which denies his power. In the Christian tradition, this involves speaking disparagingly of Christ or denying his status as God.

**catechism**
A statement of Christian belief in non-academic language, usually in question-and-answer form, used for instruction and education.

**Christology**
The theology of the nature and identity of Jesus Christ.

**confession**
(1) the admission of sin, usually made to a priest in order that he may absolve the sin and offer the sacrament of penance; (2) a statement of principles of belief, usually by one of the Protestant denominations.

**confirmation**
The renewal of baptismal vows before a bishop.

**ecclesiology**
The Christian theology of the nature of the church. (The term is also used in the nineteenth century to refer to theories about the ideal design for church buildings.)

**epistles**
The letters of advice written by leaders of the early Christian church to congregations and individuals and collected together as part of the Bible.

**Eucharist**
The ritual re-enactment of the meal which Jesus Christ shared with his closest followers on the evening before his sacrificial death. It involves sharing bread and wine which symbolize or actually become in their essentials or in a spiritual sense the body and blood of Christ.

**exegesis**
Textual interpretation, particularly of the Bible.

**faith**
Faith, in the Christian context, is not simply belief: it is the willingness to trust and to act on what is believed.

**fundamentalism**
Adherence to the literal meaning of a sacred text as the sole source of doctrine.

**grace**
In the broadest Christian context, God's favour to humanity. In the specific context of the Reformation, used particularly to describe God's gift of unmerited forgiveness and mercy.

**heresy**
False doctrine from someone within the Church – as distinct from apostasy, which is complete rejection of the faith.

**humanism**
A complex cultural movement linked with the Renaissance. Its ideas include the rediscovery of the achievements of classical culture, an emphasis on returning to the sources, and the establishment of authentic texts of classical and Biblical authorities.

**indulgences**
In the Catholic tradition, an offer of release from those penalties of sin which have not been expiated through penance. Offered retrospectively and for money, to release the souls of the dead from Purgatory, indulgences were confused with the actual remission of sin and triggered Luther's revolt against the Papacy.

**justification**
In the context of Reformation theology, being made (or being deemed to be) righteous by God.

**liturgy**
The written text of a structured religious service: used especially of the Eucharist but can apply to any other service which has a set form.

**nominalism**
A philosophy of knowledge which states that generic words ("bread", "white") are abstract concepts with no referent in reality.

**penance**
An act of satisfaction for the consequences of sin, usually imposed by a priest after confession* and absolution*. One of the seven sacraments* of the Catholic church. It is important to remember that penance is not an act of satisfaction for sin: in Christian doctrine, only Christ can do that. It is a satisfaction for the *consequences* of sin, which remain after the sin itself has been absolved.

**predestination**
The doctrine that God has chosen those who he will save ("the elect") and that humans cannot do anything to affect their fate.

**Purgatory**
In the Catholic tradition, a place of punishment after death for sins for which the sinner has not done penance in their lifetime.

**realism**
A philosophy of knowledge which states that abstract and generic words correspond to a reality beyond the specifics of appearance.

**sacrament**
A church service or rite which provides a physical channel for God's grace. The Catholic church recognized seven sacraments: baptism, confirmation, the Eucharist, penance, matrimony, ordination and extreme unction. Of these, the Protestant reformers accepted only two, baptism and confirmation, arguing that these were the only ones mentioned in the Bible.

**salvation**
Spiritual deliverance; release from sin.

**schism**
A deliberate split in the unity of the church.

**Socinianism**
An early form of Unitarianism, the rejection of the doctrine of the Trinity. It takes its name from the Italian radical reformers Lelio and Fausto Sozzini*.

**Soteriology**
The Christian theology of salvation*.

**spiritualists**
In the context of the Reformation, those radical reformers who rejected the authority of the Bible, believing instead that the Holy Spirit could speak directly to them and guide them.

**spirituality**
This has two meanings. (1) The 'spiritual estate', the clergy, as opposed to the laity; (2) The inner Christian life of prayer and devotion, as distinct from the organization and doctrine of the institutional church.

**transubstantiation**
The belief that the substance of the consecrated bread and wine at the Eucharist

is transformed into the substance of the body and blood of Christ, though the accidents (the outward appearance) are unchanged.

**Unitarianism**
Rejection of the doctrine of the Trinity in favour of the idea of a single-person God.

# Further Reading

---

*Note:* McNeill, *Inst.*: John T. McNeill, ed., *Calvin: Institutes of the Christian Religion* (Library of Christian Classics, vols xx, xxi. London: SCM Press/Philadelphia: Westminster Press, 1960).

*LW*: *Luther's Works*, ed. Jaroslav Pelikan and Helmut Lehmann (St Louis and Philadelphia, 1955).

## Sources

I have tried wherever possible to refer to works in English translations. For those with a reading knowledge of German, French or Latin, the standard edition of the complete works of Martin Luther is the Weimar edition (the *Weimar Ausgabe*), begun in 1883. The complete works of Calvin, Melanchthon and Zwingli are in the *Corpus Reformatorum* series.

Baylor, Michael B., *The Radical Reformation* (Cambridge: Cambridge University Press, 1991).

Bromiley, G. W., ed. *Zwingli and Bullinger*, Library of Christian Classics, vol. xxiv (London: SCM Press/Philadelphia: Westminster Press, 1953).

Cochrane, Arthur, ed., *Reformed Confessions of the Sixteenth Century* (Philadelphia: Westminster Press, 1966).

Hillerbrand, H. J., *The Reformation: a narrative history related by contemporary observers and participants* (New York: Harper & Row, 1964).

Jackson, S. M., ed., *The Latin Works and the Correspondence of Huldreich Zwingli, together with selections from his German works* (New York and London: G.P. Putnam's Sons, 1912–29).

Meyer, Carl S., ed. *Luther and Zwingli's Propositions for Debate: the 95 Theses of 31 Oct 1517 and the 67 Articles of 19 January 1523* (Leiden: E.J. Brill, 1963.).

Noll, M. A., *Confessions and Catechisms of the Reformation* (Leicester: Apollos, 1991).

Pauck, Wilhelm, ed. *Melanchthon and Bucer* (Library of Christian Classics xix. London: SCM Press/Philadelphia: Westminster Press, 1969).

Reid, J. K. S., ed., *Calvin: Theological Treatises* (Library of Christian Classics, vol. xxii. London: SCM Press/Philadelphia: Westminster Press, 1954).

Tappert, Theodore G., ed. and trans., *The Book of Concord* (Philadelphia: Fortress Press, 1959).

Torrance, Thomas F., ed. *Tracts and treatises on the doctrine and worship of the church, by John Calvin* (Edinburgh and London: Oliver and Boyd; Grand Rapids, MI: Eerdmans, 1958).

Wenger, John, "The Schleitheim Confession of Faith", *Mennonite Quarterly Review*, xix (1945), 243–53.

Whitaker, E. C., *Martin Bucer and the Book of Common Prayer*, Alcuin Club Collections no 55 (Great Wakering: Mayhew-McCrimmon for the Alcuin Club, 1974).

Williams, G. H.. ed., *Spiritual and Anabaptist Writers* (Library of Christian Classics, vol. xxv. London: SCM Press/Philadelphia: Westminster Press, 1957).

Woolf, B. L., *Reformation Writings of Martin Luther* (London: Lutterworth Press, 1952).

## General studies

Greengrass, Mark, *The Longman Companion to the European Reformation* (London and New York: Longman, 1998) is a recent guide with an overview of the main issues, biographical notes, glossary and a more detailed guide to further reading than that provided here.

Cameron, Euan, *The European Reformation* (Oxford: Clarendon Press, 1991) is a good analysis of ideas and social background.

Lindberg, Carter, *The European Reformations* (Oxford: Blackwell, 1996) is a more racy narrative; and

McGrath, Alister, *Reformation Thought*, 3rd edn. (Oxford: Blackwell, 1999) is an overview of Reformation theology.

Higman, Francis, *Why the Reformation?* (Geneva: Institut d'Histoire de la Réformation, 1996) packs an amazing amount of insight into what is really a pamphlet.

Pettegree, Andrew, *The Early Reformation in Europe* (Cambridge: Cambridge University Press, 1992) and

Scribner, Bob *et al.*, *The Reformation in National Context* (Cambridge and London: Cambridge University Press, 1994) are both country-by-country histories.

Also good as general histories are:

Brooks, P. N., ed. *Reformation Principle and Practice* (London: Scolar Press, 1980).

Hillerbrand, H. J., *The Protestant Reformation* (New York; London: Harper & Row, 1968).

## On the antecedents of the Reformation

Duffy, Eamon, *The Stripping of the Altars* (New Haven and London: Yale University Press, 1992).

Jayne, S., *John Colet and Marsilio Ficino* (Oxford: Oxford University Press, 1963).

McConica, J. K., *English Humanists and Reformation Politics* (Oxford: Oxford University Press, 1965).

McGrath, Alister, *The Intellectual Origins of the European Reformation* (Oxford: Blackwell, 1993).

Oberman, Heiko, *Forerunners of the Reformation* (London: Lutterworth, 1967), which translates a number of key texts.

Oberman, Heiko, *The Dawn of the Reformation: Essays in Late Medieval and Early Reformation Thought* (Edinburgh: T & T Clark, 1986).

Ozment, Steven, *The Reformation in Medieval Perspective* (Chicago: Quadrangle, 1971).

## On individual reforming movements

Edwards, Mark U., *Luther and the False Brethren* (Stanford: Stanford University Press, 1975) is a study of Luther's conflicts with those whose Protestant ideas went further than his own – with Zwingli's ideas on the Eucharist, with his former colleague Karlstadt and the Anabaptists, with the radical leaders of the Peasants' War and with the antinomians.

Goertz, Hans-Jürgen, ed., *Profiles of Radical Reformers: Biographical Sketches from Thomas Müntzer to Paracelsus* (Kitchener: Herald, 1982).

Pettegree, Andrew *et al.*, *Calvinism in Europe, 1540–1620* (Cambridge: Cambridge University Press, 1994).

Prestwich, Menna, ed., *International Calvinism 1541–1715* (Oxford: Clarendon Press, 1985).

Williams, G. H., *The Radical Reformation* (Philadelphia: Westminster Press, 1962).

## On the Reformation in particular areas

Abray, Lorna Jane *The People's Reformation: magistrates, clergy and commons in Strasbourg, 1500–1598* (Oxford: Basil Blackwell, 1985).

Chrisman, M. U. *Strasbourg and the Reform : a study in the process of change* (New Haven: Yale Historical Publications no. 87, 1967).

Crew, Phyllis Mack, *Calvinist Preaching and Iconoclasm in the Netherlands, 1544–1569* (Cambridge: Cambridge University Press, 1978).

Dickens, A. G., *The German Nation and Martin Luther* (New York: Harper & Row, 1974).

Diefendorf, Barbara, *Beneath the Cross: Catholics and Huguenots in Sixteenth-Century Paris* (New York: Oxford University Press, 1991.

Dixon, C. Scott, ed., *The German Reformation* (Oxford: Blackwell, 1999).

Duke, Alistair, *Reformation and Revolt in the Low Countries* (London: Hambledon, 1990).

Greengrass, Mark, *The French Reformation* (Oxford: Blackwell, 1987).

Karant-Nunn, Susan, *Zwickau in transition, 1500–1547: the Reformation as an agent of change* (Columbus: Ohio State University Press, 1987).

Loades, David, *Revolution in Religion: The English Reformation, 1530–1570* (Cardiff: University of Wales Press, 1992).

O'Day, Rosemary, *The Debate on the English Reformation* (London: Methuen, 1986).

Scarisbrick, J. A., *The Reformation and the English People* (Oxford: Oxford University Press, 1984).

Scribner, R., *Popular Culture and Popular Movements in Reformation Germany* (London and Ronceverte: Hambledon Press, 1987).

Zapalac, Kristin Eldyss Sorensen *In his image and likeness: political iconography and religious change in Regensburg, 1500–1600* (Ithaca: Cornell University Press, 1990).

## On individual reformers

### Bucer

Stephens, W. P., *The Holy Spirit in the Theology of Martin Bucer* (Cambridge: Cambridge University Press, 1970).

Wright, D. F., ed., *Martin Bucer: reforming church and community* (Cambridge: Cambridge University Press, 1994).

### Calvin

Bouwsma, W. J., *John Calvin: A Sixteenth-Century Portrait* (Oxford: Oxford University Press, 1989).

Higman, Francis, *Who was John Calvin? or Calvin and his Times* (University of Geneva Faculty of Theology, 1992).

McGrath, Alister, *A Life of John Calvin* (Oxford: Basil Blackwell, 1990).

Naphy, William G., *Calvin and the Consolidation of the Genevan Reformation* (Manchester: Manchester University Press, 1994).

Reid, W. S. , *John Calvin: his influence in the Western world* (Grand Rapids, MI.: Zondervan Pub. House, 1982).

Wallace, R. S., *Calvin, Geneva and the Reformation* (Edinburgh: Scottish Academic Press, 1988).

### Cranmer

Ayris, Paul, and David Selwyn, eds., *Thomas Cranmer: Churchman and Scholar* (Woodbridge: Boydell Press, 1993).

MacCulloch, Diarmaid, *Thomas Cranmer* (New Haven; London: Yale University Press, 1996).

### Karlstadt

Pater, Calvin Augustine, *Karlstadt as the Father of the Baptist Movements: The Emergence of Lay Protestantism* (Toronto, Buffalo and London: University of Toronto Press, 1984).

Sider, Ronald J., *Andreas Bodenstein von Karlstadt: The Development of his Thought 1517–1525* (Leiden: E. J. Brill, 1974).

## Luther

Althaus, Paul, *The Theology of Martin Luther*, trans. R. C. Schultz (Philadelphia: Fortress Press, 1966).

Bainton, R. H., *Here I Stand: a life of Martin Luther* (New York: New American Library, 1955).

Erikson, Erik H. *Young Man Luther: a study in psychoanalysis and history* (London: Faber and Faber, 1959).

Kittelson, J. M. *Luther the Reformer: The Story of the Man and his Career* (Minneapolis: Augsburg, 1989).

Lohse, B. *Martin Luther: An Introduction to his Life and Writings* (Philadelphia: Fortress Press, 1986).

Obermann, Heiko, *Luther: Man between God and the Devil* (New Haven; London: Yale University Press, 1989).

Pelikan, Jaroslav, *Spirit versus Structure: Luther and the institutions of the Church* (London: Collins, 1968).

## Melanchthon

Maag, Karin, ed., *Melanchthon in Europe* (Grand Rapids, MI: Baker Books, 1999).

Manschreck, C. L., *Melanchthon: The Quiet Reformer* (New York: Abingdon Press, 1958).

## Zwingli

Furcha, E. J., and Pipkin, H. W., eds., *Prophet, Pastor, Protestant: The Work of Huldrych Zwingli* (Pittsburgh Theological Monographs: New Series 11. Allison Park, PA: Pickwick Publications, 1984).

Gäbler, U., *Huldrych Zwingli: His Life and Work* (Philadelphia: Fortress Press, 1986).

Potter, G. R., *Zwingli* (Cambridge: Cambridge University Press, 1976).

Stephens, W. P., *The Theology of Huldrych Zwingli* (Oxford: Clarendon Press, 1986).

## 1 *Sin and Salvation*

McGrath, Alister, *Luther's Theology of the Cross* (Oxford: Blackwell, 1990).

McGrath, Alister, *Iustitia Dei: A History of the Christian Doctrine of Justification*, 2nd edn. (Cambridge: Cambridge University Press, 1998).

Muller, R. A., *Christ and the Decree: Christology and Predestination from Calvin to Perkins* (Studies in historical theology 2. Grand Rapids, MI: Baker Book House, 1988).

Tentler, Thomas, *Sin and Confession on the Eve of the Reformation* (Princeton: Princeton University Press, 1977).

## 2 Sacrament and Ritual

Clark, F., *Eucharistic Sacrifice and the Reformation*, 2nd edn. (Devon: Augustine, 1980).

Gerrish, B. A., *Grace and Gratitude: the eucharistic theology of John Calvin* (Minneapolis: Fortress, 1993).

Hall, B., '*Hoc est corpus meum*: the centrality of the Real Presence for Luther' in *Luther: Theologian for Catholics and Protestants*, ed. George Yule (Edinburgh: T. & T. Clark, 1985).

Rempel, John D., *The Lord's Supper in Anabaptism: a study in the Christology of Balthasar Hubmaier, Pilgrim Marpeck and Dirk Phillips* (Waterloo: Herald, 1993).

## 3 "By this book": Authority and Interpretation

*The Cambridge History of the Bible*, ed. P. R. Ackroyd *et al.*, Volume 3: the West from the Reformation to the present day (Cambridge: Cambridge University Press, 1963).

Evans, G. R., *The Language and Logic of the Bible: The Road to Reformation* (Cambridge: Cambridge University Press, 1985).

Forstmann, H. J., *Word and Spirit: Calvin's Doctrine of Biblical Authority* (Stanford: Stanford University Press, 1962).

Tavard, G. H., *Holy Writ or Holy Church? The Crisis of the Protestant Reformation* (London: Burns & Oates, 1959).

## 4 The True Church in the Protestant Tradition

Avis, Paul D. L., *The Church in the Theology of the Reformers* (London: Marshall Morgan & Scott, 1981).

Hendrix, S. H., *Luther and the Papacy: Stages in a Reformation Conflict* (Philadelphia: Fortress Press, 1981).

Milner, B. C., *Calvin's Doctrine of the Church* (Leiden: Brill, 1970).

Pelikan, Jaroslav, *Spirit versus structure: Luther and the institutions of the Church* (London: Collins, 1968).

## 5 Church and State: The Protestant Churches and Secular Authority

Blickle, Peter, *The Revolution of 1525: The German Peasants' War from a New Perspective* (Baltimore: Johns Hopkins University Press, 1981).

Cargill Thompson, W. D. J., *The Political Thought of Martin Luther* (Brighton: Harvester, 1984).

Green, R. W., ed., *Protestantism, Capitalism and Social Science: the Weber thesis controversy* (Problems in European civilization, 2nd edn. Lexington, MA.: Heath, 1973).

Höpfl, H., *Luther and Calvin on Secular Authority* (Cambridge texts in the history of political thought. Cambridge: Cambridge University Press, 1991).

Hsia, R. Po-chia, *Social Discipline in the Reformation: Central Europe, 1550–1750* (London and New York: Routledge, 1989).

Jütte, Robert, *Poverty and Deviance in Early Modern Europe* (Cambridge: Cambridge University Press, 1994).

Kouri, E. I., and Scott, Tom, eds., *Politics and Society in Reformation Europe* (Basingstoke and London: Macmillan. 1987).

Lindberg, Carter, *Beyond Charity: Reformation Initiatives for the Poor* (Minneapolis: Fortress Press, 1993).

Olson, Jeannine, *Calvin and Social Welfare* (Selinsgrove: Susquehanna University Press, 1989).

Scott, Tom, and Scribner, R. W., eds., *The German Peasants' War: a history in documents* (Atlantic Highlands: Humanities, 1991).

Tonkin, J., *The Church and Secular Order in Reformation Thought* (New York; London: Columbia University Press, 1971).

### 6 *Literacy, Education and the Popular Response to the Reformation*

Edwards, Mark, *Printing, Propaganda and Martin Luther* (Berkeley: University of California Press, 1994).

Eire, C. M. N., *War against the Idols: the reformation of worship from Erasmus to Calvin* (Cambridge: Cambridge University Press, 1989).

Hsia, R. Po-Chia, ed., *The German People and the Reformation* (Ithaca, New York: Cornell University Press, 1988).

Scribner, R. W., *For the Sake of Simple Folk: popular propaganda for the German Reformation* (Cambridge: Cambridge University Press, 1981).

Scribner, R., and Johnson, T., eds., *Popular Religion in Germany and Central Europe, 1400–1800* (Basingstoke and London: Macmillan, 1996).

Scribner, R., *Popular Culture and Popular Movements in Reformation Germany* (London and Ronceverte: Hambledon Press, 1987).

Strauss, Gerald, *Luther's House of Learning* (Baltimore and London: Johns Hopkins University Press, 1978).

Wandel, Lee Palmer, *Voracious Idols and Violent Hands: Iconoclasm in Reformation Zurich, Strasburg and Basel* (Cambridge: Cambridge University Press, 1995).

Zapalac, Kristin Eldyss Sorensen *In his image and likeness: political iconography and religious change in Regensburg, 1500–1600* (Ithaca: Cornell University Press, 1990).

### 7 *Liturgy and the Articulation of Belief*

Blunt, J. H., *The Annotated Book of Common Prayer* (London: Longman, 1903).

Fisher, J. D. C., *Christian Initiation: the Reformation Period* (London: SPCK for the Alcuin Club, 1970).

Gilmore, A., ed., *Christian Baptism* (London: Lutterworth Press, 1959).

Jasper, R. C. D. and G. J. Cuming, eds. *Prayers of the Eucharist: early and reformed*, 3rd edn., rev. and enl. (Collegeville, MN: Liturgical Press, 1990).

Jones, Cheslyn *et al.*, eds., *The Study of Liturgy* (London: SPCK / New York: Oxford University Press).

Karant-Nunn, Susan, *The Reformation of Ritual* (London and New York: Routledge, 1997).

Koslofsky, Craig M., *The Reformation of the dead : death and ritual in early modern Germany, 1450–1700* (Basingstoke: Macmillan; New York: St. Martin's Press, 2000).

Maltby, Judith D., *Prayer book and people in Elizabethan and early Stuart England* (Cambridge: Cambridge University Press, 1998).

Maxwell, William D. ed., *The Liturgical Portions of the Genevan Service Book* (Edinburgh and London: Oliver and Boyd, 1931). In spite of its title, an overview of liturgical developments in the Reformed tradition as well as a detailed analysis of Knox's Geneva Book.

Old, Hughes Oliphant, *The Shaping of the Reformed Baptismal Rite in the Sixteenth Century* (Grand Rapids, MI: William B. Eerdmans, 1992).

Ratcliff, E. C."Puritan Alternatives to the Prayer Book: the *Directory* and Richard Baxter's *Reformed Liturgy*" in M. Ramsey *et al.*, *The English Prayer Book 1549–1662* (London: SPCK for the Alcuin Club, 1963).

Repp, A. C., *Confirmation in the Lutheran Church* (St Louis, MO: Concordia, 1964).

Thompson, Bard, ed., *Liturgies of the Western Church* (Philadelphia: Fortress Press, 1961).

## 8 *Ritual and Society: The Reshaping of Popular Religious Practice*

Bell, Catherine, *Ritual Theory, Ritual Practice* (Oxford and New York: Oxford University Press, 1992).

Cressy, David, *Birth, Marriage and Death: ritual, religion and the life-cycle in Tudor and Stuart England* (Oxford: Oxford University Press, 1999).

Karant-Nunn, Susan, *The Reformation of Ritual* (London and New York: Routledge, 1997) and

Koslofsky, Craig M., *The Reformation of the dead: death and ritual in early modern Germany, 1450–1700* (Basingstoke: Macmillan; New York: St. Martin's Press, 2000) are both relevant here as well.

## 9 *Popular Belief and Folk Culture*

Cohn, Norman, *ThePursuit of the Millennium : Revolutionary Messianism in Medieval and Reformation Europe* (New York: Harper Torchbooks, 1961).

MacFarlane, Alan, *Witchcraft in Tudor and Stuart England: a regional and comparative study*, 2nd edn. (London: Routledge, 1999).

Obermann, Heiko, *The Roots of Anti-Semitism in the Age of the Renaissance and Reformation* (Philadelphia: Fortress Press, 1984).

Ozment, Steven, *When Fathers Ruled: Family Life in Reformation Europe* (Cambridge, Mass: Harvard University Press, 1983).

Reiss, Athene, *The Sunday Christ* (Oxford: BAR, 2000).

Scribner, R., and Johnson, T., eds., *Popular Religion in Germany and Central Europe, 1400–1800* (Basingstoke and London: Macmillan, 1996).

Scribner, R., *Popular Culture and Popular Movements in Reformation Germany* (London and Ronceverte: Hambledon Press, 1987).

Thomas, Keith, *Religion and the Decline of Magic* (London: Weidenfeld & Nicolson, 1971).

Wiesner-Hanks, Merry E., *Christianity and sexuality in the early modern world: regulating desire, reforming practice* (London: Routledge, 2000).

# Bibliography

Abray, Lorna Jane *The People's Reformation: magistrates, clergy and commons in Strasbourg, 1500–1598* (Oxford: Basil Blackwell, 1985).

Althaus, Paul, *The Theology of Martin Luther*, trans. R. C. Schultz (Philadelphia: Fortress Press, 1966).

Avis, Paul D. L., *The Church in the Theology of the Reformers* (London: Marshall Morgan & Scott, 1981).

Ayris, Paul, and David Selwyn, eds., *Thomas Cranmer: Churchman and Scholar* (Woodbridge: Boydell Press, 1993).

Bainton, R. H., *Here I Stand: a life of Martin Luther* (New York: New American Library, 1955).

Barnes, A. S., *Bishop Barlow and Anglican orders* (London and New York: Longmans Green, 1922.

Baylor, Michael B., *The Radical Reformation* (Cambridge: Cambridge University Press, 1991).

Bell, Catherine, *Ritual Theory, Ritual Practice* (Oxford and New York: Oxford University Press, 1992).

Blickle, Peter, *The Revolution of 1525: The German Peasants' War from a New Perspective* (Baltimore: Johns Hopkins University Press, 1981).

Blunt, J. H., *The Annotated Book of Common Prayer* (London: Longman, 1903).

Bouwsma, W. J., *John Calvin: A Sixteenth-Century Portrait* (Oxford: Oxford University Press, 1989).

Brittain, F., ed., *The Lyfe of Saynt Radegunde, edited from the copy in Jesus College Library* (Cambridge: Cambridge University Press, 1926).

Bromiley, G. W., ed. *Zwingli and Bullinger*, Library of Christian Classics vol xxiv (London: SCM Press/Philadelphia: Westminster Press, 1953).

Brooks, P. N., ed. *Reformation Principle and Practice* (London: Scolar Press, 1980).

Cameron, Euan, *The European Reformation* (Oxford: Clarendon Press, 1991).

Cargill Thompson, W. D. J., *The Political Thought of Martin Luther* (Brighton: Harvester, 1984).

Chrisman, M. U. *Strasbourg and the Reform : a study in the process of change* (New Haven: Yale Historical Publications no. 87, 1967).

Clark, F., *Eucharistic Sacrifice and the Reformation*, 2nd edn. (Devon, Augustine: 1980).

Cochrane, Arthur, ed., *Reformed Confessions of the Sixteenth Century* (Philadelphia: Westminster Press, 1966).

Cohn, Norman, *ThePursuit of the Millennium : Revolutionary Messianism in Medieval and Reformation Europe* (New York: Harper Torchbooks, 1961).

Cressy, David, *Birth, Marriage and Death: ritual, religion and the life-cycle in Tudor and Stuart England* (Oxford: Oxford University Press, 1999).

Crew, Phyllis Mack, *Calvinist Preaching and Iconoclasm in the Netherlands, 1544–1569* (Cambridge: Cambridge University Press, 1978).

Dickens, A. G., *The German Nation and Martin Luther* (New York: Harper & Row, 1974).

Diefendorf, Barbara, *Beneath the Cross: Catholics and Huguenots in Sixteenth-Century Paris* (New York: Oxford University Press, 1991).

Dixon, C. Scott, ed., *The German Reformation* (Oxford: Blackwell, 1999).

Donovan, Kevin, "The Sanctoral" in Jones *et al.*, *The Study of Liturgy*.

Duffy, Eamon, *The Stripping of the Altars* (New Haven and London: Yale University Press, 1992).

Duke, Alistair, *Reformation and Revolt in the Low Countries* (London: Hambledon, 1990).

Edwards, Mark U., *Luther and the False Brethren* (Stanford: Stanford University Press, 1975).

——, *Printing, Propaganda and Martin Luther* (Berkeley: University of California Press, 1994).

Eire, C. M. N., *War against the Idols: the reformation of worship from Erasmus to Calvin* (Cambridge: Cambridge University Press, 1989).

Erikson, Erik H. *Young man Luther : a study in psychoanalysis and history* (London: Faber and Faber, 1959).

Evans, G. R., *The Language and Logic of the Bible: The Road to Reformation* (Cambridge: Cambridge University Press, 1985).

Fisher, J. D. C., "Lutheran, Anglican and Reformed Rites" in Cheslyn Jones *et al.*, eds., *The Study of Liturgy*, pp. 154–66.

——, *Christian Initiation: the Reformation Period* (London: SPCK for the Alcuin Club, 1970).

——, *Christian Initiation: the Reformation Period* (London: SPCK for the Alcuin Club, 1970).

Forstmann, H. J., *Word and Spirit: Calvin's Doctrine of Biblical Authority* (Stanford: Stanford University Press, 1962).

Fowler, Jeaneane, *World Religions: An Introduction for Students* (Brighton: Sussex Academic Press, 1997).

Furcha, E. J., and Pipkin, H. W., eds., *Prophet, Pastor, Protestant: The Work of Huldrych Zwingli* (Pittsburgh theological monographs new series 11. Allison Park, Pa: Pickwick Publications, 1984).

Gäbler, U., *Huldrych Zwingli: His Life and Work* (Philadelphia: Fortress Press, 1986).

Gerrish, B. A., *Grace and Gratitude: the eucharistic theology of John Calvin* (Minneapolis: Fortress, 1993).

Gilmore, A., ed., *Christian Baptism* (London: Lutterworth Press, 1959).

Goertz, Hans-Jürgen, ed., *Profiles of Radical Reformers: Biographical Sketches from Thomas Müntzer to Paracelsus* (Kitchener: Herald, 1982).

Gray, M. "Ritual space and ritual burial in the early modern Christian tradition", forthcoming.

——, 'The Diocese of St Asaph in 1563', *Journal of Welsh Religious History* 1 (1993), 1–40.

Green, Ian, "Reformed Pastors" and *Bons Curés*: the changing rôle of the parish clergy in early modern Europe' in W. J. Sheils and Diana Wood, eds., *The Ministry: Clerical and Lay* (Studies in Church History xxvi, 1989).

Green, R. W., ed., *Protestantism, Capitalism and Social Science: the Weber thesis controversy* (Problems in European civilization. 2nd edn., Lexington, Mass.: Heath, 1973).

Greengrass, Mark, *The French Reformation* (Oxford: Blackwell, 1987).

Hall, B., '*Hoc est corpus meum*: the centrality of the Real Presence for Luther' in *Luther: Theologian for Catholics and Protestants* ed. George Yule (Edinburgh: T. & T. Clark, 1985).

Haller, William, *Foxe's Book of Martyrs and the Elect Nation* (London: Cape, 1963).

Hareide, Bjarne *Die Konfirmation in der Reformationszeit: Eine Unterschuung der Lutherischen Konfirmation in Deutschland 1520–1585*, Arbeiten zur Pastoraltheologie 8 (Göttingen: Vandenhoeck & Ruprecht 1971).

Heiko Oberman, *The Dawn of the Reformation: Essays in Late Medieval and Early Reformation Thought* (Edinburgh: T & T Clark, 1986).

Hendrix, S. H., *Luther and the Papacy: Stages in a Reformation Conflict* (Philadelphia: Fortress Press, 1981).

Higman, Francis, *The Style of John Calvin in his French Polemical Pamphlets* (Oxford: Oxford University Press, 1967).

——, *Who was John Calvin? or Calvin and his Times* (University of Geneva Faculty of Theology, 1992).

——, *Why the Reformation?* (Geneva: Institut d'Histoire de la Réformation, 1996).

Hillerbrand, H. J., *The Protestant Reformation* (New York; London: Harper & Row, 1968).

——, *The Reformation: a narrative history related by contemporary observers and participants* (New York: Harper & Row, 1964).

Höpfl, H., *Luther and Calvin on Secular Authority* (Cambridge texts in the history of political thought. Cambridge: Cambridge University Press, 1991).

Hoyle, Richard, *The Pilgrimage of Grace and the Politics of the 1530s* (Oxford: Oxford University Press, 2001).

Hsia, R. Po-Chia, ed., *The German People and the Reformation* (Ithaca, New York: Cornell University Press, 1988).

——, *Social Discipline in the Reformation: Central Europe, 1550–1750* (London and New York: Routledge, 1989).

Jackson, S. M., ed., *The Latin Works and the Correspondence of Huldreich Zwingli, together with selections from his German works* (New York and London: G.P. Putnam's Sons, 1912–29).

Jasper, R. C. D. and G. J. Cuming, eds. *Prayers of the Eucharist : early and reformed* 3rd ed., rev. and enl. (Collegeville, Minn.: Liturgical Press, 1990).

Jayne, S., *John Colet and Marsilio Ficino* (Oxford: Oxford University Press, 1963).

Jedin, Hubert, "Contarini und Camaldoli", *Archivo per la storia della pièta* 2 (1959).

——, "Ein Turmerlebnis des jungen Contarinis", *Kirche des Glaubens – Kirche der Geschichte: Ausgewählte Aufsätze und Vorträge* I (Freiburg, 1966), 167–80.

Jenkins, Claude, *Barlow's consecration and Archbishop Parker's Register: with some new documents* (London: SPCK, 1935).

Jones, Cheslyn *et al.*, eds., *The Study of Liturgy* (London: SPCK / New York: Oxford University Press).

Jütte, Robert, *Poverty and Deviance in Early Modern Europe* (Cambridge: Cambridge University Press, 1994).

Karant-Nunn, Susan, *The Reformation of Ritual* (London and New York: Routledge, 1997).

——, *Zwickau in transition, 1500–1547 : the Reformation as an agent of change* (Columbus: Ohio State University Press, 1987).

Kittelson, J .M. *Luther the Reformer: The Story of the Man and his Career* (Minneapolis: Augsburg, 1989).

Koslofsky, Craig M., *The Reformation of the dead : death and ritual in early modern Germany, 1450–1700* (Basingstoke: Macmillan ; New York: St. Martin's Press, 2000).

Kouri, E. I., and Scott, Tom, eds. *Politics and Society in Reformation Europe* (Basingstoke and London: Macmillan. 1987).

Lindberg, Carter, *Beyond Charity: Reformation Initiatives for the Poor* (Minneapolis: Fortress Press, 1993).

——, *The European Reformations* (Oxford: Blackwell, 1996).

Loades, David, *Revolution in Religion: The English Reformation, 1530–1570* (Cardiff: University of Wales Press, 1992).

Lohse, B. *Martin Luther: An Introduction to his Life and Writings* (Philadelphia: Fortress Press, 1986).

Maag, Karin, ed., *Melanchthon in Europe* (Grand Rapids, Michigan: Baker Books, 1999).

MacCulloch, Diarmaid, *Thomas Cranmer* (New Haven; London: Yale University Press, 1996).

MacFarlane, Alan, *Witchcraft in Tudor and Stuart England: a regional and comparative study*, 2nd edn. (London: Routledge, 1999).

Maltby, Judith D., *Prayer book and people in Elizabethan and early Stuart England* (Cambridge: Cambridge University Press, 1998).

Manschreck, C. L., *Melanchthon: The Quiet Reformer* (New York: Abingdon Press, 1958).

Maxwell, William D. ed., *The Liturgical Portions of the Genevan Service Book* (Edinburgh and London: Oliver and Boyd, 1931).

McConica, J. K., *English Humanists and Reformation Politics* (Oxford: Oxford University Press, 1965).

McGrath, Alister, *A Life of John Calvin* (Oxford: Blackwell, 1990).

——, *Iustitia Dei: A History of the Christian Doctrine of Justification*, 2nd edn. (Cambridge: Cambridge University Press, 1998).

——, *Luther's Theology of the Cross* (Oxford: Blackwell, 1990).

——, *Reformation Thought*, 3rd edn. (Oxford: Blackwell, 1999).

——, *The Intellectual Origins of the European Reformation* (Oxford: Blackwell, 1993).

Meyer, Carl S., ed. *Luther and Zwingli's Propositions for Debate: the 95 Theses of 31 Oct 1517 and the 67 Articles of 19 January 1523* (Leiden: E.J. Brill, 1963).

Milner, B. C., *Calvin's Doctrine of the Church* (Leiden: Brill, 1970).

Muller, R. A., *Christ and the Decree: Christology and Predestination from Calvin to Perkins* (Studies in historical theology 2. Grand Rapids, Mich: Baker Book House, 1988).

Naphy, William G., *Calvin and the Consolidation of the Genevan Reformation* (Manchester: Manchester University Press, 1994).

Noll, M. A., *Confessions and Catechisms of the Reformation* (Leicester: Apollos, 1991).

O'Day, Rosemary, 'The Reformation of the Ministry, 1558–1642' in O'Day and Felicity Heal, eds., *Continuity and Change: Personnel and Administration of the Church in England, 1500–1642* (Leicester: Leicester University Press, 1976), pp. 55–75.

——, *The Debate on the English Reformation* (London: Methuen, 1986).

Obermann, Heiko, *Luther: Man between God and the Devil* (New Haven; London: Yale University Press, 1989).

——, *The Roots of Anti-Semitism in the Age of the Renaissance and Reformation* (Philadelphia: Fortress Press, 1984).

Old, Hughes Oliphant, *The Shaping of the Reformed Baptismal Rite in the Sixteenth Century* (Grand Rapids, Mich: William B. Eerdmans, 1992).

Olson, Jeannine, *Calvin and Social Welfare* (Selinsgrove: Susquehanna University Press, 1989).

Ozment, Steven, *When Fathers Ruled: Family Life in Reformation Europe* (Cambridge, Mass: Harvard University Press, 1983).

Ozment, Steven, *The Reformation in Medieval Perspective* (Chicago: Quadrangle, 1971).

Pater, Calvin Augustine, *Karlstadt as the Father of the Baptist Movements: The Emergence of Lay Protestantism* (Toronto, Buffalo and London: University of Toronto Press, 1984).

Pauck, Wilhelm, ed. *Melanchthon and Bucer* (Library of Christian Classics xix. London: SCM Press/Philadelphia: Westminster Press, 1969).

Payne, John B., *Erasmus: His Theology of the Sacraments* (Richmond, Va: John Knox Press, 1970).

Pelikan, Jaroslav, *Spirit versus structure: Luther and the institutions of the Church* (London: Collins, 1968).

Pettegree, Andrew *et al.*, *Calvinism in Europe, 1540–1620* (Cambridge: Cambridge University Press, 1994).

——, *The Early Reformation in Europe* (Cambridge: Cambridge University Press, 1992).

Potter, G. R., *Zwingli* (Cambridge: Cambridge University Press, 1976).

Prestwich, Menna, ed., *International Calvinism 1541–1715* (Oxford: Clarendon Press, 1985).

Ratcliff, E. C."Puritan Alternatives to the Prayer Book: the *Directory* and Richard Baxter's *Reformed Liturgy*" in M. Ramsey *et al.*, *The English Prayer Book 1549–1662* (London: SPCK for the Alcuin Club, 1963).

Reid, J. K. S., ed., *Calvin: Theological Treatises* (Philadelphia: Westminster Press, 1954).

Reid, W. S. , *John Calvin: his influence in the Western world* (Grand Rapids, Mich.: Zondervan Pub. House, 1982).

Reiss, Athene, *The Sunday Christ* (Oxford: BAR, 2000).

Rempel, John D., *The Lord's Supper in Anabaptism: a study in the Christology of Balthasar Hubmaier, Pilgrim Marpeck and Dirk Phillips* (Waterloo: Herald, 1993).

Repp, A. C., *Confirmation in the Lutheran Church* ( St Louis, Mo: Concordia, 1964).

Roper, Lyndal, "'Going to Church and Street': Weddings in Reformation Augsburg", *Past and Present* 106, February 1985, 62–101.

Rupp, Gordon, *Patterns of Reformation* (London: Epworth Press, 1969).

Sabean, D. W., *Power in the Blood: popular culture and village discourse in early modern Germany* (Cambridge: Cambridge University Press, 1984).

Scarisbrick, J. A., *The Reformation and the English People* (Oxford: Oxford University Press, 1984).

Scott, Tom, and Scribner, R. W., eds., *The German Peasants' War: a history in documents* (Atlantic Highlands: Humanities, 1991).

Scribner, R. W., *For the Sake of Simple Folk: popular propaganda for the German Reformation* (Cambridge: Cambridge University Press, 1981).

——, and Johnson, T., eds., *Popular Religion in Germany and Central Europe, 1400–1800* (Basingstoke and London: Macmillan, 1996).

——, *Popular Culture and Popular Movements in Reformation Germany* (London and Ronceverte: Hambledon Press, 1987).

Shirley, F. J., *Elizabeth's First Archbishop* (London: SPCK, 1948).

Sider, Ronald J., *Andreas Bodenstein von Karlstadt: The Development of his Thought 1517–1525* (Leiden: E. J. Brill, 1974).

Stephens, W. P., "The church in Bucer's commentaries on the Epistle to the Ephesians" in D. F. Wright, ed., *Martin Bucer: reforming church and community* (Cambridge: Cambridge University Press, 1994).

——, *The Holy Spirit in the Theology of Martin Bucer* (Cambridge: Cambridge University Press, 1970).

——, *The Theology of Huldrych Zwingli* (Oxford: Clarendon Press, 1986).

Strauss, Gerald, *Luther's House of Learning* (Baltimore and London: Johns Hopkins University Press, 1978).

Tappert, Theodore G., ed. and trans., *The Book of Concord* (Philadelphia: Fortress Press, 1959).

Tavard, G. H., *Holy Writ or Holy Church? The Crisis of the Protestant Reformation* (London : Burns & Oates, 1959).

Tentler, Thomas, *Sin and Confession on the Eve of the Reformation* (Princeton: Princeton University Press, 1977).

*The Cambridge History of the Bible*, ed. P. R. Ackroyd *et al.*, Volume 3: the West from the Reformation to the present day (Cambridge: Cambridge University Press, 1963).

Thomas, Keith, *Religion and the Decline of Magic* (London: Weidenfeld & Nicolson, 1971).

Thompson, Bard, ed., *Liturgies of the Western Church* (Philadelphia: Fortress Press, 1961).

Tonkin, J., *The Church and Secular Order in Reformation Thought* (New York; London: Columbia University Press, 1971).

Torrance, Thomas F., ed. *Tracts and treatises on the doctrine and worship of the church, by John Calvin* (Edinburgh and London: Oliver and Boyd; Grand Rapids, Mich: Eerdmans, 1958).

Tripp, D. H.,"Protestantism and the Eucharist" in Cheslyn Jones *et al.*, eds., *The Study of Liturgy* (London: SPCK / New York: Oxford University Press).

Wallace, R. S., *Calvin, Geneva and the Reformation* (Edinburgh: Scottish Academic Press, 1988).

Wandel, Lee Palmer, *Voracious Idols and Violent Hands: Iconoclasm in Reformation Zurich, Strasburg and Basel* (Cambridge: Cambridge University Press, 1995).

Wenger, John,"The Schleitheim Confession of Faith", *Mennonite Quarterly Review* xix (1945), 243–53.

Wengert, Timothy, "Luther and Melanchthon, Melanchthon and Luther", *Luther-Jahrbuch* 65 (1998).

——, "The day Philip Melanchthon got mad". *Lutheran Quarterly* 5 (1991), 419–33.

——, "We Will Feast Together in Heaven Forever: the epistolary friendship of John Calvin and Philip Melanchthon" in Karin Maag, ed., *Melanchthon in Europe* (Grand Rapids, Michigan: Baker Books, 1999).

Whitaker, E. C., *Martin Bucer and the Book of Common Prayer*, Alcuin Club Collections no. 55 (Great Wakering: Mayhew-McCrimmon for the Alcuin Club, 1974).

Whitebrook, J. C., *The Consecration of Matthew Parker* (London: A.R. Mowbray & Co, 1945).

Wiesner-Hanks, Merry E., *Christianity and sexuality in the early modern world: regulating desire, reforming practice* (London: Routledge, 2000).

Williams, G. H., *The Radical Reformation* (Philadelphia: Westminster Press, 1962).

———. ed., *Spiritual and Anabaptist Writers* (Library of Christian Classics xxv. London: SCM Press/Philadelphia: Westminster Press, 1957).

Woolf, B. L., *Reformation Writings of Martin Luther* (London: Lutterworth Press, 1952).

Wright, D. F., ed., *Martin Bucer: reforming church and community* (Cambridge: Cambridge University Press, 1994).

Wrightson, Keith, and David Levine, *Poverty and Piety in an English Village: Terling, 1525–1700* (Revised edition: Oxford: Clarendon, 1995).

Zapalac, Kristin Eldyss Sorensen, *In his image and likeness: political iconography and religious change in Regensburg, 1500–1600* (Ithaca: Cornell University Press, 1990).

# Index